THE INSIDE STORY

THE INSIDE STORY

A Life in Journalism

Anthony Westell

DUNDURN PRESS

TORONTO · OXFORD

Copy-editor: Jennifer Bergeron
Designer: Jennifer Scott
Printer: University of Toronto Press

National Library of Canada Cataloguing in Publication Data

Westell, Anthony, 1926–
    The inside story: a life in journalism

ISBN 1-55002-375-6

1. Westell, Anthony, 1926– 2. Journalists — Canada — Biography. 3. Canada — Politics and government — 1935– I. Title.

PN4913.W48A3 2002   070'.92   C2002-901070-5

1 2 3 4 5   06   05   04   03   02

THE CANADA COUNCIL | LE CONSEIL DES ARTS
FOR THE ARTS | DU CANADA
SINCE 1957 | DEPUIS 1957

Canada

ONTARIO ARTS COUNCIL
CONSEIL DES ARTS DE L'ONTARIO

We acknowledge the support of the **Canada Council for the Arts** and the **Ontario Arts Council** for our publishing program. We also acknowledge the financial support of the **Government of Canada** through the **Book Publishing Industry Development Program** and **The Association for the Export of Canadian Books**, and the **Government of Ontario** through the **Ontario Book Publishers Tax Credit** program.

Printed and bound in Canada. ⊛
Printed on recycled paper.
www.dundurn.com

Dundurn Press	Dundurn Press	Dundurn Press
8 Market Street	73 Lime Walk	2250 Military Road
Suite 200	Headington, Oxford,	Tonawanda NY
Toronto, Ontario, Canada	England	U.S.A. 14150
M5E 1M6	OX3 7AD	

For Jeannie
who made my career possible
at the cost of her own

CONTENTS

ACKNOWLEDGMENTS

The story of my life is in many ways the story of how the lives of others have touched and ordered my own. So I acknowledge my debt to everyone mentioned in this book, and indeed to hundreds more. But in particular I wish to thank three friends who read my draft, chapter by hesitant chapter, and offered advice, dissent, and, most important, encouragement: Jack and Marie Cahill, and Peter Carver. Without them there might have been no book, and certainly not this one. My wife, Jeannie, learned proofreading as a teenaged editor of a weekly paper in wartime Britain, and she read and corrected my manuscript, even when she disagreed with what I was writing or would rather I had not written it. My sister, Diana, provided early family pictures, and my niece, Gillian Westell, provided some of the research on the Smedley family. Professor Hari Sharma told me about early and revolutionary times at Simon Fraser University.

At the conclusion of Chapter 13 I suggest that Canadians may play a role in the American Empire similar to that of the Scots in the British Empire. I owe that powerful idea to Mark Lovewell, my colleague on *The Literary Review of Canada.*

The photo on the cover was taken by a friend, the late Jan Breyer. It shows me not as I am today but at mid-life and mid-career and reading a newspaper, which seems appropriate for a book about a life spent working in newspapers.

INTRODUCTION

I was 15 in 1941, Britain was at war, and it was time to leave school. My father asked me what career I had in mind, which meant in those days what sort of work I would like to do for the rest of my life. Actually, I was hoping the war would last long enough for me to join the navy and play a part in the great adventure, but that was a couple of years away, so I said I would like to be a newspaper reporter. Looking back, I'm not sure why. I was a great reader and had swallowed whole a couple of books about the exciting lives of reporters in Fleet Street, in London, then the world capital of journalism, and at school a pal and I played at drawing front pages in which we wrote insulting stories about our teachers. One story concerned a teacher we called Sprouts because hair sprouted from his nose in bunches, and when that edition went missing we lived for several days in terror that it would be found. It retrospect, this seems a slim basis on which to start a career, but my father asked no questions and soon secured me a position as an apprentice reporter on our local daily paper.

This book is intended to be mainly the story of my life in journalism, and I had planned to begin at that point in my life when I first got a whiff of the legendary printer's ink that used to saturate newspaper offices and addict aspiring reporters. But then I realized that I ought to start further back, with the nature, nurture, and experiences that made me the person I am and shaped the journalist I became. When reporting was essentially a matter of recording facts in the order prescribed by the conventions of journalism, objectivity seemed possible. The opinions and prejudices of the reporter hardly entered into the matter. But the nature of journalism has changed, and, as I shall explain later, I had something to do with introducing those changes in Canada. News used to be about events: political speeches, accidents, cases in courts, the public working of governments, and the like. Now, those humdrum events of everyday democracy, lamentably, often go unreported, and journalists cover instead developing situations: the state of the environment, poverty, economic issues, and so on. This requires the journalist to use judgment, first about which situations to cover and which to ignore, next about which of a million facts are significant and should be highlighted, and finally on what conclusions to draw from the facts.

So journalists don't talk much about objectivity anymore. But neither do they like to be accused of being subjective in covering the news, so they claim instead to be fair, accurate, and balanced. But there are no hard and fast rules to decide what is and what is not fair, accurate, and balanced, and on any given piece of political journalism, for example, a liberal and a conservative would probably disagree. So we are back to subjectivity, or bias, if you prefer. In any event, I spent many years as a columnist with a licence to express opinions, and the reader deserves to know from whence those opinions sprang.

The first section of this book, therefore, I have entitled "The Making of a Journalist." Chapter 1, "Surfacing in the Gene Pool," discusses my ancestors, the notorious along with the virtuous, an executioner along with innkeepers and labourers, the legitimate with the illegitimate, gamblers who lost what might have been my wealth, and enough eccentrics to help me explain away some of the decisions I have made. The second chapter, "Growing Up in the Old World," explores my childhood in a motherless family in Britain before the war, now almost a forgotten world. Chapter 3, "Going to War," is about the impact of the Second World War on my youth, and my experiences in the Royal Navy in the last two years of the war. Wholly undistinguished, my service nevertheless sailed me right around the world and had a powerful influence on the political values I have carried through life.

The second section of this book, "A Working Journalist," is an account of my career, from apprenticeship in Britain to reporter, editorial writer, and national affairs columnist in Canada. While I don't want to intrude on the privacy of my wife or my children, I have discussed developments in my personal life for what they say about me and about how they influenced my career. Journalists are storytellers and I can't resist a good tale, so much of this book is anecdotal. I have described, for example, my $2.00 wedding, the way we lived and began to raise a family in ruined and rationed London, the difficulties of starting again in Canada, and our happy days in Ottawa. I hope the personal background helps to explain my journalism — and that it makes an entertaining read.

The third section, which I have called "A.k.a. an Academic," takes me from full-time journalism into life as a university teacher. Somehow, I floated to the giddy rank of associate dean of arts without ever having been a student. More importantly, I had the time to work out my ideas on journalism which seemed to me to be suffering an identity crisis, with unfortunate results for our political democracy. I developed also my ideas on social democracy and what is now called globalism. In fact, Chapter 13 is about my role in helping to move Canadian public opinion from nationalism to free trade, probably my most significant journalism. If there appears to be a contradiction between being a social democrat and a free trader, the fault is not mine, as I shall explain.

I have now to answer the difficult question of why anyone should care about my story. To write an autobiography or memoir must surely be vain unless one has played a great role in the world or is a gifted diarist, and I make neither claim. So why write? There is Socrates and his oft-quoted but little-understood, at least by me, remark that "the life which is unexamined is not worth living." I reread the story and it's not encouraging. He had been convicted of corrupting the minds of young Athenians, and addressed the jury of citizens on what penalty he might suffer. It was no good banishing him, he said, because he would be bound to go on discussing the very ideas that had already got him into trouble. But why could he not just keep quiet? Because "... the greatest good of man is daily to converse about virtue and all that concerning which you hear me examining myself and others...," there is need to examine one's life. He suggested a stiff fine, with the cheerful proviso that Plato and other friends would have to pay because he had no money. But the jury voted for death by drinking hemlock, which is of course what happened. I'm no expert on Socrates, but as I read the story he was convicted in part for examining his life in public, which is what I am about to do in this book.

So I must justify my vanity by claiming my story may be interesting and that some public good may come of it. I have tales to tell of politics not only in Ottawa but also inside the editorial offices of our great newspapers, insights to offer on political leaders from John Diefenbaker to Pierre Trudeau, and controversial issues to debate. These are footnotes to the history of our times. But a cautionary notice: I had the good fortune in 1974 to be invited to join two eminent Canadians, Davidson Dunton and David Lewis, in teaching the core seminar in the Institute of Canadian Studies at Carleton University in Ottawa. Lewis had just lost his seat in the House of Commons and was preparing to write his memoirs, and sometimes after our weekly seminar I would invite him to join me for lunch in the faculty club. I knew he was unwell because he grumbled about his diet, but I had no idea that he was seriously ill — few people did — and would press him to have an appetite-enhancing dry martini. Then, in a relaxed mood, he would grumble that he had made a mistake in accepting the research assistants offered by the university. They kept turning up awkward facts he had forgotten, questioning the way he remembered other things, and even spoiling the anecdotes he had polished over the years. They had even had the poor taste, one told me later, to find a letter which he had signed "Yours in Marx," long before he began an epic battle against Marxists in his party and the trade unions. He should, he said, have followed John Diefenbaker and Lester Pearson by telling his story to writers who could check the facts where necessary and draft a book for him to revise.

In writing this book, I have checked the facts where I was doubtful, but memory can play us false. When my wife read my account of what should have been shared memories it was rather like that song from the movie *Gigi* in which Maurice Chevalier, recalling a long-ago romance, sings, "Ah yes, I remember it well," and Hermione Gingold, as his old flame, quietly corrects every detail. In what follows, there is nothing that I know to be wrong, but I would not vouch for every dot and comma. Happily, David Lewis persisted with the more rigorous method because his political memoir, *The Good Fight*, covering the years 1909-58, and published in 1981 (MacMillan of Canada), proved to be a work of historical importance. Unhappily, he died that year without writing the second volume he had intended.

There will be no second volume for me.

THE MAKING OF A
JOURNALIST

~ *Chapter 1* ~

Surfacing in the Gene Pool

When, a couple of years ago, I researched and wrote a family history I started naturally enough with the Westells, my father's family, but they turned out to be disappointingly respectable. Poring through the 1841 records kept by British census-takers who tramped up and down the streets every ten years asking who was living in each house, their ages and occupations, and where they came from, I found a John Westall — or sometimes Westell, because not everyone knew or cared how to spell their name and census-takers wrote down what they heard — living in Bristol, then a great port in the west of England. He had been born in the village of Chilton Foliat, in the nearby county of Wiltshire, but like so many other rural workers had made his way to the city no doubt in search of work. When the census-taker found him he was a labourer living in the industrial slum of Bedminster, and married to Lucy who had been born in the neighbouring city of Bath. By the time of the next census, in 1851, John had risen in the world to become a dairyman, which could have meant that he milked cows or perhaps drove a horse and cart to deliver the milk, ladling it from shiny metal churns. Among their children was James, then seventeen and a gentleman's servant. By the census of 1861, James was a beer seller, which probably meant that he sold beer from his home without actually having a pub, and he had married a Bristol girl, Mary Gould. Another ten years, and James was foreman to a corn broker — in Britain corn meant wheat and sometimes oats — and they lived close to the docks where the grain ships docked. Here we begin to see the Westells — by then, they spelled it with an *e* — struggling upwards toward the middle class.

James and Mary had eight children, among them Henry John, born in 1863, who became my grandfather. Henry was a chemist's assistant, and it can be no coincidence that he married the daughter of a chemist, Alice Wescombe; presumably, they courted among the pills and potions.

Their only child, my father, carried both their names: John Wescombe Westell, known as Wes. When Wes was born in Bristol in 1890, Henry was still a chemist's assistant, but sometime in the following decade he went into the insurance business, and as his fortunes improved the family moved from home to better home, and then to a handsome stone house in Weston-super-Mare, a seaside resort about twenty miles from Bristol. Bracing breezes off the mud of the Bristol Channel were said to be good for all manner of invalids. The place was popular enough to draw a quip from the British wit and journalist G.K. Chesterton who declared that he would not give up any bad habit for the sake of an extra six months in a nursing home in Weston. The line was later put in the mouth of that famous fictional barrister Rumpole of the Bailey. Chesterton also remarked with equal perception that journalism was the easiest of all professions.

While the English are often said to be frozen in their class, the Westells in three generations had gone from a labourer living in an industrial slum to insurance manager living in a genteel resort, and securely in the middle class. One reason of course was the industrialization of Britain and the generation of new wealth, but even so the Westells must have had the ambition, energy, and abilities to take advantage of new opportunities. When I look in the mirror I see my father. He grew up in Weston, following his father into the insurance business and enjoying some local reputation as an amateur cricketer. Almost six feet, four inches tall, and built to scale, he was sociable, usually well-dressed, and attractive to women, although absent-minded on occasion: Walking along the main street of our city one day, he was lost in thought but noticed a woman who seemed familiar, and politely raised his hat as he passed; it was his wife. He had the fortitude to take a cold bath every morning, and he dressed his hair with olive oil, which may sound odd until you know that he kept all his hair while mine is rapidly disappearing. Despite physical similarities, I lack all his social skills — I blame that on nurture — but I hope my life will show I have inherited at least some of the genes that lifted my forbears out of the slums.

My mother, Diana Blanche Smedley, lived in Weston, a few streets away from Wes, with her widowed mother and her sister, known as Babs. Her mother, Catherine Blanche, had been born into a family of some distinction, the Woodroffes, and was proud of it. When she died she chose to be buried not with either of her husbands but with two sisters in a village churchyard thick with Woodroffes. The Woodroffe family first appeared in history in the 1300s, but the interesting part of their story began two centuries later when David Woodroffe, a haberdasher — that is, a merchant dealing in men's clothing — became high sheriff of London in 1554-5. Henry VIII had broken with Rome and established the Church of England in order to facilitate a divorce and remarriage, but his daughter Mary Tudor remained a devout Catholic. When she became Queen in 1553, she began to return the country to Roman Catholicism. That led to the persecution of persisting Protestants, which gave her the terrible name in history of Bloody Mary.

Anyone who saw a few years ago the movie *Elizabeth* must remember the horrendous opening scenes in which Protestant heretics are burnt. The man in charge might well have been Sheriff Woodroffe. In his famous *Book of Martyrs*, published in 1559, John Foxe reported that Woodroffe conducted several burnings at Smithfield in London, including those of John Bradford, a well known Protestant preacher, and John Leaf, an unfortunate apprentice who somehow got caught up in the hunt for heretics. Having described this gruesome event, Foxe continued:

> The said Woodroffe sheriff, above mentioned, was joined in office with another sir William Chester, for the year 1555. Between these two sheriffs such differences there was of judgement and religion that the one (that is master Woodroffe) was wont commonly to laugh, the other to shed tears, at the death of Christ's people ... Furthermore, here by the way to note the severe punishment of God's hand against the said Woodroffe, as against all such cruel persecutors, so it happened, that within half a year after the burning of the blessed martyr (the reference is to Bradford), the said sheriff was so stricken on the right side, with such a palsy or stroke of God's hand (whatsoever it was), that for the space of eight years after, till his dying day, he was not able

to turn himself in bed, but as two men with a sheet were fain to stir him; and withal such an insatiable devouring came upon him that it was monstrous to see. And this continued he for the space of eight years together.

Foxe described more of Woodroffe's callous treatment of Protestants sent to the fire at Smithfield, but it seems that as a high city official he still received a handsome funeral.

Despite this dubious parentage, or perhaps because of it, David's son Nicholas became lord mayor of London in 1579-80, when he was knighted, and later the Member of Parliament for London and master of the Haberdashers' Company, a powerful city guild. In 1570 his son, Sir Robert Woodroffe, bought the Manor of Ailburton (now Aylburton) in Gloucestershire, on the banks of the Severn River shortly before it becomes the Bristol Channel leading out into the Atlantic. There is evidence in stone that he was a good guy: in the village church of nearby Alvington there is to this day a memorial stone, now barely legible:

Here lies Sir Robert Woodroffe Knight, and Marye, his dear wife,
Whose lives were virtuous, just and upright; but Atropos' cruel knife
Soon cut their thread; the Fate in this being kinde,
Her hasting hence to Heaven's blisse left him not long behinde.
Both sprang from offsprings generous and just, and lying here as one
This sepulchre doth well befit, both covered with one stone.
But, Reader, understand that thou readest not this
At Heirs' or Executors' charge, but at a Dwarfe's of his,
Whose charitie her here maintained, and now they being deade
In grateful memorie, she caused this stone on them be laide.
He died XVII day of May, and she the XIIII day of March, 1609

The faithful dwarfe must have been quite a character, able to turn a neat phrase, refer to Greek mythology — Atropos was a Fate responsible for cutting the thread of life — and afford a handsome stone that has lasted four hundred years.

Sir Robert and his wife died without heir, the manor passed to his nephew Robert, and Woodroffes continued to live in the district, and around Chepstow, just across the Welsh border, for centuries. There was much intermarriage in the clan because, I suppose, there weren't that many "suitable" families in the area. That may explain the streak of eccentricity in the clan that certainly came out in Percy Woodroffe, who died in 1954, aged seventy-six, the last Woodroffe, I believe, to live in the district. He was remembered as a farmer good with animals, but a little strange. He lived at one of the family homes, Alvington Court, a notably ugly old farmhouse, probably Elizabethan with add-ons, which was supposed to have had a tunnel to the banks of the Severn River for the convenience of smugglers. When my daughter and I called there a few years ago, the current owners were aware of the story but said the only trace of a tunnel they had found was a curious depression in the ground where a tunnel might have collapsed.

In middle age, Percy married another Woodroffe, a mature second cousin from the London branch who had perhaps run out of hope of better offers. The marriage did not turn out well: Percy's wife liked to give elegant dinner parties with men in tails and ladies in gowns, but Percy would turn up in rubber boots with his pants tied up with binder twine. When they died they were buried in separate graveyards, Percy with his parents, and his wife with two Woodroffe sisters, including my grandmother, in the churchyard at the village of Alvington. An elderly woman in the village told me she once took a child riding at Alvington Court and they happened to meet Percy carrying a sick animal, prompting the child to report later, "We met Jesus, an old man with a beard carrying a lamb." Not a bad way to be remembered.

To return to the Woodroffe history, in 1852 William Edmund Woodroffe, born at Woolaston, a few miles from Alvington, married Catherine (Kate) May Bishop, youngest of fifteen children of an interesting family in the fashionable city of Bath, not far away across the Severn River. Her father, William Bishop, had been part-owner of The White Hart, not only a famous inn but the base for a network of coach lines. An old engraving I found in Bath library shows the forecourt of The White Hart crowded with coaches, which were said to be washed with hot water drawn from springs five thousand feet underground and famous since Roman times. For many years a man called Moses Pickwick owned the inn and the coach lines. According to a local legend he got his name when a lady passing through the nearby village of Wick found him as an abandoned baby — like Moses in the bulrushes — and because he was picked up in Wick, she called him Moses Pickwick. It's likely that Charles Dickens borrowed the name for his humourous stories, *The Pickwick Papers*. In one story, the central character, Mr. Pickwick, takes the coach from London to stay at The White Hart and is startled to find that the coach is operated by a Moses Pickwick. Dickens, perhaps, was acknowledging the original Pickwick.

My ancestor, William Bishop, sold his interest in The White Hart around 1850 for £30,000. That may not sound like much and to convert it even roughly into today's money makes little sense because the quality of life in terms of goods and services that could be bought then was utterly different from anything we can experience. As currency values fluctuate, converting sterling into Canadian dollars introduces another uncertainty. Nevertheless, I have tried (here and in following passages) to make a straight conversion, allowing for inflation and at today's rate of exchange, but I warn that it is at best a rough guide. So, £30,000 then would be about $4.5 million today. The family lived in a five-storey house on fashionable Pulteney Street, designed to be the most distinguished street in a city of splendid architecture. Jane Austen mentions it in her novel Persuasion, and there were numerous famous residents, including Mrs. Maria Fitzherbert who was secretly married to the Prince of Wales, later George IV; Louis Napoleon, later NapoleonIII of France; Admiral Horatio Nelson's mistress, Lady Hamilton; and William Wilberforce, a leader of the campaign to outlaw slavery. Like William's other children, Kate studied "Art, Literature and Music" in Paris, and when she was twenty-five, in 1849, received her share of her father's estate. It was probably a handsome sum because she in turn gave £1,000 (around $150,000 today) to each of her eight children when they reached twenty-one.

Kate was my great-grandmother, and by the time she married William Woodroffe he had become a wholesale wool merchant. They lived at Peckham Rye, in those days on the southern outskirts of London. During my research, I was advised not to venture into the Peckham because it was said to be populated largely by black drug dealers. But being an adventurous fellow, I boarded the familiar red double-decker bus and headed south. At Peckham, my fellow passengers were mostly elderly women of every shade, carrying shopping bags, possibly full of illegal substances. Venturing a little farther, to Peckham Rye, I walked around the park-like common and, to my surprise, found Vallance House where my great-grandparents had raised their family. But it had been converted into shabby apartments.

Their second child and first daughter was Catherine Blanche, my grandmother. On July 1, 1886, she married a second cousin — there we go again — George Smedley. I have a picture of the very Victorian wedding party on the lawn outside a rather grand house. The men are bearded, wearing top hats and frock coats, and the women are in long dresses and bonnets. Peeping out of a door in the background are two maids in aprons and frilly caps. The Smedleys were from the industrial Midlands, and the most interesting thing about them is that George's father appears to have been the illegitimate son of an Ann Smedley, of Ashover, Derbyshire, and a George Potter, of Darley Hall, Darley Dale, Derbyshire, on the edge of the famous Peak District. The illegitimate George inherited — along with his father's first name and his mother's family name — what must have been a substantial sum from an unmarried aunt because very soon he was describing himself as "Gentleman," which meant he no longer had to work for a living. He and his family moved from the Midlands to live on a small estate near Chepstow.

His son, and my grandfather, George, had not long to wait before inheriting and becoming in his turn a "Gentleman." They lived in a pleasant villa, probably Georgian, between Chepstow and Aylburton, so now the Smedley/Woodroffes were back close to where Sir Robert had established his manor in 1570. They had four children before George died in 1902, aged fifty-four. He was buried with his father, mother, and brother, all of whom died within a span of sixteen years. I view with some concern the proclivity of the Smedleys for dying young. I have already survived longer than any male relative I can trace.

At his death, grandfather George owned an impressive amount of property, mostly inherited. When the will was probated, the estate was valued at £15,843 ($1.7 million today). George left it all to his widow, grandmother Catherine, who was to maintain, educate, and bring up "in a manner suitable to their station in life" the two sons until they were twenty-one, and the two daughters until they were twenty-one unless they married earlier. But there was a proviso: if Catherine remarried, the estate was to be divided among the four children, who would then provide to their mother an annuity of £200 ($20,000 today). Catherine did in fact remarry, so my mother and her three siblings shared their father's small fortune.

But it was mostly gone within a generation. My Uncle Will married and emigrated to New Zealand before the First World War, probably for reasons of health, taking his share of the family money with him. Uncle George, apparently fleeing from gambling debts, moved to Canada before the First World War. The family tree shows George as unmarried, but there was an Aunty May; my father told me she had been the wife of the local pub keeper before running away to Canada with George to live on Vancouver Island. George lost a leg while serving as a dispatch rider in the Canadian army in First World War and drew a pension for the rest of his life. He remained a racing man, and between the wars tried unsuccessfully to introduce harness racing in England. When grandmother Catherine remarried, she moved with her new husband to Weston, taking with her my mother-to-be, Diana Blanche, known as Blanche, and Jessie, known as Babs because she was the baby of the family.

I interrupt here to deal briefly with family names. My full name is George Anthony, making me the fifth George in the line beginning with the romantic, or perhaps careless, George Potter. I regret that when my wife and I named our own children it did not occur to me to continue the tradition. As we were both journalists, we thought naturally of names that would look good in a byline, short, snappy names. It would have been awkward anyway to give them long family names because when they were born in Britain in the 1950s ration books and identity cards were still printed on austerity paper on which a pen nib could easily catch while trying to write the full name on the five dots provided. One blot, and a whole identity could disappear. So we called our children just Dan and Tracy. But all is not lost; our younger granddaughter is Annabel Woodroffe Westell.

To return to my story, it was in Weston of course that Blanche met and married the young insurance man, Wes Westell. She was from a proud family in genteel decline, with traces of eccentricity, a weakness for gambling, and a tendency to emigrate. He was from a middle class family not long risen from the slums, twenty-three when the First World

War began in 1914. He served in the Royal Engineers, rising to the rank of corporal, and survived perhaps because his unit was transferred from the Western front slaughter house to reinforce the Italians in their battles with Austrians. Right in the middle of the war, in 1916, my father and mother married in Weston, and his address on the marriage licence was British Expeditionary Forces, France. Mother must have been a lively young woman; my father liked to tell the story of how she was booed when promenading on the amusement pier at Weston wearing trousers, or rather, a sort of divided skirt she had made herself.

Babs was devoted to her older sister and heartily disliked her brother-in-law, Wes. She was family-proud and perhaps thought her sister was marrying below her station — marrying a man whose grandfather had been a servant to gentlemen like her father and grandfather. Or maybe she resented losing her beloved sister. Years later when my mother died, having named my father and Babs as executors, this rift created real problems. Wes finally won his way by threatening never again to allow Babs to see we three children, her nephews and niece. Pretty rough stuff. But Babs was eccentric, possibly with a lesbian inclination. She smoked Woodbines, the working man's cigarette, had a hairy face, and dressed in what were in her time mannish clothes, often a suede golfing jacket, slacks or a heavy tweed skirt, and flat shoes. Although well off, she rented part of her small house near the sea front at Weston and shopped in cheap stores. But she fed we children handsomely when we visited. I remember as a small boy having a whole can of sardines for tea; when we went home and my father met us at the train station my short pants were so tight on my thighs that he drove me straight to the tailor who cut them off with a long pair of scissors.

Babs eventually married a retired sea captain but they never lived together, sometimes meeting on the sea front for a walk. I put this arrangement down to her eccentricity until I saw my grandmother's will. As explained above, she had forfeited to her children her husband's fortune when she remarried, so she had not much to leave her children anyway. But she provided that Babs would enjoy the income from the small estate until she married, when the capital would be divided among three of her four children, Will having taken his share in advance when he emigrated. What that meant, of course, was that George and my mother could receive nothing until Babs married, so I assume Babs' marriage to the captain was strictly one of convenience, a generous gesture to release a little money to siblings.

When Babs fell ill, apparently because she was starving herself on some mad diet, she hired a nurse to look after her. Then the nurse fell ill and Babs looked after her. The two ladies lived together for years, but whether there was more to the relationship than friendship I cannot say. Not surprisingly, Babs doted on her sister's firstborn, my brother John. I thought I was at least acceptable as a nephew until she died in 1968. She had lived all her life on inherited money, but still managed to leave about £65,000 after death duties, perhaps $1.5 million today. My sister got the house in Weston with the contents, some of which were antiques which went to auction in London, and my brother got most of the money. I got £100 because — according to what Babs told my sister — I had not been sufficiently attentive. Well, I have already admitted that I lacked social graces, but I did not know it was going to be that expensive.

My mother had inherited the same small fortune as Babs but when she died at age forty-two she left only a few thousand pounds, including the family home. Like her brother George in Canada, she liked to go horse racing, which no doubt accounted for some of her lost capital. But she also lost money in a famous financial scandal. A promoter and public figure named Clarence Hatry went to jail for fourteen years in 1930 when he admitted forgery, causing thousands of investors to lose large sums. But my mother at least learned her lesson. Having inherited early herself and not made good use of her money, she provided in her will that her children should not inherit until each reached the serious age of twenty-five. I was twenty-five in 1951, and had been married for a year. My share of what was left of her share of the Smedley/Woodroffe money was no fortune, but it enabled us to furnish an apartment and then to make a down payment on a house, a leg-up just when we needed it and the foundation on which we have built whatever security we enjoy today. So I have no right to complain.

So there you have the gene pool from which I emerged, and which helped to shape the journalist I became. I like to think I owe most to solid, striving, respectable Westells, working their way up in the world. But as my career will show, I can make reckless, almost irresponsible, decisions, and the reader may easily find some of my ideas eccentric, all of which I probably owe to the Woodroffes.

~ Chapter 2 ~

Growing Up in the Old World

Shortly after the end of the First World War, my father got a job as an insurance agent and inspector in Exeter, the capital city of the county of Devon in the rural southwest — one county up from Land's End. My brother, Woodroffe John, was born there in 1921, I in 1926, and my sister, Diana Wescombe, in 1930. I grew up in that old city and it was part of my nurture. It has a city wall, part of which was built by the Romans, a Norman castle built by William the Conqueror, and a Gothic cathedral built by generations of craftsmen on the site of an earlier Anglo-Saxon church. Translated from Latin, the inscription under the cathedral clock warns, "The hours perish and are reckoned to our account." More cheerfully, it is said also to be the clock in the nursery rhyme:

Hickory dickory dock
The mouse ran up the clock;
The clock struck one
and down he run
Hickory, dickory dock !

John Graves Simcoe, first Lieutenant Governor of Upper Canada, attended school in Exeter, and died in a house in the ancient Close surrounding the cathedral. Exeter's Guildhall, where the city council met, is Tudor, as is Mol's Coffee House in the cathedral Close, and the nearby Ship Inn where Elizabethan sea captains swaggered with bags of Spanish gold. Sir Francis Drake, greatest of the Elizabethan exploring adventurers, is supposed to have said that after his own ship he most liked the Ship

Inn in Exeter. The city sent three ships down the River Exe to fight the Spanish Armada, and Queen Elizabeth rewarded it with its motto, Semper Fidelis, or Ever Faithful.

Among numerous churches there is St. Olave's, thought to have been originally the house chapel of Gytha, Countess of Wessex, sister-in-law of King Canute who sat on his throne on the beach and ordered the tide not to rise. Was he really trying to command the tide, or was he demonstrating to his sycophantic courtiers the limits of his power? I prefer the latter version. Gytha was also the mother of King Harold, the last Anglo-Saxon King, who died with a Norman arrow in his eye at the Battle of Hastings in 1066. The Norman conqueror, William, handed Gytha's chapel over to French monks, and built his red sandstone castle on a hill in the city. Naturally, he called it Rougemont, now also the name of a hotel. I can't say that as a child or even as a young man I was much interested in the city's history; familiarity bred not contempt but indifference. But growing up in such an environment must surely have influenced how I came to view time and change. The past was everywhere. By contrast, in most Canadian cities everything is new, or soon will be. Attention is focused on the future rather than on the past, on mastering change rather than accepting and enduring it. (I exclude from this sweeping generalization the Aboriginal and Québécois peoples who are steeped in folk history. Perhaps that is why the rest of Canada has so much trouble understanding and coming to terms with them.) Arriving in Canada when I was thirty, I was excited by the newness of the country, even if the cities were drab and the suburbs appallingly raw. But with roots in the Old World, I probably don't think about time and change in quite the same way as someone raised in Toronto or Vancouver. Europeans have been in North America for about four hundred years, which might seem to guarantee permanency unless you have grown up with the fact that the Romans remained in Exeter, which they called Isca, for about four hundred years, then marched away never to be seen there again.

When I was born my stomach was not fully developed, which meant spending a few months on a diet, preferably in a mild climate, and this led me to another and vastly important part of the physical environment in which I grew up. The kindly doctor's first idea was that mother and I might spend some months in the south of France, but my father objected that he could not possibly afford such a thing. Ah, said the doctor, then he might try a handy line of sand dunes which had their own mild weather system. This magical place was Exmouth Warren, now Dawlish Warren, the home of many rabbits in the mouth of the River Exe less than ten miles south of Exeter. The river first broadens into a mile-wide estuary, passing the deer park at Powderham Castle and villages with such splendid names as Starcross and Cockwood, and then swings around in a bay formed by the Warren sand dunes, which project from the mainland. The river flows out into the English Channel through a passage a few hundred yards wide between the end of the Warren and a resort town called, appropriately, Exmouth. Where the Warren begins at the mainland there were, and still are, golf links, and at far end, opposite Exmouth, there was before Second World War a colony of maybe thirty ramshackle summer homes. A couple were on stilts so that the tide could rise and fall beneath them, one of which always flew a line of signal flags which said, we were told, "If you can read this come in and have one." There was also the beached hull of an old sailing vessel, with windows cut in the sides to make a house, called Kate. But most cottages, as we would call them, were nestled in sand dunes, amid the tall spiky grass.

It was here that father bought a bungalow called simply The Cabin, for £200 (perhaps $10,000 today). It was built of wood, with a corrugated iron roof, with the bay in front and the sea behind. There was no power on the Warren, so we cooked on primus stoves which sometimes flared alarmingly in our wooden house, and went to bed by oil lamp. We drank rainwater collected in iron tanks and boiled, and the outside toilet was connected to wooden barrels buried in the dunes to function as a primitive septic tank. There was one large living room and a double bedroom, a kitchen of sorts and four tiny sleeping rooms, hardly more than closets. When my father bought it the furniture consisted of one table painted with a poker layout, suggesting that the previous owners had been sporting gents. The family spent fourteen summers there, with our cook and a nursemaid in the early years. There was a store of sorts which sold essentials such as candies — we called them sweets — and a mile or so along the beach, where the Warren joined the mainland, there were a couple of cafés for day trippers. But for serious shopping we had to go to Exmouth, which meant taking a boat. There were boatmen who plied for hire, rowing or sailing across the gap between Exmouth and the Warren, which could be turbulent as the tide squeezed in and out of the bay, and every Warren family had a favorite. Ours was a beery old salt who, at the start of every season, met us at Exmouth, loaded us with all our baggage into his little open boat until the gunwales were only a few inches above the water, and set off. If there was a suitable wind, he raised a tiny triangular lugsail and stuck an oar over the stern with which to steer. No breeze, and he rowed, sweating beer and grumbling. He took us as close to The Cabin as the tide would allow, and we had to to walk the rest of the way across soft sand and up and down dunes, carrying our cases. It was inevitable, of course, that we would soon get our own boat, and the first was a heavy, clinker-built — that is, the planks overlapped each other instead of being edge to edge — eleven-footer, called *Devonia*, and probably a cast-off ship's boat. Perhaps my earliest memory is sitting with my father in the stern, dressed in a blue coat with brass buttons, as my brother John rowed along the path cast by the moon on the still sea. I suppose I was three or four. We began to learn to sail in that old boat, and John went on to become a self-taught but well-known boat designer and builder.

When still in his teens — I use that word although there was no such a thing as a teenager then; you were a boy, a youth or a man — he designed and built for me, in our third floor playroom at home, an eight-foot sailing boat, with paddles for alternative locomotion. He pulled a piece of old black oak out of the rose bed in the garden and shaped it to make the prow, and for a sail we cut and hand-stitched the thick canvas of an old sailing vessel. When it was finished, he rigged a block and tackle and we swung it through the window and down into the back garden. Unfortunately, he used a composite wood for the hull, and no matter how often we painted and caulked, it sopped up water and had to be dried out every few weeks. But I still have a photo of me, aged about ten, scooting along under sail in that little boat. John's most successful design was a racing dinghy called the 505 — 5.05 metres — and they are still raced all over the world, including here in Toronto. As a youth, he loved to race with the Exmouth sailing club, and as any sailor will tell you, racing skippers who are mild ashore can become tyrants in a boat, so while I often crewed for him, I learned to detest racing — and in fact lost whatever competitive spirit I might have had. But the love of cruising has stayed with me, and with friends I have explored Lake Ontario, Lake Erie, and the North Channel of Georgian Bay. When I hear people complain that the lakes are cold even in summer, I think that they should try the English Channel at any time.

We were able to run free and wild on the Warren, in or on the water almost as much as on land, sailing, rowing, swimming, and enjoying all sorts of adventures with hardly an adult in sight. A mackerel fishing fleet went out on most days from the village of Lympstone — now the site of a huge Royal Marines base — and once they caught a small shark in the nets and brought it ashore to kill it on the beach. They told us they would sell it to a fish and chip shop, but I suppose they were pulling our legs. But what excitement! When porpoises drove millions of mackerel into the bay we could go out with no more than a piece of silver paper and a hook on a string and pull in the little fish until it became boring. Ruthlessly, we pulled soft crabs from their hiding places when they were changing shells and cut them up for bait. I couldn't do it now. But there was retribution: Once, casting with a rod and line, I managed to lodge a hook in my finger while the weight went seaward. My father had to take me in the boat to Exmouth hospital where the doctor had an easy solution; drive the hook right through the finger, snip off the barb, and pull out the shank. I had the scar for years. Airplanes were not common in those times but one day a pilot lost in the mist landed on the beach. The people in the next bungalow entertained him to lunch while we hovered enviously outside, then pointed him towards the nearest airfield, and off he went. The railway line between London and the southwest ran along the seawall on the mainland facing us across the estuary. At night we could see the lighted trains and dream of where they were bound, north and east to a London we had never visited, or south and west to Penzance near the very tip of England, Land's End.

Nowadays when my wife and I visit Britain we take the train to the south west. Just outside Exeter the line joins the estuary and it's a wonderfully scenic trip for miles, tunnelling through the red sandstone headlands, and following the coast so closely that it runs along the seafront of villages and towns. It used to be, perhaps still is, that if you took a window seat in the dining room of the Courtenay Arms Hotel in the estuary village of Starcross — Courtenay being the family name of the Earls of Devon whose castle is nearby — you could look up at the underside of the trains as they raced by a few feet away. I suppose people were so anxious to get railway service that they would accept almost any condition the Great Western Railway company demanded. The line was built by a visionary engineer with a towering reputation, Isambard Kingdom Brunel, but he overreached himself and lost a huge amount of money when he chose the stretch of line at Starcross to experiment with the madcap idea that engines could be powered by atmospheric pressure. Rather more reliable is the ferry from Starcross across the estuary to Exmouth; it has been running since the twelfth century.

We children were at the Warren in the summer of 1932 — I was six years old — when my father, who had commuted to Exeter, returned to tell us our mother was dead. She had gone into a nursing home for an operation to remove gallstones obstructing her bile duct, and died from pulmonary embolism, or blood clot in the lungs. I know no more about it than that; it was never discussed and I never thought to ask my father for information. Why a nursing home rather than a hospital? I don't know, although I believe that the middle and upper classes tended to favour private nursing homes over public hospitals. The death of my mother must of course have been a defining event in my life, but I have few memories of her. I do remember, or think I do, picking raspberries for breakfast with her in the back garden of our first home in Exeter. My father told me that when she dressed as Father Christmas and appeared in the living room, I asked why Santa was wearing Mummy's shoes — perhaps the first signs of the observant and skeptical reporter. I have a faint sense, more a feeling than a memory, of how it felt to hold her hand, sort of warm and cool at the same time. Less pleasantly, I had for some reason a horror of brown apple cores and I seem to remember her teasing me with a core, pushing it toward me. Perhaps that is why I still find them distasteful. And that's about it for memories.

There was a housemaid/nursemaid who looked after me, as was common in the middle class, so perhaps I did not see that much of my mother. But I do remember, and wish I didn't, what I thought when, having heard of her death, I went along the beach to find a friend to with whom to share the news. I thought, "I should feel sad, but I don't." My brother, aged eleven, was devastated by mother's death, but he was more aware of her than I was. She had, for example, been teaching him to play golf with a set of clubs cut down to his size. My sister was only two and unaware of what had happened. But there was I, apparently unmoved and wondering why. Was I already a detached, introspective, unemotional child, or was I instinctively raising psychological defences against a loss I could not acknowledge? Certainly, as an adult, I have never been much moved by death — except of animals. I shed no tears when my father died of a stroke at seventy; I was having breakfast in Toronto when my brother called with the news, and I went back to eating toast and marmalade. Nor were there tears when my brother died of cancer at seventy. I can rationalize my lack of feeling; death is part of life and comes to us all, so why make a fuss when a relative or friend departs? But that did not work when I took our much-loved family dog to be put down. I was with him when the vet gave him an overdose of anaesthetic and, watching him go to sleep and die, I was torn between grief — the tears came later — and the feeling that we should all be so lucky in the manner of our going. But, then, I have always been fond of dogs; they seem to me on the whole to be of better disposition than most humans: faithful friends, cheerful, good tempered through thick and thin.

In my own defence I can say that if the death of others leaves me unmoved, so does the prospect of my own death, which at my age cannot be long delayed. My brother accepted early death as preferable to the prospect of a painful old age as his incurable cancer spread, and I feel the same. I have completed a living will requesting that there be no heroic — strange word — measures to keep me from dying. But for me the troubling question remains: Was I already an unfeeling and introspective child when my mother died, or did her death make me so?

My mother was buried in Weston, perhaps because she grew up there and her sister Babs still lived there. I remember nothing of the funeral, but I do remember that when my father was driving my brother and I home to Exeter, the canvas top of the car was folded down and I was allowed to sit up on it with my head in the wind. And then we stopped halfway and I had a ginger beer. Aunty Babs came to Exeter to look after us, but that lasted only a few weeks, no doubt because of the mutual dislike she shared with my father. The burden then fell on my father's mother, Alice, a formidable widow. I have a photo of me, aged about four, with my two grandmothers. My mother's mother, Catherine, is a plump, cheerful old lady, and she has her arm around my waist. Grandma Alice is standing erect, stern-faced and in black from her enormous hat to her shoes, perhaps still in mourning for her husband who had died a couple of years earlier. I realize now what a sacrifice she made in selling her comfortable home in Weston, leaving her friends, and moving to Exeter at the age of seventy-two to run her son's household of three children and two servants. But I have no warm memories — and there I go again, coldly detached. Her main concern, naturally, was my two-year-old sister. My brother was soon sent off to board at a minor public school, as my mother had wished, and I was pretty much left to my own devices. I remember that granny scraped her fork on her false teeth when she ate, which at least has made me conscious in later life of how easy it is for adults to offend children. And she did take me to tea in a grand restaurant on my birthdays and allow me to dive into a parfait, an ice cream and fruit concoction which came in a tall glass requiring the use of a very long spoon.

She also took me to visit relatives; he was a tenant farmer and his wife was probably the worst cook ever, producing every day meals that could be eaten only with fortitude. On hot afternoons granny and I lay sweating on a featherbed while she read sad stories that reduced us both to tears. I remember being hoisted onto the back of a terrifyingly tall horse, and have never been there since. In my view, horses are too large and nervous to be trusted. And I can still see the sad, accusing eye of a rabbit shot by the farmer at harvest time. Granny died in 1940, aged seventy-nine, and my father said later it was probably a blessing because she would not have been able to cope with the difficulties of running a household in time of war — a questionable idea because she was a tough old lady who had lived through one war in which casualties were much more numerous than in World War II. On learning of her death, I did not cry.

I was a shy child who retreated to my bedroom rather than meet visitors, and while I thought I had overcome that defect when I grew up, it was pointed out that as an adult I pose for pictures, which I hate having taken, with my head on one side, apparently because I am still trying to escape notice. I never went to children's parties because I was afraid I might be

embarrassed by girls, of whom I knew none except my sister, until I went
to work at sixteen and, despite my best efforts, found them unavoidable.
Music, particularly swing, was pleasant in my ear but meant nothing to my
feet so I have never been able to dance. The last attempt was when, embold-
ened by drink, I persuaded my wife to try again. I fell over, and she said,
"Never again." I did not stay at school for lunch, or dinner as we called it,
because I was afraid I would have to eat food I did not like and would then
be sick — throw up, we would say — in public. I cycled a mile-and-a-half
home to eat, and then returned, all in about ninety minutes. That fear of
eating in public stayed with me until, as an apprentice reporter, I had to
travel to country towns and would have died of starvation had I not overcome my problem. In those early years I developed a way of coping with
fears, if not conquering them, by asking myself what was the worst thing
that could happen. I could then accept that the worst thing would not be
the end of the world — close perhaps, but not the end.

But if I was an insecure, mixed up and introspective kid, I did have
close friends, one a neighbour at home and the other at school, and with
both I still have occasional contact. And I did get on quite well with my
father. Many of his insurance clients were farmers, and he sometimes
took me in the company car to visit them, usually on market day in one
of the rural towns around Exeter. He liked to tell a story which both
amused and horrified me, and then provided the same delicious thrill for
my own children when I retold it: A farmer once took him to lunch in
the village pub where they enjoyed a hearty meal, the standard "Soup,
meat and veg., apple pie, and cheese," washed down with a pint of ale —
all of which the farmer pronounced so good that they would have the
meal again, which they did.

On weekends, father played golf at the Warren links, where in fact
he ended his days as club secretary. He often took the Exeter city clerk
as his guest, and I'm sure it was entirely coincidental that he insured the
city buses. I sometimes went along to carry his clubs, or to take our dog,
Chips, for a run in the sand dunes. It would be wrong to say that father
and I were close; I never discussed with him my feelings or problems, nor
he with me. After he died, my brother and sister discovered when going
through his papers that he had been paying maintenance for an illegitimate daughter, born in 1947. As he had obviously not wanted us to

know about it, they decided not to try to identify the mother or the child, and in fact did not for years tell me, in Canada. Somewhere, I may have a half-sister. My father had been living on his pension and left almost nothing, but my brother sent me a pair of gold cufflinks. I suppose that I never really knew my mother or my father, but at least my father and I were comfortable with each other, which is better than some father-child relationships of which I have heard.

I quite enjoyed school, which was of course a formative influence. My family was not religious; I was not christened, which could have been because of my health, but I don't recall ever going to church as a family. However, the school a few hundred yards from our first house, to which I was sent at the age of three or four, happened to be much influenced by religion. It was called Mount Radford, but was better known as Vine's, after the proprietor and headmaster, Theodore Vine, a member of the Plymouth Brethren, a form of Lutheranism combining, says my dictionary, elements of Calvinism and Pietism. There were perhaps a dozen boarders who lived in the big house with Mr. and Mrs. Vine and were mainly the sons of missionaries serving abroad. The masters tended to be enthusiastic Methodists, and the hundred or so day boys, of which I was one, were mainly the sons of shopkeepers and other small businessmen. Sons of farmers were let out early, to the envy of the rest of us, so that they could catch trains to their homes in the country. We followed the national board of education curriculum, preparing us for the Oxford school leaving certificate. But Vine seemed to me to put a special emphasis on Bible studies, with prayers and a hymn every morning, and occasional visits from missionaries who, in return for our pennies, told uplifting and sometimes entertaining stories about converting the black heathen.

Vine was an excellent teacher but an austere man who stalked about in a mortarboard and black robe in which there was a pocket for a bamboo cane, a hidden intimidator seldom used but always threatening. I was a casual student, interested in history, English literature, and composition, a class in which I somehow internalized rules of grammar and syntax which I can't articulate but which send an alarm signal when something is wrong. These days I get signals with almost every newspaper or book I read. I accept that language and usage change, and that I became obsessive about some rather silly rules, such as split infinitives. But I insist on drawing the line at misusage that changes meaning. For example, even the most respected writers misplace the word *only* in sentences and so change meaning. To explain this to students, when I was teaching at Carleton University in Ottawa, I invented a handy guide:

"Only I drink sherry in the morning," means that no one else does.
"I only drink sherry in the morning," means that I do nothing else.
"I drink only sherry in the morning," means that I drink nothing else.
"I drink sherry only in the morning," means that I do not drink it at other times.

A student once remarked that if I drank less sherry I might not have this obsession with usage, so I changed *sherry* to *coffee*. But I trust this guide will now lurk in the mind of every reader, and rise to worry them when they write a sentence using the word *only*.

I enjoyed some mathematics because numbers are so reliable — they always add up the same way, or they ought to — but science was and remains a mystery; I never did figure out whether the 2 in H_2O referred to the parts of hydrogen or of oxygen. It could be either, couldn't it? I was hopeless at French; Vine gave up in disgust after I got two marks out of fifty despite his special coaching. Maybe it was the illogicality of irregular verbs that got logical me down. And then there was the Bible. Vine taught us the Gospel According to St. Paul in preparation for our leaving exam, and it involved verse-by-verse scrutiny and a good deal of memorizing. Shakespeare, incidentally, was taught in the same way, with the assigned play in my year being *The Tempest*: all that wonderful language reduced to nit-picking analysis and mental drudgery. But I read recently that London cabbies actually enlarge their brains when they memorize "The Knowledge" of streets and addresses, which they have to do to obtain a licence, so maybe forcing kids to memorize texts did pay off.

But back to the Bible, as they say. I can't remember exactly when I came to the conclusion but, ever the detached analyst, I left school an agnostic. I should explain my reasoning, but I do not wish to give offence to those of other opinions, so let me say at once that I do not claim to know the truth. Indeed, it is precisely because I see no conclusive evidence either for or against the existence of some sort of directing or superior power that I am an agnostic. Nor do I mock faith by saying, as I think Oscar Wilde did, that faith is believing in something one knows to be untrue, or as H.L. Mencken put it, faith is having an illogical belief in the occurrence of the improbable. Faith may be given to some and not to others, and for all those capable of faith in a kindly God it must be a comfort in our turbulent and uncertain world. But that is not for me. While I am prepared to accept that there might be some sort of superior power, I see no evidence whatsoever that there is a loving God who sees every sparrow fall and has a personal interest in me — and I see plenty of evidence to the contrary. The Old Testament God was clearly far from loving. We are told that when he became displeased with his handiwork in creating the world, he drowned almost every living thing. The God of the New Testament is hardly better; he is said to have arranged matters so that his son had to be crucified in order that the rest of us might have a chance of being forgiven our sins and admitted to his presence. Some loving father.

Who Jesus was, and what he actually did and said, is still being debated after some two thousand years, but the notion that he is worthy of worship because he gave his life for us hardly bears scrutiny. Lots of mortals have endured torture and death for much less without being proclaimed gods. But perhaps Jesus has suffered the fate of many prophets: In trying to translate the master's hazy vision into regulations for the faithful, disciples become bureaucrats and the essence of the teaching is lost — or, worse, turned into a tyranny. St. Paul was perhaps the first Christian bureaucrat, mullahs seem to mess up Mohammed, and Lenin made the worst of Marx. The question remains, however, of why, if there is no God and no accountability at the end of life, we behave even half decently instead of indulging our worst instincts. The best answer I have is that it is in our own interest to treat others as we wish them to treat us, and if that comes from the Sermon on the Mount I don't think it proves Jesus to be anything more than a wise man. So, lacking conviction, I have to be content to do the best I can to make the world a slightly better place, or at least no worse than I found it, without asking or expecting divine help. But, and this is a sobering thought, questions such as these may not bother modern children who seem hardly to be aware of the Bible which, right or wrong, has been such a central part of our cultural history.

It was usual to take the Oxford school leaving exam at sixteen, but I became eligible in the winter of 1941, when I was still fifteen, and, to Vine's considerable surprise, passed with sufficient honours to have won "Exemption from Matriculation" had I had the requisite foreign language credit, the mystifying French. The explanation for my modest success was in part that I had always enjoyed exams, writing around a question to which I did not know the answer, to influence the examiner by displaying what I did know. Later in life, I used this technique in journalism to persuade editors and readers that I knew more about the subject than I really did. But looking back on the school years, I think I got a pretty good grounding in the basics. I learned also that I was hopeless in sports of all kinds. In the school yard we played cricket with balls we made ourselves by encasing a bundle of rags in a string net and soaking the result in water. The explanation for that curious custom, I think, was not poverty but respect for the school windows and a healthy fear of what damage a hard ball could do when bounced on an asphalt surface. There was a school sports field about a mile away, and there we played with the proper equipment. By appearing regularly as a volunteer to umpire games or, with others, to replace a horse in tugging an enormous roller over the wicket, I earned a place eventually in the school's cricket team. I was opening bat with the less than heroic role of dispiriting the opposing bowlers, not by scoring runs but by stonewalling their best efforts. But we weren't much good as a team anyway and always lost our annual game with the inmates of a nearby asylum, perhaps because we were distracted by the hope that they would act like lunatics, which they never did. I was as averse to competition in school sports as I was in dinghy racing, but that may have been because I knew I was without talent and would lose. In other words, I was unwilling to face defeat. Against that painful thought, when I played chess I preferred to lose a good game than to win a poor one. But for whatever reason I have never been interested in professional sports, which cuts me off from an important element in male culture, even from the Canadian national culture of hockey. I never read the sports pages in the newspapers or watch games on TV — and I couldn't care less who wins in the Olympics, which I suppose makes me an alien in today's culture, and an agnostic alien at that. So much for my childhood.

~ *Chapter 3* ~

Going to War

I was vaguely aware from childhood that war was approaching. There were black-shirted fascists handing out pamphlets in the High Street, and I was told that they scuffled with Communists on Saturday nights, even in sleepy old Exeter. After the Munich crisis in 1938, we were all fitted with gas masks, and there was much talk of civil defence against air attack with bombs that might explode, create fires, or shower us with poison gas. But life went on, and we spent the summer of 1939, as usual, on the Warren. I remember when we were shopping in Exmouth one morning seeing the front page of the *Daily Express* announcing that Germany and the Soviet Union had signed a non-aggression pact, and being told that this made war more likely. We had no radio and heard that war had been declared when a police constable pushed his bike over the sand dunes to tell us and others that we must black-out our windows. That was not a problem; we just turned out the oil lamps, but for the first time in memory there were no lights on the seafront across the water in Exmouth, and no lighted trains passing in the night. The lights did not come on again for five years.

When we packed up to return to Exeter we knew that we were losing a battle to another threat, the sea, which had been eroding the dunes year by year and was by then almost at the backdoor of The Cabin. During the winter storms in 1940, the sea finally broke through the Warren to join with the estuary bay. All the summer homes were eventually swept away and the Warren became a sandbank visible only at low tide. But years later, the unpredictable sea began to return the sand, and the Warren dunes rose again, although smaller than before. There are no buildings now and signs on the beach say, pleasingly, "Give Way to Birds" because it is part of a much larger sanctuary.

I was still at school, of course, when the war began and became probably the greatest transforming experience of my life — as indeed it must have been for everyone who was near the front lines. It changed everything, and often for the better, including social and moral values, and economic and political expectations. It is a disturbing paradox that the world was a much better place in 1945 than it had been in 1939, and reflecting on it, I realize that the social values of Britain in the war years were almost the opposite of those today. In short, they were those of the left, liberty, equality, fraternity. The national spirit was fraternal, not individualistic. We were united against a common enemy, and the struggle for liberty took precedence over everything else.

Even the famous British class system softened, and people who would hardly have talked to each other in peacetime found common cause and a measure of fellowship. The goal was production, not consumption, and in fact it was unpatriotic, often illegal, to consume more than one's equal share. Food, clothing, and petrol were severely rationed: four ounces of butter per week, an ounce or two of cheese, four ounces of bacon or ham, two ounces of the essential tea, a couple of shillings worth of meat which families pooled in order to buy a pitiful Sunday roast. One had to present a ration book to buy almost anything edible: dried and canned vegetables, rice, cereal, canned fish, cookies, candies, everything except bread, and for that you lined up at the bakery to buy the standard, greyish National Loaf. And then of course one had to queue, often for hours, for a ration book when they were issued from time to time.

The popular fish and chips were not rationed, but the shops could open only when they had cooking oil, so one went out looking for a shop with the welcome notice in the window, "Frying Tonight." The unthinkable happened when pubs occasionally ran out of beer, and Scotch whisky, like cigarettes, was mostly "under the bar," which meant that it was reserved for regular customers and no others need apply. Feeding pets was a nightmare: There were special shops selling horsemeat dyed green to prevent it from going onto the black market for human consumption, and one of my jobs as a schoolboy was to line up at a horsemeat shop and, if supplies held out until I got to the head of the queue, tuck a bloody parcel into my schoolbag for the ride home to a grateful dog. If we had known it at the time, no doubt we would have used the American saying popular during the Depression when clothes were an unnecessary expense, "Make it do, wear it out, use it up, do without." We recycled waste to an extent that makes today's programs look half-hearted. There were special bins for everything, including bones. Exhorted to give aluminum to make more Spitfires, we lined the streets outside our homes with cooking pots, learning only much later that they proved unsatisfactory for the job. Miles of old books lined the roads during paper drives, and the iron railings on our front garden were cut down and taken away, along with everyone else's.

When Winston Churchill formed his coalition government in 1940, political debate and media criticism almost disappeared. Those few critics who remained, mostly on the left, were frowned upon, even reviled. Newspapers were reduced to four or six pages and found ways to print even in the "gutters" between two pages. The BBC radio news at 9 p.m. became the national source of reliable — or so we thought — information. We know now that after the collapse of France and the rout of the British army, Churchill seriously doubted Britain's ability to survive. But at the time his defiant speeches rallied the country, and I doubt that the thought of defeat bothered many Britons. Call it stupidity or arrogance, but it probably saved us. The spirit was that of the solitary British solder, in David Low's great cartoon, holding his rifle high and saying, "Alright, alone !"

It would be wrong to say war made people happy. Life was hard, particularly for women left to raise children on their own, and it was often tedious for everybody, but war removed a lot of reasons for envy and complaint. In fact, complaining became almost illegitimate and brought a swift and sarcastic retort, "Don't yer know there's a war on?" And in a way life was fulfilling; everyone had a job to do, and most did it, which was a relief for millions after the mass unemployment of the Great Depression. This helps perhaps to explain another paradox: While we claim to hate war, history suggests that it has been a popular occupation in most centuries. When wars were declared there was more celebrating than sobbing, with patriotic crowds marching through the streets in many countries. Now, films, TV programs, and books about past wars appear every year and often are hugely popular. In my view, the absence of a popular war helped to explain the militancy of young people when they opposed the unpopular war in Vietnam and struggled for civil rights in the 1960s and 1970s. I was teaching in a university at the time and was intrigued by the fact that students dressed in military-style clothing and spoke of their protests in military jargon: a march here, an offensive there, the campaign for this or that. They were seeking a substitute for war. I understood how they felt because for me the Second World War came as an adventure, a chance to escape from the routine of normal living.

My brother was eighteen when the war began and he soon volunteered for the Royal Navy. He was trained as a coder — encoding and decoding radio messages — and volunteered to be part of a small crew taking a ship to New Zealand, a long and uncomfortable voyage. He returned to Britain in 1943 and was commissioned and trained as a meteorologist, a handy skill for a sailing enthusiast who later took up ocean racing. When invasion threatened in 1940, my father joined the Home Guard, and I was thrilled when he brought home a rifle. It was still greasy from storage, and was called a Ross rifle. I discovered much later that Ross rifles had been manufactured in Canada to equip troops serving in the Boer War, and also the Royal North West Mounted Police. Despite various improvements, however, the rifles were never satisfactory and were eventually abandoned during the First World War when the Canadian army adopted the British Lee-Enfield. But so desperate was the need for rifles in 1940, after the British army left much of its equipment on the beaches of Dunkirk, that the old Ross rifles were dug out of storage and issued to the Home Guard.

Stranger things happened in those days. Some of the brighter sparks in the Exeter Home Guard mounted a machine gun on a tiny Austin 7 car as our answer to the German Panzers. Minefields were laid across the Warren golf links to hold up German invasion forces, but there were paths through the mines so that golfers could continue to play. Tank traps were installed on the beaches at Exmouth, which made it difficult to land dinghies, but they were used mainly as racks for bathers' clothes and towels. Coastal defence guns were dug into the red sandstone cliffs to command the approaches to the Warren beaches, but as the nearest point in France was Cherbourg, about a hundred miles across the Channel, I can't imagine, in retrospect, why anyone thought it remotely possible that the Germans would attempt such a dangerous and difficult crossing.

The war was going badly at the end of 1941 when we heard on the radio that Japan had bombed Pearl Harbor. "We've won the war," said my father, with unusual prescience — and with undue optimism because it was not until several days later that Germany and Italy declared war on the United States. That bears repeating when so many people, including most Americans, are under the impression that they entered the war in Europe to support Britain in the defence of liberty and democracy. They entered in fact because Hitler and Mussolini declared war on them in support of Japan. Of course, the United States had been aiding Britain and edging toward war with Germany, but one can only speculate about what might have happened had Germany and Italy not forced the issue. Obviously, there would have been a powerful argument in the United States for concentrating its strength against Japan and leaving Europe to its own war. But my father proved to be right, and within a year or so American troops began arriving in and around Exeter.

My image of America, like those of millions of other around the world, had been shaped by Hollywood movies, but the American soldiers tended to confirm our good impressions. They were on average bigger than our own soldiers, better uniformed, better educated, and with better manners. They were instructed in how to treat British civilians, and their military police were quick to remove anyone who seemed to be causing trouble. So while there were incidents, mainly over women, most Britons tended to see Americans as saviours whose presence guaranteed victory over Germany. That may be why, many years later, I could not sympathize with the anti-Americanism of many Canadian nationalists who saw, indeed, still see, the United States not as an ally but as a threat.

I became a "Firewatcher" while still at school. The job was to watch for incendiary bombs and, if possible, put them out before they started a major fire, with a bucket of sand or a stirrup pump — that is, a pump with one leg in a bucket of water to suck, and one leg outside on which the pumper stood to stabilize the operation. Stirrup pumps were distributed by the thousand, and if they sound like an poor way to tackle a bomb, the girl who later became my wife actually made it work: she and an aunt rushed our in their nightdresses when an incendiary fell in the garden and put it out. Even more remarkably, an incendiary fell through the roof of the house next door and was promptly kicked downstairs by an old lady and extinguished. Nothing as exciting as that happened to me.

With a friend, I spent an occasional night firewatching at our school. We played chess and the headmaster came down in his dressing gown and trounced us both. At home, when air raid sirens sounded I put on my steel helmet and, with my father, turned out to patrol the crescent in which we lived. But not as promptly one night as I might have done, because I had got too accustomed to sirens when German bombers passed over, going to or from Devonport, a major naval base about forty miles away, or Bristol, an industrial centre seventy miles away. Sometimes the planes dumped their bombs on us when they couldn't find their real target, or perhaps were being chased by night fighters. There were in fact nineteen raids on Exeter between August 1940 and May 1942, most of them minor affairs.

I was in bed on the third floor of our house — on a hill about a mile from the city centre — on the night of May 3-4, 1942 and did not pay much attention when the sirens went and I heard bombs exploding a couple of miles away. But then I saw the night sky turn red and realized there was a major fire in the city. In fact, great stretches of the High Street were ablaze, including Tudor era buildings which burned all too easily. My father and I donned our steel helmets and went outside, while my sister, our housekeeper, Alice, and the dog, and a new kitten, promptly named Blitz, took shelter in a sort of store room between the sitting and dining rooms. When, a little later, I tried to check on them, I had a struggle to open the front door; blast had lifted the linoleum throughout the house, jamming the doors. I don't know what caused the blast. No bombs fell very close to us, but nearby, on the county cricket ground, anti-aircraft guns were blasting away. Or perhaps the great fire in the centre caused a powerful wind as it sucked in oxygen.

We learned after the war that 40 Junkers 88 bombers flew up the River Exe to find the little city of about 80,000 people, and dropped 10,000 incendiaries and some 160 explosive bombs to spread the blaze. About 160 people were killed and hundreds more wounded. One bomb fell through the roof of the cathedral and exploded, but they built medieval churches to last and, with a huge tarpaulin over the roof, the place survived until it could be repaired when peace came. The new library and a million books burned, much to my dismay: I was a great reader, even then, and it had been my custom to stop at the library on the way home from school to replenish the supply of books — G.A. Henty's stirring stories about boys adventuring in the Empire, and, always favourites, yarns about boys who ran away to sea. I remember the indignation of a librarian when I borrowed a short book, read it over tea, and tried to return it the same evening: Not allowed!

We didn't know at the time why the Germans had picked on Exeter, a city of little or no obvious military or industrial importance. There were rumors but censorship was tight; I had just begun work as an apprentice reporter and spent the next few days phoning our reports through to London for censoring. We were allowed to announce that there had been a raid on a place in the southwest, and to describe the damage in general terms, but not to name the city because, it was ruled, that would show the Germans, who might have been lost, where they had dropped their bombs. Actually, as we found out after the war, the Germans not only knew they had blitzed Exeter, but also why, and were boasting about it. The raid was in fact a reprisal for an attack by the Royal Air Force in March on the historic German city of Lubeck, on the Baltic. Sir Arthur Harris, chief of bomber command and known popularly as Bomber Harris, had come to the sobering conclusion that night bombing of specific German targets was so inaccurate as to have little value, and he decided to try the tactic of attacking whole German cities, setting them ablaze where possible. Lubeck was chosen as an experimental target because it could be approached over water where there were no A-A guns, and because it was "flammable," many of the buildings being medieval. The raid was a success in the sense that Lubeck was set ablaze, but Hitler, outraged at this uncivilized form of warfare, ordered that reprisal raids be carried out on historic British cities. The targets were picked from the famous German guide book, *Baedeker*, and so the raids on Exeter and other cathedral cities were called Baedeker raids.

When I told this story some fifty years later in the course of a travel article about Exeter published in *The Globe and Mail*, I was attacked by an Ontario judge who had been a bomber pilot in Britain and had taken part in the raid on Lubeck. He insisted that old city was a legitimate target because it was a port and an industrial city manufacturing U-boat components. Perhaps so, but that was not why Harris made it the target for the new form of fire bomb attack — terror bombing, as it came to be called. Similarly, the British Admiralty's chart-making division had been evacuated from London to Exeter, but that was not why Hitler ordered the attack on the city. The Germans were wrong in claiming that Exeter had been destroyed, but acres of the ancient centre were, and the city has never recovered its former charm. In the postwar rush to rebuild, more attention was paid to commerce than to history and culture.

For me, these first years of the war were a waiting time. I wanted desperately to join the armed services, preferably the navy. Why? Adventure, I suppose, a challenge, new experiences, independence in the sense of leaving home and becoming a man. I believe those are the reasons most men, and most women, volunteer in a war. It's absurd to call us heroes just because we served, or to pretend that we all marched off to defend liberty — and even more absurd to call those who were conscripted against their will heroes and martyrs. There were of course heroes, men and women who served far beyond the call of duty, displayed unusual courage, gave their lives to save others. To call us all heroes demeans those who deserve the title. I registered as a volunteer as soon as I was old enough, which was seventeen years and eight months. A close friend who also was working as an apprentice reporter volunteered with me, and we were called on December 23, 1943, two days before Christmas and four weeks before my eighteenth birthday.

The navy gathered most of its recruits in what had been a holiday camp — Butlin's Holiday Camp — near Skegness on the flat North Sea coast of Lincolnshire. In times of peace, workers and their families enjoyed cheap holidays, living in long lines of wooden huts, grandly called chalets, and eating and playing in vast, jerry built halls. Over the entrance there hung a welcoming sign that said, as I recall, "Your Pleasure is Our Endeavor," and it remained there, heavy with irony, when the Admiralty took over. Pleasure was not on the agenda for the scores of thousands of aspiring sailors who passed under the sign; basic training, square bashing, discipline, indoctrination, inoculation and immunization, and more discipline were. For a well-brought-up middle-class youth, the culture shock was severe. My shipmates — in the navy they are shipmates even in a shore establishment — came from all parts of Britain, and Ireland. There were volunteer youths of my age, and older men with families, because by 1943 Britain was calling up men in their late 30s. For the first time in my life, I was living, and suffering all sorts of indignities, with mates from the working class and with accents I could hardly understand. I have a group photo taken at the time in which I am a pudgy youth with owl-like glasses, with my head on one side, of course.

The living huts had never been intended for winter and were perishing cold. There was no hot water in the communal washrooms. And there were lots of rough sailors to shout orders at us every day. The food would have been almost inedible had the sea air and exercise not made us starving hungry. Breakfast one day a week was canned herrings in tomato sauce, a delicacy so familiar in the navy that it was known just as "herrin's in." Not many recruits could stomach them for breakfast so there was always a stack of unwanted cans at the head of the long dining tables. I got to like them, and in fact still do: On toast, they make a cheap, tasty and nourishing meal. We were tested for skills and, partly because I wore glasses and was assumed to be able to write legibly in view of my reporting skills, I was assigned to the stores branch. The navy has a nickname for everything, and we stores assistants were called Jack Dusty, presumably because we laboured in the stores where we would always be dusty. It was not the seamanlike role which I had imagined, and our uniform was a white shirt, collar and tie, with jacket and pants, not the jaunty jumper and bell bottoms of real sailors — which the Admiralty, with unconscious irony, called "men dressed as seamen." But while we might not appear to be real fighting men, in a ship we would all share the same risks.

We marched, counter-marched, and did rifle drill, which was highly recommended by grinning instructors for arms painfully swollen by vaccinations. We were tested for swimming in a huge metal tank, and those who seemed to be drowning were hooked out by a petty officer with a long pole. We were taught the rudiments of rowing a ship's boat which was firmly secured in place in one of Mr. Butlin's swimming pools. And we did all manner of manual work, washing literally thousands of dishes in the kitchens, sweeping the roadways, even labouring in the sewage farm. My favourite duty was in the guard house-cum-cell block where, after a night spent reading, rolling fags with the duty-free tobacco thoughtfully supplied by the Admiralty, and making sure the drunks in the cells were surviving, one could go up and down the rows of huts at dawn, hammering on the doors to turn out resentful shipmates. There were occasional half-day leaves, but all there was to do in Skegness was to line up at a café for eggs and chips, or sausage and chips on good days, before heading for the pub.

The friend with whom I had joined up was selected as officer material and sent off for training where he suffered perhaps a worse fate than not being selected in the first place. The navy in its inscrutable wisdom suddenly decided it needed no more officers and tossed his class back into the pool, where he became a seaman. We met again a year or two later in Hong Kong, he aboard a ship and I at a shore base. I also was a victim of inscrutable wisdom; instead of the regular three months at Skegness, my group spent five, mainly doing clean-up duties, before we ascended to Heaven, which is to say, private billets in London, and training at Highgate College, a famous school commandeered for war service. The navy, of course, had its own arcane system of bookkeeping, assigning to each of thousands of items a price which bore not the remotest relation to prices in the shops. It had probably been invented by Nelson, or around his time, and I found the study of it boring in the extreme.

However, I was kept awake — most of the time, anyway — by the arrival of Hitler's secret weapon, the V1 buzz bomb. That was a pilotless plane that went put-put-putting through the sky until it ran out of fuel and crashed, usually on London. Sitting in class, we would hear the distinctive engine noise, and if it was anywhere near us when it stopped, the lot of us, including the instructor, would sink below a desk. When I passed the course, without distinction, I was sent to the naval depot at Devonport, adjoining Plymouth and only forty or so miles from Exeter, to await further posting. Devonport barracks were notorious, some buildings dating back to the Napoleonic war. It was rumored that the Admiralty had tried to sell them to the Prison Commissioners who found them not up to standard for felons. The usual escape was to go to sea, which is perhaps what the Admiralty had in mind. But there were ancient seamen, known as Barrack Stanchions, who lived in odd corners of the old buildings, and sometimes took a free meal in a seamen's mission in the town, one of which was known as Jago's. They did not much of anything but dodge draft chits issued by the master at arms, the ship's policeman, much feared but for some reason known in naval slang as the Jaunty. (The master's deputy, a regulating petty officer, was known more appropriately as the Crusher.) The navy had a satirical song for many situations, most sung to hymn tunes and too rude to repeat, but one went like this:

O I wonder, yes I wonder
Did the jaunty make a blunder when he made out this draft chit for me
For I've been a barrack stanchion and I've dined in Jago's mansion
And now they are sending me to sea.

Eventually, and none too soon, I and the rest of an entire ship's crew, some hundreds of us, were sent by special train to Greenock, on the Clyde, near Glasgow, to commission HMS *Empire Spearhead*. She was a mass produced Liberty ship configured as a landing ship and intended for the invasion of Europe, which by then had happened. The interior included troop decks with metal framed canvas cots four or five high, and on davits along the sides she carried assault landing craft — LCAs — manned by Royal Marine crews and designed to carry forty or so men from the ship to the beach. With several other landing ships, we were going to the Pacific to show the Americans that, with the war in Europe well in hand, the Royal Navy was coming to help them defeat Japan. And so I went to war, sailed around the world, saw many interesting places, and had many interesting experiences which I would not have wanted to miss. But life in the navy was never comfortable, the arbitrary discipline was hard to endure, and the class distinction between officers and men was a hangover from past centuries. But looking back on my career as a warrior, I doubt that I made a scrap of difference to the war effort — or, if I did make a difference, I'm not sure whether it was to the advantage of the Allies or the Axis.

My first job in the *Empire Spearhead* was in the supply office where I was a clerk entering columns of figures in ledgers. That ended when, bored to tears, I made an error that took the chief petty officer days of work to discover and correct before he could balance the ship's books. One up for the Axis, I suppose. I was thereupon banished to work as a manual labourer, more or less, in the holds where the stores were kept. I much preferred it to bookkeeping. I had other duties, one of which was to mix and ladle out the lemonade which was issued instead of the traditional lime juice as a protection against scurvy. With the luck that has often attended me, I happened to be doing that job on the foredeck on a golden summer morning when we sailed up New York harbour, to dock in Manhattan — the land promised not by God but by Hollywood. After bombed, blacked-out, rationed Britain, the bright lights and well stocked stores of New York were an extraordinary experience. We worked hard to store ship for the Pacific, and to prepare to take aboard the American sailors and soldiers we were to ferry to New Guinea, but on shore leave with mates I managed to visit The Stage Door Canteen where we saw no stars but encountered a puzzle which remains to this day: On every table there was a can of condensed milk, and nobody seemed to know why.

The Americans, black soldiers and white sailors, came aboard, a band on the dock played "Anchors Away," and off we went into the wild blue yonder, or in fact south and through the Panama Canal. By that time, the Yanks, who were fresh from training camps in a land flowing with steaks and ice cream, had encountered British naval rations and cooking. There were mutters of mutiny, but the presence of Royal Marines with rifles discouraged any such ideas. As the weather got warmer, life below deck for the crew and passengers became difficult. Instead of slinging hammocks in the traditional way, we were assigned to the canvas cots intended originally for troops on short trips to the invasion beaches. The sun beating on steel decks turned the troop decks into ovens and we tossed, turned, and grilled on our cots, stacked one on top of the other. By the time we reached Bora-Bora, an island in French Polynesia which had become a refueling base for ships and aircraft, the idea of a run ashore with dusky maidens with Parisian style was attractive. But it was not of course to be. We were told that there was so much venereal disease on the island that we would be allowed no contact with the island population. Instead, the landing craft would take us to a remote beach for swimming. Better that than nothing, until I came as close to drowning as ever I have in a lifetime of swimming. As young men will, we were wrestling in the surf when a shipmate got one arm around my neck, forcing my head under water, while with the other arm he fought off another mate. All my struggles seemed to him to be just part of the game; to me it became life and death, but fortunately he let go before I expired. From Bora-Bora we went to New Guinea to launch our passengers into jungle warfare which probably made the *Empire Spearhead* look like a cruise ship.

Our next stop was Cairns in Northern Queensland, now a popular resort, but then a frontier town with raised wooden sidewalks and swing doors on the bars. Australian troops recently returned from the Middle East were doing jungle training nearby, and they didn't appreciate the fact that Americans by then were pretty much occupying their country. The arrival of the British navy added to what already a dangerous national mix in a small town. The bars had plenty of beer but few glasses so everybody had to drink out of bottles with the tops cut off, and prostitution was legal. One evening Australian soldiers who seemed to feel they had not received satisfaction for money in a brothel dismantled a large brass bed and threw it piece by piece into the street, to the applause of an admiring crowd, including me. That was more or less harmless, but there were dangerous street fights which I took care to avoid.

Our job was to pick up Australian troops and take them on training landings down the Australian coast before delivering them to New Guinea. We sent in our landing craft to bring them out to the ship, and I watched with awe as enormous men with rifles and packs, plus a mortar barrel or a piece of a machine gun on their backs, clambered up the scrambling nets we let down the side of the ship. Climbing those nets looks easy when you see it on a newscast, but the rope forming the net sags and swings and I found them difficult even when wearing swimming trunks. But I suppose that's why they did jungle training: to become tougher and stronger than I ever was or would be. The first night aboard the *Spearhead,* on the deck under the Pacific moon, the Australians sang soldiers' songs and then, inevitably, "Waltzing Matilda." Even I with my a solid tin ear was moved.

More practically, it soon became apparent that our LCAs were too small and light to ride Pacific rollers. Once or twice, embarrassingly, a roller carried one up the beach and left it stranded. So after a time we were reassigned to the scores of ships which followed the U.S. fleet into action, carrying supplies and reinforcements. In this way we participated in the invasion of Luzon in the Phillippines and observed, from a reasonably safe distance, the Japanese suicide bombers attacking U.S. ships. Crocodiles were a more immediate threat: On a swimming party on an island in a river mouth, we saw far away down the beach a Jeep racing towards us; it arrived in time to tell us that the other side of the island was swarming with crocs which liked on occasion to roll in the surf, as we were doing.

As more and more British ships arrived in the Pacific, whatever symbolic importance the presence of our landing ships might have had ended, and we headed for Sydney, on our way home. But by then I was suffering from an unheroic condition, athlete's foot, known in the navy as footrot, which kept getting worse despite the best efforts of the ship's doctor. He had in fact been more successful in treating my eyesight. I had worn glasses for years and was handicapped when I sat on and broke the only pair I had while we were in some remote part of the Pacific without an optician in sight. The best the doc could do was to say that in the ship's little library there was a copy of a book called *Better Sight Without Glasses*, by Aldous Huxley, as I remember. The basic idea was that poor eyesight was caused by lazy muscles that wouldn't focus the eyes properly, and that eye exercises could correct that. Without specs, the alternative to falling down a hatchway or some other shipboard disaster was to make my eyes work better, and they did. It was years before I again needed glasses.

But no such luck with the footrot, and at Sydney I was discharged into the skin disease ward in a naval hospital, right next to Rose Cottage, the navy's name for the venereal disease ward. Life in the hospital was a good deal better than on a ship, and some of my fellow patients spent hours every day irritating the skin disease the doctors were trying to cure. Rubbing the milled edge of coins into the skin was supposed to work a treat. We enjoyed the presence of female nurses although it was entirely understood that they reserved their social life for officers; played cards on a bedspread in which the incriminating evidence of gambling could be swept up and hidden in a second, read, yarned, and took our treatment every day. My treatment was soaking my feet and ankles in some concoction which gradually brought the disease under control, although it could not cure it.

When I was allowed shore leave — the navy goes ashore even from a hospital on land — I was commissioned by the ward to smuggle back bottles of cheap wine, called plonk. It was winter in Sydney so I wore my issue raincoat and concealed bottles in the deep pockets. The problem was that tropical rain and heat had weakened the stitching and I feared that unless I kept hold of the bottles they might easily fall through. That of course entailed keeping my hands in my pockets, which further entailed meeting no officers I would have to salute. Somehow I managed. But the time came when the doctors decided they could do no more and that I would have to return to a cooler climate. Equipped with salves and potions, I was discharged into the temporary Royal Naval barracks built on a dusty plain on the outskirts of Sydney, supposedly to await a passage home. But the United States dropped the atom bombs and Japan quickly surrendered.

I was in Sydney on VJ Day, August, 15,1945, always the lone and interested observer rather than a participant in the celebrations. Within a day or two I had the awaited draft chit — but to go to Hong Kong rather than back to Britain. The Japanese in Hong Kong, and no doubt elsewhere, were ready to lay down their arms, but not until there were British or American forces to protect them from the civilian populations they had mistreated. The Royal Navy scrambled to sweep up all the spare bodies it could find and ship them off to former colonies now to be reoccupied. With hundreds of others, I went from Sydney to Hong Kong on an aircraft carrier, arriving when the actual surrender was still underway and the colony was in turmoil.

During the Japanese occupation, the harbour ferry service between Hong Kong island and Kowloon on the mainland had fallen into disrepair, and there were even pirate junks operating in the approaches to the harbor — pirate junks being in the main regular trading junks which saw an opportunity for a little private enterprise on the side. I was assigned to a party based in the old British naval dockyard in Kowloon, on the mainland, with the task of running a small boat ferry service across the harbour for a month or so until the regular service could be restored. My job was to arrange to feed and fuel the fifty or so men in the group, and the problem was that there were no supplies and no place to cook anyway. I scrounged food off ships in the harbour, but attempts to cook over an open fire, using the top of a metal depthcharge container as a large pan, were not successful.

Equally or more serious, there was no rum. When he was first lord of the admiralty — that is, civilian minister in charge of the Royal Navy —

Winston Churchill was asked by a pompous officer to remember the traditions of the service, and famously replied that the traditions were rum, buggery, and the lash. The lash was no longer in use during my service, I'm happy to say, and the occasional incident of buggery of which I was aware, although nominally a serious crime, was ignored. But rum was almost a religion, and it fell within the responsibilities of the supply branch. Ratings aged twenty and above were entitled to one-eighth of a pint of rum a day, mixed with two-eighths of a pint of water to make grog, the idea being that grog could not be hoarded because it would not keep for more than a day. Chief and petty officers got neat rum, while commissioned officers had a private bar in which pink gin was the favored tipple. The rum was bought in barrels and tended to vary in strength depending on where it came from, but it was always stronger than the pub rum we know today. So at age twenty men who might never have tasted spirits before were issued every noon with three eighths of a pint — six ounces — of potent grog.

It was easy to make it a habit — almost a precondition of eating the unappetizing naval lunch, or dinner as it was called — but it was more than that. The daily issue was a secular ceremony of almost mystical importance. "Spirits up" was piped throughout the ship, the rum and water measured exactly into a wooden tub under watchful eyes, and the grog issued to a representative from each mess who would be found in grave default by his mates if it were short even a drop. So it was not enough to dip a measure into the tub and fill it more or less; the level in the measure had to be convex — filled to the fullest extent possible. And every drop of rum in the ship had to be accounted for, which created real problems because the stuff tended to evaporate from the barrels. Anyway, there I was in Kowloon with no rum for sailors demanding their rights. Japanese brandy made from pine needles, which I discovered in a store in the dockyard, was sampled, but found to be no substitute. Nor were the sailors comforted by the knowledge that in lieu of rum they would receive sixpence a day. But the navy knew a crisis when it saw one, and rum was somehow procured after a day or two.

Shortly, catering was turned over to Chinese contractors, known as compradors, who, amazingly, could make both passable meals and a profit out of the naval ration allowance, and I was ordered back to the main base on Hong Kong island. It was a fascinating time, almost like living in a rip-roaring, lawless frontier town. Although the war with Japan was over, the Chinese civil war was still raging, and much of the country was devastated. The United Nations Relief and Rehabilitation Commission (UNRRA) was sending in freighters loaded with food which was off-loaded onto queues of waiting junks to be carried up the Pearl River to Canton — although the occasional junk scooted off in the wrong direction, causing much shouting and fist-waving. Divisions of Chinese Nationalist troops passed through, on their way, aboard American ships, to Shanghai to fight the Communists. The Happy Valley racetrack, which had served as a Japanese internment camp for civilians, reopened for business, amid dark suspicions that all the races were fixed. If they were, I saw one sailor who must have been on the inside: Coming away from the track, his shirt was stuffed to overflowing with HK dollars.

The former civilian internees began to trickle back from Australia where they had gone for rehabilitation and were much annoyed to find that their colony had not reverted to prewar customs. Imagine, the insolent soldiery did not automatically step aside on the sidewalks. The securities markets reopened to wild speculation, and it was said that someone had made a killing by tapping the telegraph line to Shanghai and inserting false information. Because many things were in short supply, the black market boomed, a predictor, I suppose, of the remarkable cowboy capitalism that has since made Hong Kong an economic dynamo. Luxurious restaurants reopened, and for a short time even common sailors could afford to eat in them. Japanese officers — mostly, it appeared, short, fat, middle-aged men in stiff, high collared uniforms — were made to run through the streets on their way to be tried as war criminals. But, again, routine health problems removed me from the scene. I was struck down by fever first diagnosed as malaria but then as the much less serious sand fly fever. For some reason, recent cuts and sores reopened and had to be drained by lint wicks soaked in some strange mixture of Epsom salts as I lay on the floor of a primitive sick bay. Then, running closely behind a mate to catch a tram, I went straight into an iron lamp standard which he dodged around. After several days of insisting that it was nothing worse than a strain, a naval doctor conceded that I had broken a small bone in my wrist, and as I couldn't take care of myself in barracks with my right arms in a cast, I would have to go to hospital. Such luck!

A few more pleasant weeks of leisure, during which I solved the puzzle of why there was a yellow line on the grass all the way around the building: The rumour had got around that the yellow tablets we were supposed to take daily to ward off malaria were in fact a drug to suppress sexual desire, so instead of swallowing them the patients were dropping them out of the windows, and they dissolved in the grass. With my arm out of cast but weak, I was sent to a convalescent camp, once and now again, I hear, a famous resort. And then, after nine months in Hong Kong, I was shipped home to Britain — via the Suez Canal and the Mediterranean, which meant I had circled the world — as a working passenger on a mighty battleship, to await my turn for demobilization. I spent those last few months in what had been a harbour defence base near Devonport, where the important task was to try to get the quantity of stores on hand a little closer to the quantity shown on the books. That involved various tricks for writing off more food and materials than we actually consumed, and the problem, as usual, was rum. It sometimes took several sample tots for a warrant officer to decide that, yes, this gallon jar had gone off, and to sign the necessary papers. When my turn for demobilization came I handed on the task to my successor, and he no doubt to another, and so on until the books were balanced.

I left the navy in the fall of 1946, two years and ten months after I had joined, aged twenty but a "veteran" in today's absurd terminology. We were offered none of the benefits provided to Canadian and American servicemen and women, but we could choose a suit of civilian clothes from a mass-tailored range. I chose a grey pinstripe suit, natty shirt with a blue weave printed on one side, herringbone overcoat, and a distinctly conservative trilby hat. For years, you could identify former servicemen, including me, by their demob clothes because replacement clothing was still rationed. But if little in my material circumstances had changed, I was not the shy, awkward, naive youth who had joined up. I was leaner, without specs, more worldly, and with a durable shell around the soft centre of shyness.

I was not then much interested in politics but my experiences had shaped my response to the political wars already raging in what we called "civvy street." Many of my shipmates were from the working class in regions of Britain where the Labour Party and the dream of socialism were strong, the sort of people who would never have been my friends in peacetime. And the sharp division in the navy between officers and men — far sharper, I think, than in the army or the air force — made me resentful of the sort of class distinction between bosses and workers that I might have accepted as natural in civilian life. The landmark election of July 1945 had occurred while I was still in some remote corner of the Pacific, and it had made little impact on me. I was too young to vote anyway, but I remember that the petty officers, conservative to a man, were deeply concerned that the Labour Party might win and bring their familiar and hierarchical society crashing down.

The Labour Party had helped to make Churchill prime minister, and faithfully supported his national government. But with the war in Europe won, it withdrew from the coalition, forcing an election. At once, ferocious party warfare resumed, and Churchill contributed with an extraordinary attack on the Labour leaders, many of whom had served in his Cabinet: They would, he charged, if elected, introduce "some form of Gestapo" to enforce their plans, and their socialism would lead inevitably to totalitarianism. The press also resumed the prewar party warfare with most national dailies supporting the Conservatives, but Labour won in a landslide, despite Churchill's immense personal popularity. The vote, I think, was essentially a vote for the values that had been established during the war, for fair shares instead of class and privilege, for a planned and directed economy that would guarantee full employment instead of relying on a market that had in the 1930s produced massive unemployment; in short for liberty, equality, and fraternity, a.k.a. socialism. The war had shown what government could achieve in organizing the national resources of labour and materials, and now we could set about building that famous land fit for heroes. To the extent that it was a negative vote, it was not against Churchill, but against the Tory party which was held to blame for the prewar depression, the years of appeasing Hitler, and for leading the country into war so ill-prepared that we came to the brink of defeat and disaster.

I shared those values and ideas, so when the time came to choose sides in the postwar political wars, I chose Labour. That displeased my father, a typical-middle class Conservative with no confidence at all in the ability of the working class to govern itself, let alone its betters. When the august

Times newspaper, which sold for three pence when other dailies cost a penny, supported the Labour government in its early days — as in fact it thought proper to support all new governments — the businessmen's club to which my father belonged declared it to be a mere "threepenny *Daily Worker*," the *Worker*, of course, being the Communist daily. Indeed, any hope that the wartime spirit might continue was soon shown to be hopelessly naive. Nevertheless, having found my political home — what we now call social democracy — all those years ago, I have never seen cause to change. It seems undeniable to me that democratic government is the best, perhaps the only, agency through which ordinary people can hope to make progress against capital and privilege. By progress I do not mean merely higher incomes, but fuller and more equal participation in a society that raises the quality of life along with the quantity of goods and services we are able to buy. This does not mean I have always supported a party calling itself social democratic. In Canada I have voted for the CCF/NDP, the Liberals, and the Conservatives when that seemed the best way to advance social democratic ideas. The war years did not make me, but they shaped the attitudes I carried into journalism.

A
WORKING
JOURNALIST

~ *Chapter 4* ~

Funerals, Fleet Street, Family Man

Having laid my genes, nurture and experiences as a youth face up on the page, as it were, I can now begin the substance of this memoir, which is my life and good times as a journalist. When I left school in 1941, at age fifteen, my father explained that there was no money for further education — my brother had been at a boarding school until he was seventeen — and when I said I would like to be a reporter he might well have objected because in those days it was not really a career for a middle-class boy in Britain. There were basically three ways into the business: As an inky copy boy of fourteen hoping to get a chance to move up to reporting; as an apprentice training to be a reporter; or by way of Oxford or Cambridge and family connections for the few chosen to be editorial writers or foreign correspondents on a major paper. The fact that there were apprentices and unions revealed that it was a trade or craft rather than a respectable profession like law or medicine or accounting. In fact, the newsrooms of most papers were "closed shops," meaning that you couldn't work there unless you were a member of the National Union of Journalists. The phrase "gentlemen of the press" was intended ironically because reporters were mainly from the lower middle or working classes and certainly not gentlemen in the sense of class. Except for a few stars, they were poorly paid, and the pub was their club. As one cynical poet put it:

You cannot hope to bribe or twist
Thank God! the British journalist.
But seeing what the man will do
Unbribed, there's no occasion to.

Nevertheless, my father arranged for me to have an interview with the formidable lady who was a part-owner — the other owners being a London-based chain — of the local afternoon paper, the *Express & Echo*. She agreed the paper would take me on as an apprentice for five years, not, I suspect, because I was such a promising lad but because there was a manpower, even a boypower, shortage, in the war years. Terms of apprenticeship, or indentures, varied in the different trades and crafts. Under some, in the nineteenth century, the apprentice's parents paid for his training and upkeep by his master, and others which I came across during my family research forbade dancing, drinking, fornication, even marriage. Of course, it wasn't that strict for me, although under the union agreement, apprentices started out at a few shillings a week — perhaps $20 in today's money. And there wasn't much training because most of the senior reporters were away at the war, and those who remained were old or unfit. We did have an able "district man" who covered rural affairs, but he had the bulbous nose of a drinker, and when he came into the office he often carried a fishing rod and had a collection of flies in his hat. He was not above borrowing a few shillings from a junior if he could, and had a beguiling way of asking: "Would you care to increase my indebtedness to you ?"

The paper's building was in no better shape than the staff. The exterior was black oak Tudor, and the interior a warren of corridors and offices, some of which were braced by two-by-fours, no doubt because when the presses ran the whole place shook. Here, the week after my sixteenth birthday, I joined two other apprentices who, like me, were waiting to enter the forces, and being older left before I did. We worked in what was called the junior reporters' room, and the chief reporter had a cubicle in the corner. We were required to learn shorthand and typing in our own time, which meant evening classes at a secretarial school. I had no trouble with typing, or rather, I soon learned to type very fast with two fingers, as I am doing now. But my handwriting had always been messy — now it is illegible even to me, unless I print — and I never did learn to write neat shorthand outlines, correctly positioned on the line. I lived in dread of the occasional days when the chief reporter would call one of us into his cubicle and dictate the leading editorial from *The Times* or *The Daily Telegraph* which we would then have to read back from our shorthand notes. I survived by reading the editorials every day and memorizing enough to help me over illegible words and sentences in my shorthand.

To emphasize the importance of shorthand, the chief reporter, a kindly old gent we referred to behind his back as Father, liked to tell us the cautionary story — quite true, he insisted — of the young reporter who had the misfortune to be in the assize court in the middle of an important trial when the official reporter making a shorthand record could not continue. The judge — and they were awe-inspiring figures in wig and robes with almost unlimited power in their courtrooms — was under the mistaken impression that all reporters could write shorthand, and he more or less drafted the young reporter into taking the official note. As bad luck would have it, there was a query that afternoon about exactly what had been said just before, and the reporter was asked to read out the disputed passage. When the judge saw the young man was flustered and in difficulties, he instructed him to retire to the chamber adjoining the courtroom, study his notes, and return when he was ready. After an hour, the judge sent his usher to find out what was happening; the usher returned and whispered in his Lordship's ear; the window to the street was open and the reporter was gone, no doubt having decided that flight was the better part of having to tell the judge that he couldn't read his notes and incur some imagined but dreadful punishment. The chief reporter supposed that to avoid such humiliation we would be more diligent in our shorthand studies, but it merely persuaded me to resist any and all pressure to take an official note at any time. Eventually, I did learn a sort of bastard shorthand, some as invented by Mr. Pitman and some by me, which served, barely, until I came to Canada where, I discovered to my delight, shorthand was considered an advantage but not a necessity.

The first job of the junior reporters on Monday was to call on each of the movie theatres to pick up publicity handouts on the week's films, and write brief digests — not reviews. These were a service to readers who wanted to know "what's on," and a free advertisement for the theatre. Well, not entirely free because they provided two free press tickets which could be picked up at the box office for each movie program. These not only saved us money, but also provided a little prestige; one felt

like a real newspaperman when asking for "the *Express and Echo* tickets."
There was of course no TV in those days and as the city was full of soldiery who had girlfriends and so required not only entertainment but a
warm, dark place in which to snuggle, movies were immensely popular.
Each three- or four-hour show included two movies, news, and cartoons,
and the program might change in midweek. In the grander palaces, a
mighty organ flashing coloured lights would rise from beneath the stage,
and the organist would lead a singsong, a popular attraction when the
community spirit of wartime was strong. Movie houses were always full,
the shows ran continuously, and as it was often necessary to queue and
wait for a seat to become vacant, one might enter at any point in a film
and remain for the next showing to see what one had missed at the
beginning. Film notes were the first thing I wrote for a newspaper.

Reporting funerals was another job for junior reporters, and I covered
scores. A paid death notice would appear in the paper, along with
announcements of births, weddings and deaths, on the page popularly
known as "Hatches, Matches and Dispatches." No matter how insignificant
the departed, if the family so requested the funeral would be reported.
After all, this was local news that many would read. I or some other junior would first go to the home to express polite regrets and obtain enough
details to write a short and laudatory obituary. At first, I was reluctant to
intrude on private grief, but I soon learned, long before Andy Warhol, that
everyone wants their few minutes of public attention, and for ordinary
families death was one of the few opportunities they had to get their name
in the paper. Very often, we reporters were pressed to admire the deceased
in a coffin in the front parlor, and invited to borrow any family photo we
thought would reproduce well. The next stage was to attend the church
and take the names of all the mourners, which provided another lesson;
get the spelling right because people can be very touchy about their
names, and — horrors — might complain to the editor if it were wrong
in the paper. If the family wanted the list of wreaths published with the
funeral report they had to pay by the line, but it was the reporter's job to
make a list of names and notes on the "floral tributes."

Funerals of course soon became boring, but there was sometimes a
cash reward. If the undertaker pressed a few shillings into one's eager hand
— almost a week's pay — one would attach a note to the bottom of the

report, "Funeral arrangements by ...". The busiest undertaker in Exeter sixty years ago was H. Bidgood — see how readily the name comes to mind after more than fifty years — and he enriched me considerably. Nobody ever questioned this arrangement, so I suppose it was just an accepted bit of graft, like the movie tickets. Occasionally, a local dignitary would die, and then the chief reporter would turn out the entire staff to make sure we got every name at every door of the church, or perhaps even at the cathedral, and fill columns with them. Names made news, and I expect they still would if papers deigned to cover such mundane events.

The daily courts in which minor cases were tried were called police courts in those days because the police not only gathered the evidence but conducted the prosecution. The chief reporter showed me the the ropes, but soon I was covering them myself. There were also county courts and, occasionally, assize courts at which a real judge and the barristers who travelled the legal circuit would appear. As an innocent youngster I listened with keen interest to messy divorce cases, some of which went on for days. The London papers were always ready to pay for a bit of scandal, but we were allowed to report only the evidence the judge mentioned in his summing up. There was keen disappointment when, after a sexy case, a spoilsport judge would grant a decree without reviewing the evidence in open court. Looking back on it now, I wonder that the paper allowed such a neophyte as I to report courts when it would have been easy for me to make a costly mistake, but I suppose I learned quickly the simple formula most journalists used to report the courts: name, verdict, charge, sentence, evidence. In Britain in peacetime when there was plenty of paper, courts were extensively reported, sometimes with key evidence given almost verbatim and filling column after column, and I was surprised on coming to Canada to see how little attention was paid to courts. After all, even minor cases can provide tragedy, comedy, or sometimes drama.

Our circulation went far beyond Exeter and juniors were assigned what the chief reporter called a "parish," meaning a rural town to which we had to travel from time to time to cover council meetings, courts and other events. As the most junior, I got the parish furthest away, Okehampton, a town on the edge of Dartmoor about twenty miles as the train steamed from Exeter. So at the end of a day of work in the city, or sometimes on a Saturday morning, I would take the train to my parish. Twenty miles doesn't sound much now, but wartime trains were so crowded that getting a seat was a bit of luck, and one never knew when the local passenger train would be shunted onto a siding to make way for something with higher priority, perhaps a troop train. If there happened to be an air raid warning in effect in Exeter when I was returning at night from Okehampton the train would be parked on a branch line to await the "all clear." Then I had to go into the office to write my copy. It sounds terrible, but I loved every minute of it — or most minutes anyway. I learned mostly by reading the papers to see how various types of stories were handled, but one subeditor — what we would call a deskman — seemed to take particular pleasure in correcting my English; I remember clearly when he stormed into the junior reporter's room and said, "Westell, if you confuse *accept* and *except* once more, I'll personally fire you." I don't think I have ever since used either word without checking to see I had got it right, so I suppose I should be grateful to him, but at the time I thought him a tyrant. I described earlier the bombing of Exeter in May, 1942, three months after I had started work. While the fire which consumed so much of the High Street was stopped before it reached our offices, the explosions upset our presses, and production of the paper was shifted that very day to Torquay, about twenty miles away, where the chain had another daily. Our editors went by bus to Torquay every day to produce our paper, leaving we reporters, senior and junior, with even less supervision than usual. And the paper became, if that were possible, even less enterprising in covering the news.

One day in 1943 my father passed on a tip that Bob Hope and his company, who were touring to entertain American troops would be arriving that night at a local hotel he was frequenting at the time, contemplating, I think, marriage to the sophisticated blonde lady behind the bar. I took a seat in the hotel lobby that night and waited for Hope, who arrived eventually. Rushing up, I sought an interview. He, seeing a scruffy seventeen-year-old before him, asked if I was from the "college paper," to which I replied with all the dignity I could muster that no, I was from the local daily paper. I asked a few no doubt banal questions, and he tossed off a few cracks, and so I had my interview, and rushed back to the office to write up the scoop, making as much of so little as I could. It did appear in the paper, savagely cut in length, and I was advised that the *Express & Echo* was not much interested in American movie stars. But I'm sure it was one of the best-read items in the paper that day.

Soon after, when I was twenty months into my apprenticeship, there came the eagerly awaited call to join His Majesty's navy. On demobilization — in my case almost three years later — one of the few benefits offered to servicemen was the right to get their old job back, so in 1946 I returned to the *Express & Echo*. At the paper, not much had changed except that the prewar editor had returned, having risen to the rank of captain in the army, and was even more conservative than his wartime replacement. To relieve the housing shortage, the government was buying aluminum homes prefabricated in factories that had previously produced aircraft. The houses were small, but well equipped, and a score or so were assembled on sites in Exeter. I discovered somehow that there was a problem with ventilation, causing moisture to freeze on the inside walls during the cold winter of 1947. So tenants were existing in a sort of igloo, or ice house. I wrote an excited story but it never got into the paper; our editor said that if there was anything to it the problem would be on the agenda of city council's housing committee and we would report it then.

Speedway, or motorcycle racing, began in Exeter around that time, and I was assigned to cover this dubious new sport. For a small city, the crowds were large and the interest high, but the paper refused to print more than a few paragraphs. So I conceived the idea of starting a speedway weekly — called *Fanfare*, naturally — and persuaded a couple of other young reporters to work on it with me in our spare time. It paid its way and survived for several years after I left Exeter, so was I an entrepreneur in the making? I think not; I was restless, looking for new challenges and inclined to a sort of reckless optimism, a pattern which has recurred in my career. A year or so later, frustrated by the *Express & Echo*, I abandoned my apprenticeship which had more than a year to run, and moved to a larger city. I was at first concerned about breaching my contract, but I reasoned that the *Express & Echo* had never fulfilled its side of the bargain by providing training. And when I heard that the editor had complained that I was leaving just when I was becoming useful, I thought of the countless hours of cheap and reasonably competent labour I had given the paper, and departed with a clear conscience.

I would have preferred to have gone straight to London but could find no opening in Fleet Street, so I went to Bristol, the next city up the country from Exeter, where there were two afternoon papers in fierce competition, and a sluggish morning paper. All career changes alter the direction of one's life, but that one had larger consequences than most. A few days after I started work at the *Evening World* a young woman returned from holiday, Jeannie Collings, and we were neighbours at the huge reporters' table. I can't say I paid her much attention, but she soon noticed that I was something less than a snappy dresser. I was quite like-ly to have a hole in the elbow of my jacket, and the collar of one of my few shirts was too tight to button up because I had bought it from a smaller colleague in Exeter who needed to raise a few shillings. Such things did not bother me then, and they still don't. Nature, eating, and drinking made me apple-shaped and clothes, no matter how expensive, don't sit well on apples. In those days, men could get away with being scruffy, but women journalists were expected to dress respectably, often with hat and gloves, which was quite a feat when wages were low and clothes were rationed. All we young, single reporters lived in rooming houses, some better than others, but Jeannie had a particularly dismal room with no running water. She contrived nevertheless to emerge every day like a butterfly, with clean gloves and starched blouse, having done her laundry in a bowl on the gas ring.

The city itself had been devastated by bombing and the centre was still mostly in ruins when I arrived there in 1948. Food was rationed and while restaurant prices were controlled we could afford them only on special occasions, so we ate our main meal every day in the office can-teen at midday. After a few pints in the pub in the evening, we would devour suspicious "meat" pies bought on the street. But we were young, the paper was lively — too lively in fact for the solid citizens of Bristol — and we put out several editions a day in fierce competition with our bigger, duller, and richer rival, the *Evening Post*. We learned much later that our efforts had been in vain because the *Post* in effect controlled the *World*, and eventually closed it down. The editor while I was there was a small man who relaxed at his huge desk by resting his feet in a bottom drawer. He also spent too much of his time on his knees in the neigh-bouring church, and if he was asking for editorial guidance, he didn't get it. I met him years later in Toronto where he had a job better suited to his abilities: receptionist at his wife's hairdressing salon.

One of our daily tasks was to check on the previous day's crimes, and that meant getting a list of reported robberies from the police. To show me how this was done, the regular police reporter took me with him to the police station where we made our way to the offices of the special branch, the counter-intelligence cops who were much concerned, of course, with the local Communists. The understanding was that they would hand over a list of robberies and we would pass on to them any news or gossip we had picked up while covering political and trade union meetings. I was dismayed, and resolved there and then to avoid crime reporting, which I managed to do for some fifty years. I appreciate that the police have a difficult job, but there is something about their them-and-us culture which bothers me still, and I would hate as a reporter to be dependent again on the goodwill of police officers, as I was that day in Bristol. But it was all fun while it lasted, and my neighbour on the table, Jeannie, and I were attracted to each other, more and more as each month passed. It was a memorably happy time in my life, and half a century later I still have friends in Bristol. But after hardly more than a year I was again restless and on the move.

The *World* was part of the Northcliffe Group of ten provincial papers, and I inquired about a job in the group's small London editorial office — a half-dozen editors and reporters. Once again, I was in luck, and in 1949 I headed at last to Fleet Street, the generic name for a cluster of streets and lanes in which all the major newspapers and news agencies had their offices. By then, Jeannie and I knew without ever discussing it that we were moving towards marriage. Neither of us was closely attached to home or family, and ours was not a romantic declaration of love but a private union of good companions who shared, in addition to the normal passion, a passion for journalism. It was my form of romance, unsentimental, but durable. I had ranted against marriage in office canteen arguments, but the underlying truth was that while I had a good impression of myself as a journalist, I had poor opinion of myself as a social being, and dismissed marriage because I could not imagine anyone wanting to marry me. When that proved to be wrong, I did not hesitate for long.

When I moved to London the plan was for Jeannie to follow in a few weeks. I rented two rooms — with running water! — and a gas ring in a pleasant house in Bloomsbury. Such "bedsits," as they were called, were home to many thousands in London before apartments were available and affordable. My room had just about enough space for a bed; Jeannie's was larger and brighter, with not-very-easy chairs, a dining table, and a bed that folded into a box on the wall. We decided to marry with the minimum of fuss, which meant telling no one. On January 10, 1950, we went to St. Pancras Town Hall, paid seven shillings and sixpence for a licence, hired two doormen at half-a-crown (two shillings and sixpence) each, and were wed. The whole enterprise cost twelve shillings and sixpence, about $2.00 in those days, a cost we have amortized at four cents a year which seems a reasonable bargain, at least for me. She wore a grey suit which served for years, both before and after, and I had a new suit bought on the instalment plan — the British called it "the never-never" — from a company which advertised "Wear While You Pay the Willerby Way." Romantic as ever, I neglected to buy a ring, prompting Jeannie to buy one for herself, second-hand because new rings were of poor quality gold. We almost lost it when it rolled down a mouse hole, but peering down we could see it balanced on a joist and were able to hook it up with a wire clothes hanger. We celebrated our marriage with a drink at the once-famous Criterion bar, where we read the three afternoon papers, followed by lunch at the once-famous Trocadera restaurant, and a movie, *Al Jolson Sings Again*, and I moved into Jeannie's room.

The following day we went back to work; Jeannie had a job in public relations. Marriage brought me the generous affection I had not received, at least since my mother died, but my own personality, cool and detached, did not allow me to reciprocate as I should have, and in fact wanted to. Jeannie and I have been married now for fifty-two years, and I owe her a great deal. But she has always refused to be an appendage to my professional life — for example, to attend public events simply because she is my wife — and for that reason I am not going to invade her privacy by writing much about her, or about our two children. But I do want to describe our life in London, and the society of which we were a part, in the early 1950s, because it was the context in which I first became a political journalist. Britons had emerged from the war as victors who now wanted to enjoy the spoils. We did not realize that it was the end of the country as a great power, the last of the famous victories — which is why, half a century later, Britons are still lost in nostalgia for those war years. In reality, the country was bankrupt. While Canada and the United States had got rich producing the materials of war, Britain had got poor by cashing in overseas investments to pay for the materials, and by running down the infrastructure on which the economy depended — the railways, ships, roads, even the factories themselves. The European countries that had been conquered and looted by the Germans were in no better physical shape, but they had no illusions about the rewards of victory; they were prepared to work hard to rebuild. That was even truer in Germany where survival itself depended on a united effort to rebuild the cities and restore the economy. In Britain, with the end of the war and the election of a social-ist government deeply threatening to powerful interests, the country plunged back into divisive, class-based party politics. Instead of ending, food rationing became tighter, and there was an acute shortage of hous-ing. In the bitter winter of 1947 coal was rationed for the first time. The Labour Government had not only failed to deliver on what had always been unreasonable expectations that peace would bring plenty, but had to start educating the country about basic economics. In those days the aver-age person knew little or nothing about the balance of payments, the necessity of exporting, devaluation, and inflation. The major newspapers carried "City news" — news about activities in the financial district of London known as the City — but the national economy was something else again, an abstraction until hard times made it a pressing reality.

Our standard of living would seem like poverty to today's young peo-ple, but for us life in our bedsit was luxury after rooming houses in Bristol. There was a gas fire which would work when we put a shilling in the meter, and Jeannie cooked for both of us, and even for dinner guests, on a gas ring, often using a pressure cooker with three divisions for different foods. She supplemented our rations with strange foods such as whale meat, a canned fish which the Ministry of Food tried unsuccessfully to market as Snoek, and off-ration items including "Mock Duck" which we bought at a delicatessen in Fleet Street. It neither looked, walked, nor quacked like a duck, and what it was we never found out, which was perhaps just as well. We shared a bathroom and a toilet with other tenants, being allowed one bath a week in no more than five inches of water to save energy, and Jeannie washed our clothes in the corner basin in our room.

We became friendly with a young man, Tom Bottomore, living above our bedsit, who had served as a captain in the army Intelligence Corps and was then studying at the University of London and teaching for the Workers Educational Association. He was awarded a Rockefeller Scholarship for $1,000 to study in the United States, a big deal, but was refused admission to the country on the grounds that he had as a boy sold the *Daily Worker*, the Communist paper, on the streets and was therefore a danger to security. To its credit, the foundation allowed him instead to study in Paris, and we took care of some of his belongings while he was away. Some twenty years later, Tom was head of the new and radical department of Sociology, Anthropology and Political Science at Simon Fraser University in Vancouver when New Left students set out to "democratize" the university. They demanded equal power with faculty and the administration, and when Tom became involved in a dispute with three senior students he was denounced, and decided to return to Britain. So this academic Marxist who was too radical for the United States was not sufficiently radical for the revolutionary students at SFU. Incidentally, Bottomore went on to become an internationally known sociologist.

Another friend in the building was a Polish woman with a past that seemed to us extraordinary, although I suppose it was ordinary in the sense that there were millions like her displaced by the war. In 1939 she was living a comfortable middle-class life in the large Jewish community in Lvov in Eastern Poland when the Red Army arrived, carving up Poland in partnership with the Germans. Fortunately, her daughter was at university in Britain, but her husband was arrested— she never saw him again — and she was put on a train to Siberia. Somehow she survived, and after the war made her way across Europe, heading for Britain and her daughter. Soon after she arrived, her daughter died, apparently of a disease caught in her own research laboratory. When we became friends, Lucy was trying to make a new life, coping with our strange English ways and working as a child-minder for better-off Polish families. In a sense she was lucky because when the Germans attacked the Soviet Union they captured Lvov and massacred almost the entire Jewish population, and in fact while Lucy hated Communism, she carefully distinguished between Nazis and Communists. Nazis, she said, were cruel by policy and design, while the Communists were cruel by indifference and incompetence. She was not persecuted, she explained, but merely put off the train in Siberia and left to fend for herself. We kept in touch with Lucy after we emigrated to Canada, but one day a letter came back marked "Deceased." She had survived a sudden and catastrophic disruption of her life and lived into old age, and I have often wondered how I would cope in similar circumstances. Not well, I fear.

Almost all the new housing was being built by municipalities with subsidized rents for low income families. It was called council housing then, but we would call it public housing. Rents on private properties were controlled, but if you were lucky enough to find a vacant apartment there was always some sort of "key money" involved. For example, you would be asked to pay hundreds of pounds for "fittings and furniture" worth nothing. A family of four we knew actually could not live together because they could not find a place they could afford. Eventually they emigrated to Canada and then moved on to the United States, where they have done very well indeed. Their elder daughter is now a dean at an elite American college for women. We had no luck looking for an apartment until a report ran through Fleet Street that the London County Council was building what was grandly called Upper Income Group Housing, in Camberwell in unfashionable south London. I hurried to County Hall to apply, and in 1951 we moved into a brand new, two-bedroom apartment with a kitchen, our own bathroom, and even a balcony. Almost every other tenant in the building was either a journalist who had, like me, got an early report, or a doctor from King's College Hospital just down the road. For our one room in Bloomsbury we had been paying £3 a week, and the rent for the apartment, although unsubsidized, was about the same. It's interesting to consider that when we return to London now we take a studio apartment in a basic block in Bloomsbury near our old room and pay £350 a week, a bargain in today's London.

Once in our own apartment we lost no time in starting a family, and our grocer was among the first to know. Pregnant women got a special green ration book entitling them to extra food, and when Jeannie presented hers to our cheery Cockney grocer, he responded with, "'Ere, 'ere, what's been going on." But he did produce eggs above and beyond the call of the ration book. Now here comes an awkward question I can't answer. On May 6, 1952, I left for work, and later Jeannie called an ambulance to take her to St. George's Hospital at Hyde Park Corner, now converted into a hotel. No pacing the floor for me; when she gave birth the following morning, I was again at work. I found out we had a son by calling the hospital from a phone in a press room at the House of Commons and, for want of another piece of paper, wrote down the birth weight on a corner of my union card, which I still have: 7 pounds, 6 and a half ounces. Did I put work before family? Perhaps. Was I simply cold and indifferent? I don't think so, because I soon proved quite good at tricky jobs like bathing the baby. The best explanation — excuse if you like — was that I was, and still am, reserved to the point of being unable or unwilling to show emotion at birth, as I have been at death. And if I can skip ahead of my story, somewhat the same thing happened when our second child was born, in 1956. Jeannie elected to have the baby at home, and having summoned the two midwives, I left for work; it was after all budget day in the House of Commons. I learned that we had a daughter when Jeannie telephoned me that afternoon at the press gallery.

To return to 1952, the last of the great London smogs came down that winter, fog carrying smoke and particles from millions of coal fires. It was dark when it was time for me to go home and the trams and buses — there were no underground trains to Camberwell — had stopped running. But many were stationary with their lights on, which guided me as a I walked out through the mean streets. When I reached Camberwell Green I had to strike off the main road into the dense fog, and only with difficulty found the right hill to climb out of the Thames Valley. Halfway up the hill my head suddenly emerged from the smog and it was as if I were standing up to my neck in water. But by the following day the smog had crept up to the level of our apartment, and Jeannie had to keep cleaning coal dust out of our new baby's nose and ears, and off the crockery. When more electricity became available coal fires were banned, and Sherlock Holmes, who seemed to thrive on London fogs, would not have recognized the old place.

TV was just becoming available in Britain in the early 1950s, and the BBC offered the only British radio programs. So the primary medium of news by far was the Fleet Street press, and it was into that exciting and intensely competitive industry that I moved in 1949. There were a dozen national daily papers, seven national Sundays, and three London evening — we would say, afternoon — papers competing edition by edition to hit the streets first with the latest. There has been nothing like it since, and probably never will be again. There were three quality broadsheets, including the magisterial *Times* which still had classified ads on the front page; four middle-market papers mixing news with bright features and political causes; two tabloids; the specialist *Financial Times*, the Communist Party's *Daily Worker*, and even a daily for pub- keepers. The most popular paper was the brash tabloid *Daily Mirror*, selling more than four million copies a day. It featured a comic strip in which a blonde named Jane frequently mislaid her skirt, and it motivated its reporters with a sad tale that went (as best as I can recall): "Jenny is sitting at the kitchen table after dinner (we would say lunch) on a wet Saturday in Scunthorpe (a dreary industrial town). Her husband has left for the football game, and then he'll go to the pub with his mates, and he'll probably be drunk when he gets home. The table is covered with dirty dishes that have to be washed. The baby is crying and needs to be changed, and Jenny has just discovered she's pregnant again. She picks up her *Daily Mirror*. What have you written that will interest her?"

But the *Mirror*, which supported Labour, also worked to popularize serious news. For example, it reported the annual *Economic White Paper* with a two-page spread of few words but many charts, tables and graphic symbols. I remember the despair of its political correspondent when he was given seventy-five words in which to explain something called the European Payments Union. The *Mirror* also packed a mean political punch; during the 1951 election campaign it raised the issue of whether nuclear weapons should be entrusted to Labour leader Clement Attlee or Tory leader Winston Churchill, and on polling day its entire front page was given to a drawing of a revolver with the question, "Whose Finger on the Trigger?". It was widely agreed that this graphic message gave Labour the edge, but it was not enough; Labour won the most votes, but the Conservatives won the most seats. The socialists were out, and Churchill was back — just.

Most of the papers were conservative in outlook, and *The Daily Telegraph*, biggest of the quality papers, was almost the voice of the Conservative Party. Another reason for its popularity with the middle class may have been that under discreet, one-column headlines it carried the most detailed accounts of sexy divorce cases. The largest of the mainstream papers was *The Daily Express*, owned by Lord Beaverbrook, formerly the Canadian financier Max Aitken. He made a surprising, decisive and ultimately amusing appearance in my career, as I'll explain later, but for the moment it is enough to say that he bought the *Express* before the First World War to promote his own brand of conservative imperialism, and made no secret of it. When he appeared before the Royal Commission on the Press, he was asked for what purpose he owned newspapers, apparently with the intent of trapping him in some false claim. Instead, Beaverbrook answered, "To make propaganda." With his flair for propaganda, he called his crusade Empire Free Trade when what he proposed in fact was tariff protection against goods produced by countries outside the Empire. The trend toward free trade after the Second World War dismayed Beaverbrook and he ordered that the symbol of a Crusader, with sword and shield, printed in red on the front of the *Express* should be draped in chains— apparently to express his own growing sense of political impotence. But it was also another example of his flair for dramatic journalism which made the *Express* so popular.

When I joined the London office of Northcliffe Newspapers in 1949, I was on the fringe of this exciting journalistic community gathered in and around Fleet Street, a district that dated from medieval times. The Northcliffe offices were on Carmelite Street, named for the Carmelite order of friars who once had their house there. They wore white robes, and so the next street was called Whitefriars. Nearby was the Blackfriars bridge and railway station, named for the Dominican friars who wore black robes. We had four reporters, and two desk editors, of which I was one, who handled mainly enquiries from our ten provincial papers. It was not exciting work, although I did get out of the office occasionally to cover a major story. One such story was the trial of Klaus Fuchs, the German-born British scientist who passed secrets to the Russians while working on the development of the atomic bomb at Los Alamos. I was intrigued by the evidence of the British security agent who interrogated Fuchs and led him, almost like a priest, to confess. Fuchs was a committed Communist who went to live in East Germany after serving his time in prison and apparently never repented. So what led him to confess? I couldn't figure it then, and I can't now. But soon I was focused on new interests when my luck struck again and I began my career as a political reporter.

~ *Chapter 5* ~

Getting Started in Politics

In 1951 British MPs returned to the House of Commons chamber from which they had been driven by bomb damage — good timing for me, as it turned out. In rebuilding and remodelling the House, more accommodation had been provided for the press, both in the gallery for parliamentary reporters overlooking the chamber and in the space behind the scenes, as it were, for political reporters who covered the Cabinet, the political parties, and the Whitehall bureaucracy. These political correspondents were then, and still are, called Lobby correspondents because they had access to the MPs' lobby just outside the chamber, making it easy to chat with ministers and backbenchers. The public and journalists who were not members of the lobby had to seek out MPs in the vast central lobby where police officers controlled the crowds. Through this lobby every day passed the Speaker, in wig and robes, attended by officials including the sergeant-at-arms wearing a sword, on his way to open a sitting of the Commons. It was a sight so impressive that when one day an MP spotted a friend across the lobby and called his name, "Neil," people began to fall to their knees before the Speaker, to general embarrassment.

More space in the new Commons meant that many provincial papers were allowed for the first time to appoint Lobby correspondents, and I was one of two appointed to represent the ten papers in the Northcliffe Group. After barely more than a year in London, I found myself in the Lobby which had previously been the mysterious preserve of senior correspondents. I say mysterious because the Lobby was an essential part of the way in which government and opposition managed the news. The older members of the Lobby representing the national and major provincial dailies, who usually dressed in the black jackets and striped pants affected by MPs and civil servants, were concerned about the influx of young reporters from obscure provincial evening papers who might not understand the rules. They presented us with a small, leather-bound book, with the House of Commons seal in gold on the cover, entitled *Lobby Practice*. Among other things, we were instructed that while one could gather information, with which to write informed news, when talking to MPs in the Lobby, on no account could one identify a source or quote from a conversation. To quote would be "to reduce Lobbying to mere reporting," an idea that struck we reporters as curious.

But this rule of "not for attribution" extended far beyond the Lobby. We went on most days to 10 Downing Street, the home and offices of the prime minister, to be briefed on the government's views and intentions by the official spokesman, but the source could not be given. On other occasions, ministers and opposition leaders met the Lobby in a remote room in the rambling Palace of Westminster to discuss events on a "background only" basis. We reported that "it is understood" that this or that is thought, or will be done, a formula that made us sound like insiders, and seemed to impress even our editors, although we were mostly mouthpieces.

The source was often the prime minister's press officer, a new position created when Clement Attlee became prime minister in 1945. The first press officer had difficulty in persuading Attlee that a news ticker tape machine should be installed in "No.10," the popular name for 10 Downing Street. His winning argument was that it would provide the prime minister with up-to-the minute cricket scores. Of course, it carried much more news, including the stories we wrote out of the briefings. Attlee snuck out of Cabinet one day to check on the cricket scores and was surprised to find instead a report on what Cabinet was thought to be discussing. "Why," he asked the press officer, "are the Cabinet minutes on my cricket machine?" The answer is not recorded. When Churchill returned to power he wanted to abolish the position of press officer, but had to settle for a compromise by appointing a civil servant rather than a former journalist and insisting that his office not be in No.10. But soon the spin doctor, as we could call a political press officer today, was back in Downing Street and still unquotable. One of the provincial journalists who went into the Lobby with me became Prime Minister Harold Wilson's press officer and was knighted for his pains, which must have been considerable.

The job of course was always political, but in the early years the press officers felt a responsibility to the journalists from whose ranks they were often recruited. Among these was William Clark, spokesman for Anthony Eden when he succeeded Churchill as prime minister. We met many years later in New York when we were both presenting papers at a conference on foreign policy and secrecy, and Clark told the best cautionary tale on security I have ever heard — and which I insert here for no other reason than that it remains a good story. He had been press attaché at the British Embassy in Washington just after the Second World War, and was summoned one day to the new head of chancery to be lectured on security measures. This high official noted that Clark had not signed the necessary form acknowledging that he was aware of the terms of the Official Secrets Act. So would he please sign now? Cark asked if perhaps he could first read a copy of the Act, but was told testily that that was unnecessary. The important point was that he must not give information to unauthorized persons. Clark then asked if journalists were included in the category of unauthorized persons, pointing out that if they were he could not possibly do his job. But no, he was assured it was alright to give information to "good journalists," but he should watch out for the French who always leaked, and keep in mind that the Americans bugged embassy phones. Thus instructed, Clark signed the form and went about his work. Some ten years later, the head of chancery skipped to Moscow hours ahead of the spycatchers: He was Donald Maclean, and when he briefed Clark on the importance of security he was also busy stealing secrets for the Soviet Union.

To return to Downing Street, as media became ever more adversarial, the job of press officer came to be that of a political adviser to the prime minister and a partisan warrior in the political wars who was often unmasked and criticized in the opposition press. Prime Minister Tony Blair's press officer finally accepted the inevitable and went public, admitting TV cameras to the briefings, as they do at the White House.

It was yet more luck for me that when I entered the Lobby in 1950 politics were at a fever point. There was lots to report, and an eager audience. Labour had survived the 1950 election with only a tiny majority of six seats, and the Conservatives set out on a physical campaign to tire the government into defeat and another election. Procedural rules were used to keep the House sitting late night after night, and while back-benchers could sleep-in the next day, ministers had to be at their desks. Labour MPs in hospital were carried to Westminster on stretchers to sustain the government in vital votes. As Opposition leader, Churchill led one debate that lasted twenty-one hours, and he finished with a huge breakfast followed by whisky and soda and a cigar. He was seventy-six and perhaps needed to demonstrate as much to himself as to the people that he still had the energy to win the next election and serve as prime minister. Doctors were already telling him that his brain was deteriorating, although neither press nor public knew anything of that at the time.

When Britain sent troops to join the UN force in Korea in 1950, the government offset some of the cost of rearming by imposing charges on false teeth and eye glasses provided by the new National Health Service. This led to a Cabinet revolt and the resignation of three ministers, including Aneurin Bevan, known as Nye, the architect of the NHS, and one of the best orators in the Commons. The left-wing Bevanite group inside and outside the party became a significant influence, but it wasn't all plain sailing for Nye. He was married to another firebrand MP, Jennie Lee, and when sympathizers urged him to return to the Cabinet and fight from within, Bevan objected, "But you don't have to go home and sleep with Jennie." The Conservatives also were divided, between what we would call Red Tories — Margaret Thatcher later dismissed them as "Wets" — of which R.A. (Rab) Butler was a leader, and the traditional Tories led by Churchill and his designated heir, Anthony Eden. Butler's researchers at party headquarters were churning out progressive policy papers, and when one was offered to Churchill as he was about to board a train, he declined it, saying politely, "I prefer non-fiction for journeys." Worn down by the Tory tactics in the Commons and by the divisions in his own party, Attlee called a new election in 1951 and, as I have already mentioned, Churchill was returned to power.

Most of my work in those years concerned MPs from the cities and regions served by the Northcliffe papers, but I got an introduction, as it were, to the *Sunday Express*, a popular national paper, through a friend who had been hired to write editorials and a column called "Crossbencher." The column was closely watched at Westminster because Lord Beaverbrook occasionally used it to air his opinions about politicians and events. My friend introduced me to Charles Wintour, the political editor and a rising man in the Beaverbrook press, and I freelanced by selling him interesting scraps of political news and gossip of no use to the Northcliffe papers. When my friend went on holiday, Wintour hired me to stand in for him, and as I was going to be entrusted with writing in a space identified with his Lordship, I had to be vetted by his son, also Max Aitken. He had been a wartime flying ace and was running the Sunday paper for his father. He asked me what my politics were and I did not hesitate to say Labour because I knew Beaverbrook made a point of hiring bright young socialists and introducing them to the pleasures of money. Some were seduced and became his political followers, others enjoyed what he had to offer but remained socialists. Nye Bevan, for example, enjoyed Beaverbrook's champagne and was mocked as a "Bollinger Bolshevik" but remained on the Labour left. Michael Foot, who had edited the *Evening Standard* for Beaverbrook, became a Labour MP and edited *Tribune*, a vitriolic left wing-weekly around which the Bevanites organized — and which was secretly subsidized by Beaverbrook to make trouble for Attlee. Foot went on to become the leader of the Labour Party, although not a successful one.

I was nowhere near that league, but although I was working for the *Express* only at weekends — when I had finished at Northcliffe — it was my stepping stone into the real Fleet Street. Beaverbrook was usually out of London and his instructions arrived by phone to which several people listened in order that not a word be missed, or on a disk from a primitive recording machine. When a disk arrived, Wintour would assemble several of us to listen to the scratchy and still-Canadian voice, two or three times if necessary to be sure exactly what he was saying about whom. Then a researcher would go to work, and next I would settle down to write as "Crossbencher." When I had drafted the column, usually on a Saturday morning, it was scrutinized by Wintour, and then vetted by a lawyer because there were often personal snippets about political figures that verged on the edge of Britain's tough libel laws. The son of a hell-fire preaching Presbyterian minister, first in Maple, Ontario, and then in Newcastle, New Brunswick, Beaverbrook was familiar with the majestic language and cadence of the King James Bible, and "Crossbencher" had to be written with that flavour, using archaic words and phrases such as "wherefore" and "for why?"

Beaverbrook himself wrote standing at a lectern as if delivering a sermon, and produced several well received books of history. One, titled *Friends*, was of particular interest to me because it was published after I had moved to Canada (Heinemann, London, 1959) and was about a political figure in Canadian history and was published just when I was becoming interested in the subject. The book told the story of Beaverbrook's almost lifelong friendship with R.B. Bennett, who entered municipal politics in New Brunswick with Beaverbrook's help and rose to become prime minister. He was a successful lawyer in Calgary before going to Ottawa and made a fortune by investing in Beaverbrook's dubious company promotions in Canada. How he acquired his second fortune was, wrote Beaverbrook, a true story "stranger than fiction." In his youth in Chatham, N.B., Bennett had been friendly with Jennie Shirreff, a woman ten years older than he. She became nurse to E.B. Eddy — who, wrote Beaverbrook, was "a maker of matches, pails, pulp, paper and money"— and married him. When Eddy died, she inherited the company, and when she died she left a chunk of her fortune to Bennett. Bennett also inherited from Jennie's brother and wound up with a company worth many millions — which he subsequently sold to the Weston empire in Britain. What was the relationship between Jennie and Bennett? Beaverbrook insisted that although romantics back home in New Brunswick thought Bennett would have made a better husband for Jennie than old Eddy, there was no romance. Maybe it was just friendship, but I still chuckle at Leonard W. Brockington's summing up of the story. First president of the CBC, a director of *The Globe and Mail*, and much else, Brockington was the wittiest of speakers even when confined to a wheelchair, and he put the story this way, neatly adapting Shapespeare:

There is a tide in the affairs of men,
Which, taken at the Eddy, leads on to fortune ...

But I have digressed for the sake of a good story, and must return to my efforts to write in the Biblical style preferred by Beaverbrook. I suppose I met his requirements because I received no complaints. In fact, "writing in the style of" had been one of my strong points at school, and I fell easily into Crossbencher. For somewhat the same reason, I suppose, I enjoyed also writing punchy editorials despite the fact that Beaverbrook's opinions were far from my own. It was a game, an exercise, and one which I found myself playing again when I wrote editorials for the *Globe* and then *The Toronto Star*, about which more later. The money earned from the *Sunday Express* encouraged Jeannie and I to think about buying a house, and that meant moving to the country because London property was too expensive. Before we could househunt I had to learn to drive — Jeannie had learned in Bristol — and buy a car. I passed the driving test and I don't think it was really necessary to slip the examiner a ten shilling note, but my instructor said it helped. But there was a long waiting list for new cars and we wound up with a clapped-out prewar Wolsey. I would not have dared to kick the tires, and to drive any distance was to break down, or at minimum to have a puncture. On one long trip with the baby in the back I thought the steering strange; the service station found that the steering gear was held together by caked mud and oil, vital pins having sheared through. But we chugged around the countryside near London and eventually struck gold. A large country house near Cobham, Surrey, had been divided into two parts, and we bought the smaller part from the owner, a London butcher, for the staggering sum of £3,000, then about $10,000. Years ago, we heard that our old house had sold for £350,000, and now it is worth perhaps £500,000, or well over $1 million at today's rates, which is roughly what I earned in thirty-five years of work in Canada. Such is the strange magic of the markets we keep hearing about. Anyway, the house was up a broad rustic drive and stood among trees, close to a famous golf course. It was called, grandly, Wood Manor, on three floors with four bedrooms, and we moved there in 1953.

It had been occupied by Canadian troops during the Second World War, and the marks of their boots were still visible on the freshly painted window sills. Apparently they preferred windows to doors. The surrounding woods had grown over the fences into the garden, and amid the trees there was an excavation that looked like a machine gun pit. When I started to dig I turned up ammunition clips and many empty bottles. Inside we had other problems. The postwar austerity was easing — although food rationing did not end until 1954 — but we still couldn't afford carpeting to cover the rough wood floors. Then we saw an advertisement offering for sale the blue and gold felt that had covered the floor of Westminster Abbey for the coronation of Elizabeth II. We bought yards of it, and while the dark blue served well enough, the gold proved no match for a leaky toddler. For the stairs, we bought something called Yugoslavian rag rugging which I laid with far less than complete success.

We now needed our old car to get me to the railway station three miles away, and on cold, wet mornings, which seemed to be most of them, it was often reluctant to start. We tried hanging a warming oil lamp under the hood at night, but when that didn't work Jeannie had to push me down the sloping drive until the engine caught. Sensitive fellow that I am, I didn't feel entirely comfortable shouting at a pregnant wife to push harder and faster. For a year or so a pleasant Canadian family rented the larger part of the original house, and while they eyed our old Wolsey with amusement, we eyed with envy their new Plymouth shipped from Canada. New cars were still in short supply and the purchase tax was steep, but the wily butcher from whom we had bought our house explained how to get around that. Panel trucks, as we would call them, were not taxed because they were intended for business use, so the plot, which we followed, was to buy a used truck and have windows cut in the sides and a bench seat from a junk yard installed in the back. Jeannie managed all that while, naturally, I was travelling on work in Europe. She met me with the new car at Heathrow airport and we drove home in style. Such was life in Britain in the early 1950s — or perhaps I should say that's the way it was for us, and we were considered quite well off.

My career, meanwhile, was prospering. Wintour moved from the *Sunday Express* to be deputy editor of the *Evening Standard* and in 1954 he invited me to join his staff as diplomatic correspondent and deputy political correspondent. That meant that the Foreign Office was my primary beat, and again my timing was perfect — perfectly lucky, that is. Stalin had died the previous year, and 1955 was a year of musical chairs. Churchill retired and was replaced by Anthony Eden who had made his reputation as foreign secretary; Attlee retired as leader of the Labour party and was replaced by Hugh Gaitskell; and in the Soviet Union the new team of Nicolay Bulganin and Nikita Khrushchev took over and emerged into the world as travelling salesmen for communism. West Germany rearmed as a member of NATO, and plans were afoot for the first postwar summit conference of the leaders of the great powers, then the United States, Britain, France, and the Soviet Union. The focus of news was shifting from domestic to international affairs, and for the next couple of years I had story after story on the front page, often two or three on the same day as edition followed edition.

My working day started at about eight o'clock at home in Wood Manor when, having read the morning papers delivered to the door, I phoned in a story for the first edition. It was often about some meeting or event that was to occur later in the morning but would have happened by the time the paper reached the reader. That required the use of an ugly but ingenious construction covering future, present, and past tenses. For example, "The Cabinet was expected to meet this morning and decide to ...". Then I would take the train to London and update or change the story through the day, phoning from the Foreign Office, the Commons, or wherever the news was happening. The three "evening" papers published their first editions at around 9 in the morning and their last at about four in the afternoon, unless there was a "Special Edition." Because most of their sales were on the streets speed was almost everything, and to beat a rival by one edition was a triumph. In Canada, when a reporter phones in news it is usually to the rewrite desk, where fast and skilled journalists turns the raw facts into a polished story. In Britain, the person on the other end of the phone was not a journalist but a copytaker, and the reporter was expected to turn in a finished story that could be slapped straight into the paper. I got so used to this that I seldom again typed a story until I came to Canada, where my ability to write on the phone, as it were, was much admired, as we shall see.

The Foreign Office managed news in much the same way as Downing Street did. There was an on-the-record daily briefing at noon every day for any journalist who wanted to attend. But as some of the foreign journalists were obviously working for their governments, very little of importance was said. For smaller groups of trusted correspondents — one group being we three from the evening papers — there were private briefings from which the information could be used but not attributed.

It was not unusual to attend a private briefing on the British government's views on some event, and then attend the public briefing at which the same spokesman would say something rather different. Because we three competitors were receiving the same briefing, the trick was in getting to a phone fast and then dictating a coherent story. The story was usually pretty much what the FO wanted to say because there were few other sources; on matters of importance, foreign governments spoke through their own press or dealt directly with the British government rather than through ambassadors in London. The system of news management obtained even at international conferences. Each government briefed its own press, putting its own spin on what had transpired in private talks. This created a problem for the *Daily Worker's* reporter when the Soviet Union was involved. He needed to hear Moscow's line but that did not always turn into a story for British readers. At a meeting of foreign ministers, including Moscow's V.M. Molotov, in Geneva, which I covered, the dignified Foreign Office spokesman was in the middle of his briefing when the *Worker* correspondent slipped in. "Welcome Sam," said the spokesman," but shouldn't you be at the Soviet briefing?" "Nah," replied Sam," it's all Molotov, Molotov, bleeding Molotov." Appalled at this indiscretion, the FO man instructed us crisply, "Nobody heard that, right ?" It was not reported partly because the media were not news in those days as they are now, but also because while we knew the *Worker* correspondents had their own political agenda, they were also our colleagues. There was a waiting list for phones in London in the 1950s, as for so many other things, and when I mentioned one day in the press gallery that I was having difficulty getting a line, the *Worker's* Lobby correspondent advised me to become a security risk; when he moved houses he got a phone right away because the spooks wanted to tap it.

Churchill had been seeking a meeting with the new Russian leaders, hoping to pull off a triumph of personal diplomacy to cap his career. But his own Cabinet was not keen and, more importantly, neither was President Dwight Eisenhower. Talks on other matters continued at the foreign minister level which meant for me assignments to Paris and Geneva, both pleasant escapes from austere Britain. On my first trip to Paris I obtained quite by accident the reputation of being a tough operator. The *Standard's* correspondent in Paris was a legendary Australian called Sam

White. From his reserved seat at the Hotel Crillon bar, he covered the political and social life of the city in a sparkling, sometimes startling column. One such column was based on an interview with the wife of a French Cabinet minister who was so indiscreet as to alarm the editor of the Standard when he read White's copy. He called White to make sure the piece was well founded, and asked if White had made clear to the lady that her remarks were to be published. "Oh yes," said White. "And what did she say?" asked the editor. "She fainted," replied White. This was a man I was anxious to meet, and as I did not know Paris, I asked the news editor to get White to book me a hotel room, which he did. I met and dined with White, and when I was checking out of the hotel the next day I assumed in my naivety that as he had booked the room he would pay my bill from the bureau account. The hotel clerk was suspicious but my French and his English were limited, and somehow I wore him down. When I got back to London I discovered that White had phoned the news editor to say with rueful admiration that I had stiffed him. So are reputations made.

Then the new Russian leadership proposed four-power talks on European security, suggesting Vienna as the site. Eisenhower and Eden agreed, but shifted the venue to Geneva, home of the old League of Nations and a traditional site for diplomatic negotiations. Foreign ministers began to meet to prepare for the summit of their masters, and the pattern, happily for me, was for the Western three to meet in Paris before going to Geneva to meet Molotov — who arrived, I observed by chance, in a sort of cargo plane equipped with an iron bedstead. Another character writing for the Standard at the time was Randolph Churchill, who laboured under the burden of being the son of his famous father. He was not a popular figure, given to booze and bluster, and earned part of his considerable upkeep by writing articles for Beaverbrook, as Winston had done when out of office in the 1930s. Also like his father, he wrote well, but he lacked the authority of any substantial achievement in his own life. On my way to the Summit in 1955, I went from home to Heathrow and flew to Paris. When the plane landed I was alarmed to see a man waving a notice with my name on it, with the message to phone the editor at once. Wondering what crisis had occurred, I wrestled with the French phone system and eventually got through to the editor who, somewhat aggrieved, said that he had expected to see me in the office before I left because he had instructions for me. Randolph would be at Geneva to write articles but I was to take no notice because they were relying on me for news coverage — and on no account was I to advance him money. In the event, I don't recall that we even met amid the swirling mob of journalists covering the great event.

And it was a great event at the time, although now it has almost passed from the history books, an unprecedented public meeting in peacetime between the leaders of the Free World, so called, and the Communist world. Eisenhower was accompanied by hundreds of American media people and of course his own security men. We Europeans thought of secret services as being secret, and when I asked a U.S. official about a button in his lapel I was bemused to be told it was the badge of the Secret Service. We all now know of course that Secret Service is the curious name given to the highly visible White House security service. TV news coverage was in its infancy, and I felt myself very daring when I decided that the best way to cover some events would be to watch Swiss TV. It was apparent that if I joined the mob watching the leaders enter the hall to begin their conference the chances of getting to a free phone fast would be small. So I stayed in my hotel room and was able to phone an "I-was-almost-there" story well ahead of my rivals. Now we all know that TV cameras often provide a better view of events than an eye witness on foot at the scene. In those days we used the phone when we were up against deadline, but filed overnight by telegraph, using our press credentials to send copy collect, usually at the special press rate per word but occasionally at the more expensive "Urgent" rate. Histories of journalism are full of stories about the use and abuse of telegraph wires to transmit the news, but my favourite is about an incident said to have occurred in Geneva when the League of Nations was meeting in the 1930s. A wire service correspondent was having a row with his editors in London who threatened to fire him, and he replied with a classic, "Fire me, and I'll send you the Bible, collect, at Urgent rates." It ought to be true.

At the 1955 summit, while their husbands conferred to achieve little of immediate importance, the wives of the great men competed to entertain each other. The Eisenhowers had rented a magnificent villa with a private dock on the lake — it belonged to the Cartier family of jewellers — and Mamie upstaged the other ladies by inviting them to an afternoon on the lake in a private yacht the size of small liner. The media were admitted to the grounds of the villa to see the ladies embark and it was, predictably, a mob scene. To obtain a clear view photographers climbed on priceless pieces of statuary on the vast lawn, but the prize for initiative was taken by two French magazine journalists who attempted to swim into the harbour in frogmen's suits but were somehow detected and hauled out by security guards.

Like many summit meetings, the conference did allow the leaders to get to know each other, and Eden took the unusual step of inviting the Russians, Bulganin who was nominal head of government and Khrushchev who held the real power as party boss, to visit Britain, which they did in April of 1956. Now that world leaders jet hither and thither across the world, it is hard to imagine how unusual, almost sensational, was the visit of the Communist leaders — and in the middle of the Cold War. Soviet leaders were expected to hunker down in Moscow, seldom to be seen by their own people, let alone the outside world, and never, never to hold a press conferences. B and K, as the headlines called them, broke the pattern. They went first to India where they made rude remarks about Britain's colonial past. Much offense was taken in London and there was talk even of cancelling the visit, but the Foreign Office had its own way of fighting back. When it was announced that B and K's security chief, Col.General Ivan Serov, would be coming to London to make security arrangements, the FO slipped me a copy of his curriculum vitae, as it were — a long list of decorations received for oppressing, suppressing and/or terrorizing various unfortunate peoples. As a result of the story, he was hounded by reporters when he arrived and his protestations that he was just a policeman cut no ice. As part of the security plan the government refused to release, or even show editors, a schedule of B and K's engagements, arguing that it would be a sort of Assassin's Guide to Where to Be. So when one morning I read just that schedule tucked away as a short story in the back of the *Telegraph*, I had a story which I phoned in for the first edition: Was the FO retaliating against B and K for their insulting behaviour in India, perhaps even discouraging them from coming to Britain? Later that day, an embarrassed FO answered: No, the schedule had been issued by mistake, which made another story.

The big event for me and for other reporters was to be B and K's press conference, an unimaginable opportunity to question Soviet leaders. The media interest was huge and the rule was that once admitted to the press conference reporters would not be allowed to leave until the end, which would be mid-afternoon at the earliest. This presented problems for evening newspapers, particularly so because it was obvious that every public phone in the area would be swamped as hundreds of journalists rushed from the hall. The *Standard* was allotted two seats; I got one to cover all the news, and the other went to Randolph Churchill who, the *Standard* advertised, would confront the Soviet leaders with the ugly truths about Communist rule. On the day, Bulganin began by reading a long statement that said little, but nevertheless caused me to scribble furiously until my hand ached. When he finished it looked as if they were going to depart, but a journalist jumped up with a question, Khrushchev replied, and I was scribbling again, and nervously watching the time as the editions slipped by. When the press conference finally ended, I squeezed out of the crowd and ran as fast as I could to the Commons press gallery where we had a private line. "How much do you want?" I asked the news editor. "Everything," he replied, "including colour and items for the *Diary* " — the "Londoner's Diary" being a popular, full-page feature which purported to be an insider's diary of London life. So I started to dictate, and went on dictating for, I suppose, half an hour. When the next edition appeared, my copy was all over the paper, much of it under my byline. There was nothing by Randolph, but by the last edition his name was in the paper — over copy that was in part mine. Outraged, I called the news editor who apologized and explained that Randolph had not delivered on time what the *Standard* had promised in its ads, and my copy was the only available substitute. Ah, well, such is fame, and, anyway, I was getting ready again to move on.

~ *Chapter 6* ~

Small Head, Big Feet Lead to Canada

My career was blooming, Jeannie was pregnant with our second child, and as my income grew so we were able to make Wood Manor more comfortable — even to look forward to central heating in what had proved to be a chilly house. And, following a familiar pattern, I began to think of making a change. It was irrational and I'm not at all sure I can recall my thought processes. But certainly, by the end of 1955, I was beginning to find the *Standard* job too easy, not boring because the news was always interesting, but insufficiently challenging, requiring only facile reporting skills. It looked to me also as if I had at thirty reached an elevated level of journalism but one on which I was likely to remain on for the next thirty-five or so years. Indeed, some of the young journalists with whom I entered the Lobby in 1951 remained there for the rest of their careers, a fate I would have found intolerable. Another nagging notion was that my success had been largely the result of good luck, being in the right place at the right time, enabling me to build success on only average ability. Certainly I had enjoyed luck, as I have shown in this record, and I wondered what would happen if I started all over again. That seemed to be an intriguing challenge, but for a journalist in Britain there was nowhere better than Fleet Street, so I would have to leave the country. It would have to be an English-writing country, and Canada was closer than Australia and looked less foreign than the United States. There was also the fact that at Wood Manor we had Canadian neighbours who encouraged me in the idea of emigrating. Jeannie had always wanted to live in the United States, and was ambivalent about Canada. In reality, neither of us knew much about the country. She wanted to return to journalism at some stage, and there seemed to be a chance that we could get jobs together in Canada. But with a toddler and a large house to care for and a baby on the way, she was probably too distracted to think seriously about Canada.

Then the problem of what next seemed to be solved when Wintour said he wanted to send me to New York to be the Standard correspondent, as White was in Paris. But first I would have to be approved by Beaverbrook. So an appointment was made and off I went to his penthouse apartment in Mayfair. I was wearing my best heavy brown brogue shoes, which may have been a fatal mistake. Beaverbrook asked how my wife would like the idea of going to New York, and I replied she would be enthusiastic, adding that in fact we had already been talking of going to Canada. The conversation was brief and seemed to me to be routine, but when I got back to the office Wintour told me there would be no New York, and while I could stay at the *Standard* there would be no further advancement in the Beaverbrook press: I had expressed an interest in Canada, and there I should go. It was only much later, in Ottawa in 1973, that I discovered what had really happened. The Parliamentary Librarian, Erik Spicer, had the courteous custom of sending me new books which he thought would be of interest, and in this way I received a book by Wintour, *Pressures on the Press: An Editor Looks at Fleet Street* (Andre Deutsch, London, 1972). Writing of the pressures exerted on him by Beaverbrook, Wintour recalled:

> In assessing character he had one weakness: he placed too much reliance on the size of people's heads. Once I brought a promising journalist to see him, hoping he would accept that the young man deserved accelerated promotion. "Small head, big feet. Won't do." That was the crushing and final verdict when the interview was over.

I wrote to Wintour to confirm that this was about me, and he replied:

> You are indeed the central figure in the anecdote you mention. I was furious with Beaverbrook at the time; it was typical of the irrational way his mind worked sometimes. He and Lloyd George both used to judge people on the shape of their heads.

Beaverbrook had served as minister of information in Prime Minister David Lloyd George's Cabinet during the First World War, and there was a further connection: both were small men with large heads and small feet. My head is about average and I take a size10 shoe, but encased in stout brogues they probably looked big that day as we sat on his rooftop patio. However, Beaverbrook may have been seeking a reason to turn me down for the New York job for he soon appointed his granddaughter, Lady Jean Campbell. She was successful as a reporter but less so in love. She had a notorious affair with Norman Mailer, and I have sometimes reflected that had my shoes been smaller I might have had an affair with Mailer. Seriously, having neither social graces nor interest in café society, I could not have been a correspondent on the model of Sam White or Lady Jean, so Beaverbrook's decision to reject me was probably for the best if for the wrong reasons. Luck had served me again.

There is another reason why it was just as well that I did not continue in Beaverbrook's empire. Ambition blinded me at the time, but I can see now that I didn't like him, his politics, or his journalism. He had a compelling personality and great wealth, and gathered around him a court of admirers, sycophants, protegés, and women, many much younger than he, who became his lovers and were then disappointed to be relegated to the role of dear friend. I could not have been part of all that. His impish personality expressed itself in politics in making mischief, for both conservatives and socialists, always hoping to promote his own imperial agenda. He served well as a minister in two wars, but I think history will find him to have been a divisive and malign influence on British affairs. (Auberon Waugh, a caustic wit, was said to have remarked that he believed in the Devil because how else could one explain Beaverbrook.) He was a brilliant journalist with a populist touch, but he had entered the business for the wrong reasons. Newspapers have always been political; some in fact were started by political parties, and several publishers in Canada became leading party politicians — for example, George Brown of *The Globe,* now *The Globe and Mail.* Other proprietors have been in the business primarily to make money, which for them takes precedence over politics — for example, the late Roy Thomson in Canada and Britain, and Rupert Murdoch with his world-wide media empire. The third type of proprietor makes his fortune elsewhere and then buys a newspaper or several as a way of gaining political influence and power. He sees journalism not as a public service, but as a vehicle for propagating his own ideas — for example, Randolph Hearst in the United States, Beaverbrook in Britain, Conrad Black in Canada. It is a way of buying influence and would not be allowed in an ideal democracy.

In a famous speech in 1929, British Prime Minister Stanley Baldwin, a Conservative, denounced both Beaverbrook and his rival, Lord Rothermere of the *Daily Mail*. They wanted power, he said, "... but power without responsibility — the prerogative of the harlot throughout the ages." He meant that they used their papers to make propaganda for their causes and to attack opponents, but did not accept the responsibilities of governing. Anne Chisholm and Michael Davie, in their splendid biography, *Beaverbrook: A Life* (Hutchinson, London, 1992), say that Baldwin's stinging attack is thought to have been written by Rudyard Kipling, formerly an adviser to Beaverbrook, and they note that the *Express'* biased reporting of the speech merely confirmed the charge of dishonest journalism. By my time, Beaverbrook's influence had waned, and he wound up at retirement lamenting that he had been a failure. His admirers dismissed the very idea as absurd, but he was right in the sense that the Empire Crusade, which he had entered the newspaper business to promote, had gone nowhere. In some measure, Black follows in Beaverbrook's footsteps. Like Beaverbrook, he made his fortune as a financier in Canada, and then bought an influential British paper, *The Daily Telegraph*, which made him an instant player in British politics. His cause is to persuade Britain to join Canada, the U.S., and Mexico in a free trade area instead of committing itself fully to Europe. His intervention as a relative newcomer in the critical debate on Britain's future is resented by Conservative politicians who favour Europe, just as Beaverbrook was resented when his Empire Crusade split the Tories. The difference is that Black's *Telegraph*, unlike Beaverbrook's *Express*, is a quality paper practicing serious journalism in its news columns. Unfortunately, the same could not be said of the *National Post* when Black launched it in Canada to promote his political agenda and attack opponents in a style of journalism Beaverbrook would have understood.

A week or two before I saw Beaverbrook, Jeannie had given birth at Wood Manor to our second child and first daughter, but that did not deter me from pursuing Canadian prospects as soon as I knew I had no future with the Beaverbrook papers. Roy Thomson at that time owned *The Scotsman* and a few other provincial papers in Britain, and I arranged to see him at his London office. I explained that I was interested in emigrating to Canada with my wife who wanted to return to journalism, and I asked if he might be able to provide jobs for both of us on one of his papers. He said he thought he could, but asked how much I was earning at the *Standard*. I told him £30 a week plus generous tax-free expenses, and I remain grateful for his honesty when he said: "I don't pay that sort of money. You'd better go to *The Globe and Mail*." Had he been less frank, Jeannie and I might easily have landed up as a team of two running a small weekly. As it was, he arranged an interview for me with the Globe's managing editor, Tommy Munns, who was visiting London that summer.

But first another distressing problem arose. Our four-year-old boy was diagnosed as a diabetic who would be dependent on insulin for the rest of his life, and whose diet would have to be carefully managed. He was kept in Guildford Hospital for six weeks, so we were shuttling between the new baby at home and the toddler in hospital. Surely this should have persuaded me to put Canada on hold at least until the implications of diabetes became clearer, but instead I argued that insulin had been discovered in Toronto and so it would be a fine place to go. When I met Munns and he offered me a job, and the die was cast. I was giving up a senior reporting job with a good income in London for an insecure general assignment job in Canada at less pay. To suit my agenda, my wife was to leave a country house she was growing to love and her community of friends, at a time when she was nursing a baby and learning how to give injections and weigh out food for a four year old, all to begin a new life in who-knows-what housing among strangers in a new, cold land. I, who have always prided myself on being rational and responsible, can perhaps put some of the blame on the strains of eccentricity and recklessness in my genes, but I am being too kind to myself. The unpleasant truth is that I was selfish. Certainly I was seeking a new challenge in journalism, but I failed to see, or turned a blind eye to, the reality that I was forcing on my wife a challenge she neither needed nor wanted.

We began to make plans to sell up and sail, and then another big story broke. Egyptian President Gamal Abdal Nasser was rearming with

Soviet equipment and making military alliances with other Arab states that posed a threat to Israel. Suddenly, in July, he nationalized the Suez Canal, which Britain had controlled and saw as vital to its own commerce and that of many other countries. Prime Minister Eden had made his reputation in the 1930s by opposing appeasement of Hitler, and he saw Nasser as a new Hitler who had to be stopped. The United States and even some of Eden's ministers were less bellicose, and diplomatic efforts to find an international solution dragged on through the summer into fall, which meant that there were lots of stories for me to write. We had with us that summer a French au pair girl, and one evening at Wood Manor she received a phone call and chattered happily away in French. The call was from her uncle, a French paratroop officer, she explained, and he had just arrived in Britain to plan some sort of operation with the British. There were already rumors that Britain, France, and Israel were planning action against Egypt if diplomacy failed, but the next day I could get no confirmation of our girl's story. But of course she proved correct. In October, Israel made what was called a pre-emptive strike against Egypt, and Britain and France sent troops to occupy the Canal Zone. There is little doubt now that the whole affair was cooked up by Britain, France, and Israel, to provide an excuse for invasion to destroy Egypt's military power and recover the canal.

While this was going on, we were applying for immigration permits and booking a passage to Canada. One of my friends in the Lobby was Drew Webster, brother of Jack who was already a rising star on *The Vancouver Sun* and went on to become a national radio and TV personality. In fact, I first met Jack when he came to Britain to do a story for the *Sun* on how much B.C. lumber Britain was going to buy that year, and he was obviously doing so well that it raised my interest in Canada. We met several times in Canada, including once on a plane going to Britain where Jack and his wife were to seek a child they had given up for adoption years before. He told me the sad story that day, but the ending was happy and he wrote a book about it later. Drew somehow knew the general manager of the Thomas Cook travel agency, and through him I was able to reserve a stateroom for the four of us on the main deck of the SS *Homeric,* an Italian liner known to many thousands of immigrants. We sold Wood Manor to another friend in journalism for £3,500. We had spent some money on the house beyond the £3,000 we had paid for it and did not believe in seeking a profit from a friend. Advised that our furniture would dry out and split in Canadian central heating, we sold it, which proved to be a mistake because we have never again found such comfortable easy chairs. Now Canadians are eager to buy Victorian and Edwardian pieces imported from Britain.

Late in October we sailed from Southampton, and I read in the ship's newspaper that Israeli, British, and French forces had attacked Egypt. That story was behind me. As soon as we cleared Ireland we ran into an autumn gale, which was not fun in the North Atlantic — worse in fact than anything I had encountered steaming around the world in the navy. We all took anti-seasick pills, and Jeannie passed some on to the baby in her milk. In any event, the baby slept peacefully through long days and nights, with the waves climbing and falling around our porthole. Our main concern was that if our boy got sick he would not be able to eat to balance the insulin we were injecting every day. So we insisted on going for meals when we would rather have stayed in our bunks, and we probably passed some sort of crisis on the first morning of the storm. There were few passengers in the dining hall and our son was beginning to look pensive. But when the ship plunged a jar of syrup slid across the table and poured into my lap, a cause of much amusement to the boy who forgot about being sick. Back in our cabin, I drew with chalk on a canvas suitcase a game that had no ending, and so we passed time for almost a week. The worst moments were during lifeboat drill on the open deck: Jeannie discovered that when wearing a fat life-jacket she could not get her arms fully around the baby. I discovered during the exercise that our son was having an insulin reaction and had to rush him off in search of sugar. What would have happened in a real shipwreck did not bear thinking about.

The weather eased when we entered the Gulf of St. Lawrence, and off Gaspé, our first sight of Canada, a pilot came aboard. Then, on the other side, we saw Labrador, and it was not welcoming; this was November, there was snow among the black trees, and only occasionally a lonely figure to be seen. We were "landed" as immigrants on November 8, 1956, at Quebec City — I still have the blue card — but disembarked at Montreal the next day, hours late because there was a dock strike. As we waited on the dockside, our daughter was sleeping in her carry-cot, under a warm blanket but with no hat, and an official sternly warned us, "Cover that baby's head" — another reminder that this was not England. We had reserved a bedroom on the night train to Toronto, quite unlike any train or carriage we had seen before, and arrived at Union Station at breakfast time. A friend of Jeannie's who had immigrated a little earlier met us, and our first concern, as usual, was to get some food into our son to balance the insulin we had injected, which we did at the station restaurant, our first meal ashore in our new country. Our friend had booked us into the King Edward Hotel, and we drove there through the cold grey morning with the cab driver cheerfully informing us that there was snow up north.

That afternoon, while Jeannie rested and fed the baby, I took our boy in search of a toy shop which I thought would give him a happy introduction to his new country. Unfortunately, I turned south through the financial district, which was deserted, this being Saturday, and I began to have doubts: Was this cold, bleak provincial city really where I wanted to be? Toronto in 1956 was an undistinguished city, with no high rises and in fact few buildings of interest. But there was no turning back, and I reported to the *Globe* on Monday and began at once a search for an apartment because the King Eddy, while comfortable, was rapidly running through the small amount of money we had been able to bring. I was advised that apartments were hard to find and that I should not be fussy, so I took a two-bedroom walk-up on Wilson Avenue, just north of Highway 401 and with a fine view of a gas station. I was scared that after Wood Manor the apartment would not seem a good swap so I warned Jeannie not to expect much, but because her expectations were already low and I had lowered them further, she was not displeased. At least it was warm. It was probably more of a wrench for our son who no longer had his sandpit and chums to share it with. He stood at the window with his thumb in his mouth watching, I suppose, the plastic flags fluttering on the gas station. I went to work.

When I reported to managing editor Munns he said that in view of my experience he would pay me above the union scale — $111 instead of $110, as I recall. He was a cautious man working for a parsimonious publisher and putting out a conservative provincial daily with circulation and financial problems, so the *Globe* could have proved a dull place to work. But my luck was still running strong and big changes were on the way. The previous owner, George McCullagh, had died in 1952 — by his own hand, but that was hushed up for years with the connivance of the chief coroner: such things could be done by the well-connected in Ontario of that time. For three years the paper had been run under the stifling hand of trustees and it was still in the end of that era when I arrived. But it had been bought the year before by a Montreal millionaire, Howard Webster, for no better reason, he said, than that he liked it. Later events suggested that he had become tired of buying and selling corporations and wanted a more exciting life. In effect, he had bought for something over $10 million a press card that admitted him to a new world. In 1957 he appointed a new publisher, Oakley Dalgleish, known as Dal, who had been editor-in-chief. Dal was an energetic, experienced journalist — he had worked in Fleet Street and reported from the Spanish Civil War in the 1930s — with a vision of what the paper could become. He had lost an eye as a child and wore a black eyepatch that gave him a piratical appearance; he is said to have been the inspiration for a famous figure in advertising at the time, the Hathaway Shirt Man, who wore an eye patch. With Webster's support, Dal began to transform the *Globe* from a provincial into a national paper with an international presence. He even launched a short-lived weekly edition in Britain, and went to Red China to negotiate a deal under which Canada admitted a Chinese correspondent and China admitted a *Globe* correspondent at a time when the U.S. government forbade its own reporters to go to China. When the first *Globe* reporter emerged from China, where he had been exploring the possibilities, he had to give a press conferences for eager but frustrated American journalists.

Before most people, Dal saw the potential of news about business and launched in 1962 the "Report on Business," section which, over time, eschewed the familiar company handouts in favor of reporting, and eventually earned enough in advertising to underwrite the expansion of the rest of the paper. In time, I came to work closely with Dal and although we disagreed about almost everything — he was a devout Tory, I a social democrat — I grew to like and respect him. But before those days, I had to earn my spurs on a new paper in a new country. I was of course on general assignment, covering lunch speeches, fires, accidents, whatever came along. As a new man, I got night shifts, sometimes working until 2 a.m. and then taking the subway and a bus in the depth of winter to get home. It was a come-down from covering international crises, but reporting is always an education and I needed to get to know about Canada. One of my first jobs was to cover pre-Grey Cup celebrations at the Royal York Hotel, and I had first to ask nervously what the Grey Cup was. On another occasion I covered a fire and came back with a story about frozen firemen covered in ice, and the city editor had to explain that it was hardly news.

Jeannie too had problems adjusting. She had only a thin, cloth coat, and soon hated and feared the cold. When we bought a used car, it proved to be a lemon, and when she took the driving test the gearshift on the steering column kept jamming, which meant she had to get out in traffic, raise the hood and free the linkage as the examiner waited. She would have survived that, but just to make things more difficult heavy snow was falling and, when parking, she neglected to clear the rear window and gently nudged the car behind. So no licence that time. However, she was much impressed with the Sick Kids hospital where she took our diabetic son for check-ups — so relaxed and informal after starchy British hospitals. But on the other hand she had to struggle with new foods, measures and recipes to keep him on his strict diet. We began to think about buying a house, but in the city only conventional mortgages on older homes were available and we couldn't muster a large enough down-payment. We might have been better off to have looked for a bigger and better apartment to rent in a downtown district, but buying seemed the thing to do, and that decision had a large impact on our lives.

So we began to explore the suburbs where federal housing policy provided large, cheap mortgages on new homes. But we discovered that to buy even the most basic new house on the far edge of development in the eastern suburb of Scarborough — we thought that there were probably bears, certainly wolves, beyond — we would have to make up the down-payment by taking a second mortgage, which meant in effect a short-term loan. Always financially conservative — many would say tight — I was reluctant to borrow on the salary I was earning. But one of my colleagues on the *Globe* was another British journalist, Michael Cope, who had arrived in Canada, via Australia, with wife and child and they also were in need of a house they couldn't afford. Neither of us was a handyman but we decided nevertheless that I would take a loan and buy a house into which we would cram both families while we built a basement apartment. He would pay me a small rent with which I would pay off the second mortgage. He would save money toward a down payment, and when we had both saved enough we would move into separate houses. Miraculously, that creative financing worked, although the apartment, on which we laboured clumsily day and night when not at the *Globe*, was far from being a professional job. The house was about the cheapest we could find — $13,600 — and essentially a small brick box with unpainted interior walls, sitting on a bare earth lot. We bought used appliances from Eaton's warehouse and came to appreciate the wonderful service on which the store had built its success. When the beat-up old fridge we had bought for a few dollars proved unsatisfactory, Eaton's sent us a better one, delivered to our distant suburb, at no charge. There was no public transit or convenient highway to downtown and work. We had to drive through the docks, but on the other hand parking on the waterfront cost only fifty cents a day. On top of our work at the *Globe* and on the apartment, Cope and I began to freelance to raise cash, calling ourselves the Canada News Agency (CNA) and selling news around the world by mail, cable and phone, but mainly to British papers which in those days were interested in Canada. Nowadays for some reason Canada is stereotyped as terminally boring. Cope did most of the work, but I had lucrative connections in Fleet Street — the *Standard* even sent me to Ottawa and Montreal in 1958 to cover a Commonwealth economic conference, and to Vancouver for a business story — and we did surprisingly well. When Cope lost his job at the *Globe*, we were able to more than make up his salary.

I had the idea that suburban papers were the coming thing and we invested a few thousand in a struggling weekly, which enabled Jeannie to return to journalism, working from home while caring for the children. I worked on editing and layout when I got home from the *Globe*, and we had the naive idea that our free labour would make up for lack of capital. I was right about the potential market but others had the same idea and we found ourselves competing against a weekly with mysteriously large resources — mysterious, that was, until we discovered that it was owned by *The Toronto Star* the largest and wealthiest paper in Canada. Jeannie laboured mightily and even at one desperate point put on her hat and gloves and went out to collect overdue accounts, something I could never have done. When the printer demanded cash to produce the week's issue, we borrowed at the bank against my salary, but nothing worked. Jeannie's years of work went for nothing, and we lost some thousands of dollars which made life leaner and meaner than it might have been.

For Jeannie, those years were mostly a bleak experience, isolated in the suburbs, with little social life, and always short of cash. About the only redeeming feature was that the children made good starts in good new schools and had plenty of friends in a safe environment. Today's parents would be horrified, I suppose, to know that we sent them off to play in a wooded ravine with a stream and didn't see them until the next mealtime. I wonder sometimes if the various threats to children have really increased or whether we are simply more aware of them and made fearful to the point at which kids are so programmed and protected that they have no time to be just kids free to play as they wish.

~ *Chapter 7* ~

Good Times at the *Globe*

T hings went better at work where, in 1958, I was appointed to the City Hall bureau. It was the end of an era, the last dying days of the sensational style of journalism dramatized in the famous play, later a movie, *The Front Page*. City politics were just breaking free from the grip of the fiercely Protestant Orange Order imported from Ulster. Mounted on a white horse, "King Billy," usually a city politician, still led a popular parade every year to celebrate the Battle of the Boyne in Ireland in 1690 at which King William III's Protestants decisively defeated a smaller Catholic force. But Italian and other Catholic immigrants were pouring into the city, and the *Toronto Telegram*, as the voice of the Orange Order, no longer controlled City Hall, where once it had elected as mayor one of its own journalists. By miraculous accident or brilliant design, the election of a Jewish mayor, Nathan Phillips, pointedly calling himself "The Mayor of All the People," marked the end of Protestant dominance without aggravating the religious divide. Also, effective governance was moving from the City Council to the new Metropolitan Council which included suburban mayors and reeves.

But the daily battle between the afternoon papers, the Liberal *Star* and the Tory *Telegram*, helped to keep politics lively at City Hall. Looking back now, I think of the cynical comment on academic politics that could have been applied equally well to City Hall: the reason they were so bitter was that so little was at stake. On one occasion when not much was happening, the *Tely* reporters took the mayor to a theatre, long since gone, which featured strippers between the movies, and had him, deeply shocked, denounce sex shows in Toronto the Good. More often, the *Tely* or *Star* reporters would provoke one of the four controllers into criticizing another, then run with the criticism to the offended party to get a response, and before you knew it there would be a front page lead story about the great row raging at City Hall. I watched bemused for a time and then asked my city editor, Bob Turnbull, if I should match the afternoon paper stories. "No, no sport," said Bob — he called everyone sport — "Just report the news up there." All three papers did in fact report council committees and agencies and meetings of the board of control, and gave extensive coverage to meetings of the full council. Any citizen who wanted to keep in touch with city government could find the record in the three papers, which is more than can be said today.

When we reporters weren't covering meetings, we relaxed in the cramped press room, napping on the old leather couch or playing cards, sometimes with lawyers who wandered in from the courts between cases. Most of them were Ontario Conservative Party pols who smoked cigars, wore their hats on the back of their heads, and had all the latest gossip from the wards. To a man, they were hoping for a patronage appointment to the bench. In that press room, I learned crib and hearts and other useful skills for living. We usually lunched with Mayor Phillips and the four controllers at a restaurant on Yonge Street where I was introduced to strawberry shortcake, compliments of the chef, which I found to look much better than it tasted. When time for the World Series came around, my journalistic colleagues begged, borrowed, or possibly stole a television set, installed it in the press room, and instructed me in the arts and crafts of baseball. I didn't understand then, and I still don't. None of us was earning much and relations between politicians and the press were very different from the puritanical standards of today. We considered it a fringe benefit when a council committee adjourned for dinner in a restaurant and included us on the tab, or when we were invited to a reception at which the rye and ginger was free. It seems in not very pleasant memory that everyone then drank rye and ginger. I was told that if I were good and came to be considered reliable, I would be invited to an annual event at which the chief film censor showed all the naughty pieces that had been cut from movies, but maybe that was just a story because I never received an invitation. Mayor Phillips, known as Nate, liked to give reporters little presents — hockey tickets, a tie sometimes with a gravy stain, and the like — and his wife sent presents to reporters' wives. When I politely refused these gifts, Nate was offended and said his wife too would be upset. He told a colleague that I was implying that he was doing something wrong, and asked sadly, "How can you trust a fellow like that?" I heard indirectly that other reporters who took the gifts also felt that I was putting them in a bad light.

That colleague, incidentally, was Stanley Westall, a near namesake but no relative. When Munns hired me he said it was possible only because another Brit with a similar name had just left: a Westell and a Westall on the staff, he said, would have been just too confusing. Stan had left to return to Britain but things did not please him there, and he was back in Toronto on the *Globe* only a few months after I arrived. Confusion there was, and it continued for years — once involving even bank accounts — because Stan and I worked together in Toronto and Ottawa, became good friends and sailing pals, and still are. One critical confusion occurred when another colleague, Ron Haggart, left the *Globe* for a much better job at the *Star* and said he would see what he could do for me. Soon he told me he had spoken to the *Star's* formidable publisher, Beland Honderich, and I could expect a call. Nothing happened, but sometime later Stan mentioned that he had been surprised when, out of the blue, Honderich had asked him in for a chat and offered him a job he didn't want. No doubt Bee, as Honderich was called, was surprised too.

Returning to the subject of press-politician relations, my wife called me at City Hall just before Christmas one year to say that a railway truck had delivered a case of canned raspberries and a large cheese. There was no note attached, but the name on the box was that of a well known construction company. She was feeding us on a very tight budget and was, I think, a little disappointed when I said I had not ordered the foods and they would have to go back. She bundled the kids into their snow suits and got them into the car, loaded the canned fruit and cheese, and drove to the nearest railway station which was in the village of Agincourt north of our house. At the station, she got the kids and the foods out of the car, and staggered up the icy steps to the office. Wrong station; there were two stations in Agincourt, one for Canadian Pacific and one for Canadian National, and now she had to repeat the whole loading and unloading process at the second station before she could return the foods, collect. She was not a happy wife. When I mentioned the incident in the press room, I was told, "Oh, those gifts are from Lampy. The guy who owns the construction company is his friend." Lampy was Allan Lamport, a popular former mayor who had begun the greening of good grey Toronto by introducing Sunday sports, and was by then the chairman of the Toronto Transit Commission. Much was forgiven Lampy because he was always good for an amusing quote, intended or otherwise. My favorite was his puzzled answer in council to an alderman who accused him of awarding contracts to help his friends: "So who else should you help?"

I heard tales also of reporters in the provincial press gallery at Queen's Park receiving $100 every year as a "stationery allowance," and being engaged as secretaries by committees of the legislature they were supposed to be reporting. I encountered questionable conduct when I was pulled out of City Hall in 1959 and assigned for a week or two to cover a provincial election campaign. Provincial governments were not considered very important in those days and coverage was often sketchy, but why I, who knew almost nothing of the province, was assigned to help cover the election I never did quite understand. Perhaps it was a further step in the *Globe's* education of Tony Westell. Anyway, it turned out that there were to be four reporters following the leaders — one from each of the Toronto dailies and one from the Canadian Press wire service — and as I had the largest and most powerful car, a Ford with an interior the size of a drawing-room, I was drafted as driver for the press. It proved to be quite an experience because the Liberal challenger, John Wintermeyer, was being chauffeured at high speed by a stockcar driver and we spent days racing through Eastern Ontario, often at night on roads I had never seen to towns I had never heard of. But nothing untoward happened until I switched candidates to cover Premier Leslie Frost in Northern Ontario. We arrived one night at a small city only to be told that the local hotel would be honored to put up the premier and his party but had no rooms for the press. One of Frost's aides took the innkeeper aside, whispered in his ear and at once rooms could be found, immediately. I asked another reporter how it had been done. "Oh," he said, "He probably just told him that if he couldn't find rooms he needn't bother to apply for renewal of his liquor licence." Or there may have been a more innocent explanation. There was another curious incident a day or so later. Setting off in the morning, we were told that there had been a change in the premier's plans, and we were all to be driven to a nearby lake where we would be picked up by a float plane and flown to a summer cottage occupied by Roy Freuhauf, owner of an American company that made truck bodies. When we landed — curious word, come to think of it, for a plane on floats — on a lake bordering a palatial cottage, the pilot taxied us to a dock, tied up and then disappeared. By the time we had walked up and been greeted by Freuhauf, the pilot was behind the bar. We were entertained while the premier and the tycoon talked— about what we weren't told and didn't ask — and then we flew away to resume the electioneering schedule. I was intrigued, but taking my lead from the natives, I said and wrote nothing.

Most newspapers in those times happily accepted rail passes from the railway companies, free holidays for travel writers, free plane seats from the political parties during elections. In those times, also, at the *Globe,* Dalgleish was in close touch and sympathy with Premier Frost. As Richard J. (Dic) Doyle, editor in chief, wrote later in his book *Hurly-Burly - A Time at the Globe* (Macmillan of Canada, 1990), "What you saw was what you got — a Tory premier with a Tory editor close beside him." There was supposed to be a firewall between the editorial page, which expressed the opinions of the paper, and the news department, which was "objective," but it was not always flameproof. Today, most newspapers protect their credibility by avoiding even the appearance of a conflict of interest.

The *Globe* normally had an editorial page editor who presided over a board of four writers and a cartoonist. When one of the writers was on vacation a reporter was drafted to the board, and it was my turn in 1959, which proved to be another step up in my career. The page editor at the time, in practice if not by title, was Richard J. Needham, known to us for some reason as Bob. He was a remarkable wordsmith, able to write at lightning speed on any subject, and he claimed that his model was a New York journalist who wrote editorials for both the conservative *Herald-Tribune* and the Communist *Daily Worker.* But when later he began to write his own column he turned out to be a libertarian, almost an anarchist, and with style, wisdom and humor he built a large following, particularly among young women. For himself, he preferred single ladies of a certain age who were said to be suitably grateful for his attentions. He claimed to live in a Chinese rooming house, and when he retired from the *Globe*, I was told, he refused to accept a pension and worked as a bicycle messenger. His private life was very much his own, but on one occasion when we were working together he began to talk about problems with a daughter in hospital. I was embarrassed by these uninvited confidences and cut him off, and regret to this day that I was so unsympathetic. But there again was my cooly detached style.

My first day on the editorial board, fresh from City Hall, I was assigned to write a brief editorial on a city subject, and produced a couple of snappy paragraphs with a sting in the tail for the mayor. Before sending all the copy up to Dalgleish for approval, Bob showed me that he had written on my brief: "I think we have found an editorial writer." So it proved, and I spent five mostly happy years on the board. We met around noon, by when we were supposed to have read all the papers and have ideas on topics the page should address that day. Dalgleish, who had run the page for years before becoming publisher, often attended our meetings, and when he was in town always approved all editorials. When he was absent, his assistant, Jim Cooper, would represent him. Cooper had come to Toronto originally as a Beaverbrook press correspondent, which gave us something in common, but I got on well also with Dal. Sitting on a table in the editor's large office where the board met, swinging his legs and snapping the elastic on his eye patch, he loved to argue about policy, and found in me a willing respondent. Sometimes he kept the meetings going for so long that he cut seriously into writing time, to the alarm of the editor.

Occasionally he would invite the board to lunch in the executive dining room, and on special occasions such as an election night he would take us to dinner at Winston's restaurant, then next door to the Globe on King Street. We were paraded also to meet and, it was hoped, impress top businessmen who were of course advertisers. In his book *Hurly-Burly*, Doyle has an amusing account of one such affair when Dal was trying to alert Premier Frost and business tycoons to the growing nationalism in Quebec:

Westell summed up the paper's perception of crisis. He did it brilliantly. No one I knew was better equipped with voice or countenance to convey impending disaster. It was his talent to conjure up The Flood with a mere mention of dew. He might have been the good humour man as far as Leslie Frost was concerned.

Curiously, I have no recollection of the event, but Doyle assures me he has the written evidence on a menu. I do, however, remember another such occasion when I was seated next to the great E.P. Taylor, a leading financier and racehorse owner. His son, Charles, was then *Globe* correspondent in China, and E.P. asked me in the deepest confidence if it were true that his boy had a Chinese girl friend in Hong Kong. He hastened to explain that he was not at all concerned, but his wife was worried. I was able to say I knew nothing of such an unseemly affair.

These of course were heady times for me, only a few years in Canada but already a member of an editorial board of an influential paper and dining with what sociologists might have called the Power Elite. But I could see another side of the situation. Dalgleish, and later Doyle when he was editor, treated the board as if it were important because, I suppose, it suited their purpose to project the image of heavy-duty thinkers debating and deciding Globe policy. But I and some, if not all, of my colleagues had no such illusions. We knew whose opinion would prevail on important issues, which for Dal ranged from great affairs of state to the deplorable condition of the roads his chauffeur had to drive on between the office and Dal's home in the country. We were hired writers who would be allowed to argue about policy, and might even win the day on minor matters, but whose true value was an ability to present any case in compelling prose, within the space allotted, and by deadline. To me, it was an enjoyable exercise, although many of the opinions I was required to present struck me as reactionary. One of my colleagues was Stuart Shaw, legally-trained in Alberta, a splendid writer despite the fact he could hardly see the typewriter keys and suffered from an ailment which caused him to nod off to sleep at awkward moments, sometimes in the middle of an urgently needed editorial. He and I did not take ourselves as seriously as might have been wished, and we spent a few lunch times designing a training program for *Globe* editorial writers, based on the Parable of the Good Samaritan. The first lesson taught how to defend the robbers who fell upon the traveler; they were entrepreneurs seizing upon a business opportunity, although their capitalistic high spirits were perhaps a trifle too boisterous. The second lesson justified the priest who passed by the injured man on the other side of the street; he was looking after Number One, as should we all in an individualistic and competitive society. The final test for graduation and a seat on the board was to mount a convincing attack on the Good Samaritan who bound the injured traveller's wounds and paid his bill at the inn; he was a typical bleeding heart liberal whose good intentions turned the traveller into a dependent victim.

After a few months on the board I found myself going with Needham to the composing room every night to make up the editorial page. Union rules were strict and we editorial workers were not permitted to touch the lead type on pain of an instant walk-out by the members of the International Typographical Union (ITU). As the lines of type were fitted into the steel frame of the page, we indicated where we wanted a line cut, a word changed, a "widow," which was a line with only one or two words, tidied, sometimes a paragraph rewritten to make things fit — and often we were reading the type upside down and backwards, a skill quickly acquired. Then we read proofs to catch errors — Dalgleish permitted no errors in his precious page — and read them again to make sure that in correcting errors we had not committed new errors. It was editing the old way, labour intensive but certainly more accurate and probably faster than today's electronic systems. It was also part of the romance of newspapering; I can still smell the hot lead. Becoming Needham's assistant in that way made me, in effect, his deputy, and I began to go in on Sunday to consult with Dalgleish by phone, write a new leader if necessary, and put out the page. One Sunday I got a call at home from Needham announcing that after a disagreement with Dal he was leaving and I had to be prepared to take his place the following morning. I commiserated and asked where he was going. To Los Angeles, he said; he had his flight booked. When I went to work the next day I told a colleague what had happened, and that our leader had gone to L.A. Strange, he said, because he had just seen him on the street. It transpired that Needham had called so many people to announce his departure that he missed his flight, thought better of it, and went and got a job on the *Star*. I filled in until Dalgleish appointed a new page editor from among the ranks of old *Globe* hands in the newsroom, and life continued. The new editor did not want the job and did not last long after he failed to get the point when Dal bounced into the editorial conference one day waving an umbrella to make some argument about a weakness in foreign policy. The editor was mystified. Dal, exasperated, cried, "You know, Chamberlain," referring of course to the umbrella-carrying former British Prime Minister, Neville Chamberlain, who had attempted to appease Hitler. The editor, still puzzled, enquired, "You mean the United Church PR man?" and soon he was back in the newsroom. Needham returned to the *Globe* several years later: The *Globe* was like that then, a writer's paper to which writers tended to return after finding other papers less accommodating.

By 1962, having been away from Britain for almost six years, I was well enough established on the editorial board to ask if I might go to London to write editorials from an important conference of Commonwealth prime ministers. Prime Minister John Diefenbaker was to oppose the British government's wish to enter the European Common Market because it would make it tougher for Canada and other Commonwealth exporters to sell in Britain. I intended also of course to see friends and family. The plan was approved by Dal, and as it turned out he was to be in London at the same time. "I'll be at the Savoy; see me there," he instructed, so I did not escape the editorial leash. When we met in London, he was full of good humour and wanted even to press on me a pair of cufflinks which, he said, would admit me to an exclusive nightclub. His wife, known as Del, wisely persuaded him that it would not be a good idea. He had on occasions a mischievous sense of humor, sometimes directed at our proprietor and his friend Howard Webster. He liked to tell an anecdote about an incident when he and Webster were visiting London. They had a favorite restaurant and decided to lay on a special lunch for one of Webster's business associates, Gene Tunney who had been world boxing champion. Tunney arrived from the U.S., and the fawning restaurant proprietor explained that in his honour they had had his favourite corn-fed steak frozen and flown from Chicago, and had taken instruction from his favourite restaurant in New York on how he liked it cooked, and now they were about to serve it. "It's Friday," said Tunney, and in those days Catholics did not eat meat on Fridays. Another of Dal's stories concerned Webster's first visit to London as owner of the *Globe*, with Dal of course in attendance. In recognition of the fact that they had just arranged to buy the London *Times* news service, they were invited to lunch at the proprietor's country house and Webster was seated next to Lord Kemsley, a famous press baron who owned dozens of papers. Kemsley introduced himself to Webster and said conversationally, "I understand you have just bought *The*

Globe and Mail," to which Webster replied, "Oh yes, and what do you do?" Kemsley allowed as he too owned a newspaper.

At the Commonwealth conference, the prime ministers solemnly agreed, as usual, that their discussions would be in private, and an official would brief the press in only general terms, with no names named. Diefenbaker was an Anglophile and took the secrecy talk seriously. He was surprised and alarmed, therefore, when the British papers ran stories which purported to reveal what was happening in the conference, putting both him and his case against Britain in a poor light. Who could be leaking such inaccurate information? Certainly not those admirable Brits with their famous sense of fair play. But as a graduate of British news management, I knew exactly what was happening, and confirmed it with former pals at Westminster. The anonymous Downing Street source was briefing the press on the way British arguments were prevailing at the conference over those of the hick from Canada. I tried to explain the process to the Canadian Cabinet secretary, Bob Bryce, but the black arts of spinning were unknown to him, and I doubt that Diefenbaker ever understood how he had been shafted.

Back in Canada, he was in trouble from another source and an election was looming. Both the North Atlantic Treaty Organization (NATO) and the North American Air Defence Command (NORAD) planned to use nuclear weapons in the event of a Soviet attack. As a member of the alliances, Canada had tacitly accepted the nuclear strategy without itself acquiring nuclear weapons. U.S.- made Bomarc anti-aircraft missiles had been deployed in Canada, but it was not until 1961 that it became clear that they were to be armed with nuclear warheads. A great debate over nuclear weapons began between those who believed in collective defence through the alliance system and its nuclear weapons, and those who wanted Canada to be an independent voice for peace and disarmament. The debate raged at many levels, from grassroots "Peace" movements to the Cabinet which was hopelessly divided. External Affairs Minister Howard Green was hot for nuclear disarmament; Defence Minister Douglas Harkness for honoring nuclear commitments to allies; Diefenbaker was undecided, but highly suspicious of the United States and tempted always to wrap himself in the flag of anti-Americanism and spit in the eye of President John F. Kennedy whom he disliked personally. Curiously, while the Cabinet was still unde-

cided on nuclear weapons, the RCAF was running visits for opinion leaders to NORAD headquarters at Colorado Springs and to a Strategic Air
Command bomber base in Nebraska. As the *Globe's* representative on the
Canadian Institute of International Affairs, I went on one of those indoctrination visits, organized by Wing Commander William Lee, the top PR
man in the Defence Department. (Make what you will of the fact that
when the nuclear issue eventually defeated the Conservative government,
in 1963, Bill Lee left the airforce and became a political assistant to the new
Liberald defence minister, Paul Hellyer, and later worked for prime ministers Pierre Trudeau and John Turner.) I had no need of nuclear indoctrination because both I and the *Globe* firmly supported collective security. In
fact, the series of editorials I wrote on the nuclear issue won me in 1963
my first National Newspaper Award. But the trip to the United States had
one unexpected consequence. When our RCAF plane landed on a secure
U.S. base, an officer came aboard and said casually he assumed we were all
Canadian citizens. Embarrassed, I had to admit I was not, and I resolved
there and then to correct that defect, which I soon did. Fortunately, my
British citizenship was acceptable to the American security people.

As a Tory, Dalgleish had welcomed Diefenbaker when he narrowly
defeated the Liberals in 1957 and then won a huge victory in 1958. But his
enthusiasm soon began to wane when the new prime minister proved to
be better at politics than at government. One among many disillusionments
occurred when Webster, whose father had been a senator, decided that he
wanted to talk to Diefenbaker about Senate reform. Dalgleish made the
appointment and went with Webster, but not much was achieved. As Dal
told the story, when they entered his office, Dief said, "Ah yes, you want to
talk about the Senate; well, I'll tell you what I'm going to do about the
Senate; I'm going to appoint an Indian." And that was more or less that.
Incidentally, he did appoint an Indian who, like other senators, fell victim
to the combination of too little work and too much whisky. But as the 1962
election approached Dal had to choose between Diefenbaker and supporting a return of the reviled Liberals. He summoned Doyle, then managing
editor and his protégé, and me to his office to review the issue. Both Doyle
and I made our cases for supporting Lester Pearson and the Liberals, mainly because Diefenbaker seemed a hopeless case, but Dal said that just for the
sake of argument he would make the case for the Tories. He had on his side

the fact that the *Globe* had been campaigning for tax reform — some things never change — and Diefenbaker had announced on the first day of the campaign that if re-elected he would appoint a royal commission to propose change. There was no doubt that it was a sop to the *Globe* because the Ottawa bureau chief told us that Dief admitted as much in a private aside, but Dal was not discouraged. Neither was Doyle who pronounced himself converted by Dal's arguments. I was not, but it was now the publisher and the managing editor for the Tories and I for the Liberals, so we endorsed the Tories and I dutifully wrote some of the arguments. There was, however, an ironic outcome. Dief won, with only a minority government in daily danger of defeat, but he did honour his promise by appointing a Toronto accountant, Kenneth Carter, to head a tax commission, thereby seeming to justify Dal's decision. After an exhaustive inquiry, the Carter commission produced in 1966 a six-volume report proposing radical reforms that would have raised taxes on the wealthy and on some businesses, including farmers, and lowered them on the poor. This frightened the *Globe* and most of the business community half to death, which in turn frightened the Liberal government of the time, so eventually nothing much happened.

Diefenbaker's minority government was defeated on a vote of confidence in the Commons in 1963 because he simply could not make up his mind on nuclear weapons and managed to unite against him opposition parties on both sides of the issue. So now Dal had to face again the decision of which party to support — unless by some miracle Diefenbaker could be replaced by a new and more credible Tory leader. There was in fact a plot under way by disaffected Cabinet ministers, of whom George Hees was a leader, to persuade Dief to resign as prime minister and become chief justice of the Supreme Court — a preposterous idea because his legal career had been as a crusading counsel, not as a judge or legal scholar. Dal was privy to the plot and happened at the time to be in hospital for an operation for hemorrhoids, which did nothing to improve his disposition. (The unfortunate hospital orderly who served him was of German descent and Dal irritably insisted he was a former U-boat commander.) When the plot failed and Hees and others emerged from the Tory caucus to announce that they were all united behind their beloved leader, Dal summoned me to his bedside for instructions on what to say in a lead editorial, the most powerful, I think, I ever wrote:

When the members of the Cabinet emerged from the Conservative Party caucus in Ottawa on Wednesday they assured reporters that there was no truth in reports of a revolt against Prime Minister John Diefenbaker's leadership. "The party was never more excellent," said Finance Minister George Nowlan. "We've never had a more united party," insisted Trade and Commerce Minister George Hees. "Nothing but a hallelujah chorus," added Senator Wallace McCutcheon who denied any intention of resigning from the government. Others made similar comments.

These men were not telling the truth. It is a matter of fact that some Ministers of the Crown who on Wednesday declared their allegiance to the great leader had, only two days before, their resignations ready in their pockets. It was to be the Prime Minister's resignation or theirs.

Today the Prime Minister is still in office and the rebels, having deserted their cause, are still in the Cabinet. They have purchased their jobs, for a few weeks, doubtless to "preserve" the party. So now these men lead their tattered party into the election with lies on their lips and a dual standard of morality. They have one set of morals for church-going and for the children's hour, and another for the smoke filled rooms...

There can be nothing among them now but more turmoil, backbiting and suspicion.

Such is the sort of leadership they are asking the public to endorse.

When I read my handiwork in the morning I had only one regret. The first paragraph was a low key recitation of the facts. The second as I wrote it opened with abrupt change of pace and a shocking charge, "These men were lying." But the cautious editor of the page had changed it to the gentler, "were not telling the truth," which took some of the pace and punch out the piece. Nevertheless, we heard from Ottawa that Hees had turned pale on reading the indictment.

Dal called me to his office on one occasion to commend my work and to say that my turn as editor of the editorial page would come. It was not to be: that summer of 1963 he died suddenly of a heart attack, aged fifty-three. I was surprised to find myself moved by his death. While disagreeing with his politics, I enjoyed jousting with him and admired the way he made the *Globe* a much better paper than it had been when he took over as publisher, and on track to become even better. His death meant change at the top, and before long change for me. Webster became publisher for the time being, Cooper editor-in-chief, and Doyle editor, running the editorial page himself and the news department through his old friend Clark Davey, who became managing editor. Doyle and Davey had worked together on a small Ontario daily, *The Chatham Daily News*, and as he moved up through the *Globe* Doyle took Davey with him — not that Davey was not an able journalist in his own right. The two became known to the staff as the Chatham Mafia, particularly when a third Chatham boy, Colin McCullough, who had been an assistant to Doyle, became assistant to the publisher. Three journalists from one small town in top jobs at the *Globe* seemed beyond coincidence.

But despite the fact that I was not from Chatham, Doyle made me his assistant on the editorial page and chief editorial writer. This meant in effect that I was editor of the page when he was absent, which proved to be rather more than either of us had expected when the International Typographical Union went on strike against the three Toronto dailies. I have already explained how we put together the editorial page every night, working with the craftsmen who received copy from the editorial department, set it into lines of lead type on linotype machines, and then fitted them into page forms. Early in 1964, it became known that computer technology was coming that would send the copy directly from the editors to a computer and then to automated machines that could set type at several times the rate of a manual worker. There were lengthy negotiations between the ITU and the employers, with some give and take, and the men I worked with — long-service craftsmen attached to the *Globe* — were not expecting a strike. But suddenly the strike came, apparently because the union headquarters in the United States had chosen Toronto as the field of battle for all North America.

The rank and file members rallied to their union, in part because the union controlled their pension rights, and the men we had worked with were walking picket lines around the three newspaper offices and jeering those of us who crossed. There were security men in the lobbies and we had to show passes to go to work in what had been an easy-going place. The question was whether the members of the Newspaper Guild, to which I and most Toronto journalists belonged, would decide to refuse to cross the lines. Managers and non-unionized employees could man the composing rooms and put together some sort of paper, but with no journalists there would be little interesting copy to fill the paper. We Guild members met at the Royal York Hotel to decide what to do. I had always been a union member and had seen how journalists' unions had improved our living and working conditions, but I couldn't see how the ITU could stop technological advance, or even that it should try. The employers were offering job security to the ITU men, although in different jobs, and that seemed to me the important issue. There was also the fact that Guild had signed contracts with the papers and I thought that we should honour our obligations, just as we expected the employers to honour theirs. Unaccustomed as I was to public speaking and keenly aware that my position as assistant to the editor would make me suspect, I did join the debate at the Guild meeting, to some effect, or so I was told. I pointed out that we were lucky to have three dailies in Toronto when many North American cities were down to one, and that a prolonged strike might well mean that the most vulnerable, the *Telegram*, would not reopen. The warning was not idle; the *Tely* did close a few years later. The meeting voted overwhelmingly to keep working, but that did not mean doing the work of the strikers.

Back at the office, Cooper, Doyle, Davey, and every other executive in the building was working in the composing room. They did not ask Guild members to join them, but some did anyway. I was left to run the editorial page and what we called the op-ed page, the facing page on which we ran articles. There was of course some hypocrisy in my position; I wasn't doing the work of strikers, but I was doing in addition to my own the work the work of others who were thereby freed to replace strikers. But I thought the strikers' cause was not only wrong but lost, and in fact many of them never returned to their jobs at the *Globe* when the strike eventually petered out.

While Doyle and I had worked well together it would be in both our interests if I moved on and was no longer arguing about policy and looking over his editorial shoulder. He asked if I would like to go to Ottawa as bureau chief, and the offer was as welcome as it was unexpected. After less than eight years in Canada, I was being offered one of the top reporting jobs in the country. And Jeannie and I had already decided it was past time to leave the suburbs so that we and the children could enjoy more of urban life. She had heard bad things about Ottawa, but a summertime visit, with the kids, convinced her that it would be a much better place to live than Scarborough, or perhaps even downtown Toronto. Our plans were delayed by the strike and also by the difficulty of finding a suitable house in Ottawa. We sold our Scarborough house to a colleague on the *Globe* not long arrived from Scotland at a no-profit price: in fact, in another piece of creative financing, I lent him the money to pay me the downpayment. In Ottawa we found a three-storey, five-bedroom house in the Glebe, a pleasant old residential area within walking distance of Parliament and good schools. It had been renovated enough to make it possible for us to walk right in, and we bought it for $24,000. I worried about how we would ever repay such an enormous mortgage.

~ Chapter 8 ~

Making a National Name

O ur real estate agent welcomed us to Ottawa with a warning about the climate. He was working on a novel, he said, which began, "It was early spring in Ottawa and pretty soon the nights would be drawing in." Nevertheless, he had chosen to settle in the city on retiring from the U.S. Consular Service, and we too survived the brutal winters to enjoy life in a small capital. In fact, the next fourteen years were the best in my life — so far — and when after a few years the managing editor called to tell me, "You're going to Washington," I politely but firmly refused. It was the first, and perhaps the last, occasion in my life when I refused an opportunity to "move on." I was not persuaded even by the prospect that after Washington I could reasonably expect to be appointed to London. I didn't want to uproot my family again, and anyway I was only just beginning to know my way around the federal government.

The fabulous "Sixties" were dawning — they ran from about 1965 to 1975 — and everything seemed possible. It was an age of confidence, optimism, and experimentation, and unlike some parents we welcomed it. Our house became Action Central for kids growing into their teens, mostly because my wife welcomed them, enjoyed their company, and served them Earl Gray tea — not drugs, as some less popular parents seemed to believe. On several occasions when kids could not get on at home they came to live with us until the problems could be sorted out. When our daughter and her friends were threatening to drop out of high school, we helped them plan a free school and then take their proposal to the Ottawa School Board, where it was turned down by reactionary trustees who accused them of being revolutionaries. I was afraid that might disillusion the youngsters with the democratic process, but instead most of them went back to school to graduate. Schools were not only peaceful but creative centres for student life, one of the great achievements of Canadian society, and one I fear is fading into history. The best teachers became, and some remain, friends who inspired high standards rather than acting as taskmasters, or should I say taskpersons.

We soon acquired a new member of the family, a mongrel puppy bought for $2.00 and named Chipper, who became better known in the district than we were. Our back-fence neighbour at the time was Mario Bernardi, conductor of the National Arts Centre orchestra, and Chipper was a regular gate crasher at his barbecues — and sometimes an invited guest at his small daughter's bedtime baths. In fact, he established secondary homes with several families where he could drop in for a snack. Much too late, I read that a dog will become leader of the pack unless firmly put in his place when a puppy. Chipper became leader of our pack, coming and going as he pleased, except for occasional encounters with the dog catcher, and for years our house was organized around his convenience. But how I loved that dog, and how I wept when, after a last jog together, we had to take him, at age fourteen and in poor health, to the vet for a lethal overdose of an anaesthetic. Shortly, our old cat became ill, and the vet advised us that she too was grieving for Chipper.

But I must not pretend that I was a major player in this vibrant home life. I was working too hard, and I reserved home for my private life. As I recall, the only politician to cross the threshold was Flora Macdonald who, out for an evening run, arrived panting on our doorstep in need of refreshment, which we took on the back porch. I don't mean to say that I had no social life with politicians; I sometimes took them to lunch or attended their parties. It was just that I preferred to draw a line between my private and professional lives. I may have forfeited good contacts and much gossip in that way, but on the other hand I preserved a certain distance between myself and those on whom I reported, and I thought that desirable. However, my knack for being in the right place at the right time held good. The period of 1965-1968 was probably the most exciting there has ever been in Canadian political life, and I had first-rate colleagues in the bureau. Any bureau chief's reputation rests as much on the work of the staff as it does on his or her own. I inherited a strong bureau, but among the coming and goings of the next few years I remember, and owe my thanks, to two in particular. Geoffrey Stevens arrived from Toronto soon after I did, and we developed a remarkable partnership. We covered many major stories together, sharing a byline, and our editors said they could not discern where Geoff's copy ended and mine began. I was less than excited when informed that the owner's nephew, Norman Webster, was to join us. I needed a reporter who had been appointed on merit, and it took me some days to overcome my prejudice and realize that Norman more than met the bill. We were extremely busy when he arrived and I set him to work day and night. He was willing and able, and it was only after several days that he mentioned that his grandparents lived in Ottawa and he would like an evening off to visit them. Norman lived in a sort of rooming house around the corner from my house, and on occasions when we worked late I would take him home around 11 p.m. and expect my wife to feed us both. One morning she answered the door to a young American woman who said she was going to marry Norman and that he had suggested she talk to my wife to find out what being married to him might entail. My wife can't have been too discouraging because Norman and Pat are still married. He went on to become editor-in-chief of the *Globe*, with Geoff as his managing editor.

A few weeks after I took over as bureau chief, a scandal struck the Liberal government, and other scandals followed one after the other for a couple of years. There were Mafia men and ministerial assistants, call girls and Cabinet ministers, spies and speculation about every sort of skullduggery. Much of it was more sensational than serious, but it made wonderful headlines. More importantly, there were general elections in 1965 and 1968, and both the Liberal and Conservative parties changed their leaders. Lester Pearson gave way with dignity to Pierre Trudeau; John Diefenbaker was removed struggling to make way for Robert Stanfield. Federal-provincial negotiations to reform the constitution began in 1967 — initiated by Ontario, in case you have been blaming Ottawa — and the Parti Québécois was formed in 1968, raising for the first time a serious threat of separation. And then of course in there were the country's centennial celebrations in 1967, including the Expo world fair in Montreal. With all that and much more on the Ottawa news agenda, it's not surprising that now my children sometimes ask me, jocularly

I hope, "Where were you when we were growing up?" Most of the time I was in the parliamentary press gallery, and my byline on the front of the *Globe* became known across Canada. The competition for attention was much less intense then than now. When I joined the press gallery there were only about fifty members covering the daily news: thirty years later, the number was more than two hundred, including the TV crews. Newspapers were still the dominant medium, and as bureau chief for the paper read by most politicians and top civil servants, not to mention other journalists, I had standing and access long before I had earned it. The *Globe* was one of the few papers with an office off Parliament Hill, but we still did much of our work in the press gallery "hot room," strategically located between the Commons and the Senate. Desks for reporters from the major papers and news organizations overflowed the allotted space and, to the alarm of the fire marshall, some members piled bound volumes of Hansard in the corridor to wall off cubicles.

At one end of the hot room there was a lounge-cum-library which served also as cardroom and, occasionally, as overnight accommodation for those who couldn't, for one reason or another, go home. At the other end was a sort of "speakeasy," operated by the clerks who also answered phones and handed out free stationery. Liquor by the glass could be obtained at reasonable prices, and a pop machine had been adapted to serve cans of beer. This scandalous state of affairs was frequently exposed by investigative reporters in need of a story — not our members, of course — but as thirsty MPs found our facilities useful, nothing was ever done. And as we often worked until after the Commons rose at 10 p.m. or later, reporting debates and votes, and filing every day two columns of verbatim reporting from Hansard, the bar was much appreciated. CP and CN telegraph agents handled most of our copy right from the gallery. We also had access to the parliamentary dining room where excellent food was served at subsidized prices, and we came and went on Parliament Hill as we pleased. Prime ministers often talked with reporters off the record, confident they would not be betrayed, most ministers were readily available, backbench MPs of course clamored for attention, and even senior bureaucrats, the legendary mandarins, talked privately with reporters they knew. This easy-going relationship changed later when membership in the gallery ballooned with TV and radio reporters and their accompanying technicians, the civil service mushroomed, security became a serious concern, and some journalists came to believe that there could be no confidences between politicians who were all suspect and the news media carrying the sword of truth on behalf of the suffering taxpayers.

Every year the gallery organized a dinner and put on a show, mostly original songs lampooning the politicians. To suggest the flavour of the occasions, let me recall the best song I heard. It was by George Bain who dealt seriously with serious matters in his column in the *Globe* on most days but lapsed on other days with even more success into comic essays and verse. The song was sung by a tubby reporter dressed as a blonde German prostitute, Gerda Munsinger, who, in one of the scandals of the era, had been linked by rumor to Conservative Cabinet Minister George Hees, who could not fairly, or safely, be named at that stage of the affair. But Hees in his youth had played football for the Toronto Argonauts, and the refrain of George's song was, "Mein Gott, that handsome Argonot." I should add that on another occasion George lampooned me, but I have forgotten what it was about, which is perhaps just as well. The dinner was the social occasion of the political year. Gallery members invited their publishers and editors, and such politicians and business tycoons as they wished to please; invitations were eagerly sought. The Governor General and party leaders made speeches, often witty. Everything was strictly off-the-record. In fact, when Prime Minister W.L. Mackenzie King announced at a dinner his intention to retire, the gallery executive felt they had to go to see him the following morning to ask if they could report what he had said. He agreed. At the first dinner I attended, as a guest before moving to Ottawa, Governor General George Vanier explained that he wanted to speak about relations between Quebec and the rest of Canada, but as that would verge improperly on political issues he would discuss instead relations between two imaginary islands in the Arctic, which he did with his customary wisdom. Not a word was reported.

But a great deal was drunk, often far too much, before, during and after the dinner, and I came face to bottle with this in my first year as bureau chief. We had invited our owner, Howard Webster, and our editor, Dic Doyle, and my first engagement of the day was to host a lunch for them to which we invited also politicians, civil servants and others. By mid-afternoon, we had all had quite enough to drink, but Webster, who had a deep thirst, wanted to go on to another event, and so I took him to a reception being given by *The Wall Street Journal*. At five it was time to change into dinner jackets for the pre-dinner cocktail reception. I went home and was struggling into my starched shirt and rented tux when my wife took me aside and said the children were asking why daddy was talking and walking so funny. I drank no more that day and became soberer while others got drunker, a revealing evening. When I went home in the early hours some revellers were heading for the National Press Club for a pre-breakfast pick-me-up. (I interrupt my narrative here to note that few reporters in those days owned a dinner suit and the custom was to rent one as necessary and charge it on expenses. I persuaded the *Globe* that it would be more convenient for all if those of us who wished bought evening dress and amortized the cost by charging "rental" when we wore it. This sensible arrangement worked for a quarter century until William Thorsell became editor and scrapped it. His argument was that evening dress should be part of every journalist's working equipment. I think that said more about Thorsell's elevated social life than about the lives of most of his staff. But something of the old arrangement survives; with suitable expansions, I'm still wearing the suit I bought in 1965.

The boisterous nature of the gallery dinner was one reason, I suppose, why women were not invited — not even the two or three women members of the gallery or the women MPs. But consciousness was rising in the 1960s, even in the press gallery, and I and a few others staged a coup at the gallery's annual meeting and carried a surprise vote to change the policy and admit women to the dinner. Our cause was not helped when our most prominent woman, Joyce Fairbairn — later an aide to Prime Minister Trudeau and then a Senator and minister — said she didn't want to go to the dinner anyway. Some of the older hands were outraged by our outrageous procedural tactics and announced that they would call an emergency meeting to reverse the vote. I thought I might be able to head them off by immediately inviting Judy LaMarsh, a formidable Cabinet minister: Would they dare to tell her that the policy had been changed and her invitation cancelled? I called Judy at home and was told she was being interviewed at a local TV station where, as it happened, one of my *Globe* was recording a program. So then I called the station, got my colleague on the phone, and asked him to invite Judy on my behalf. "I'll invite her myself," he said, and she accepted. He got his reward a few years later when Judy, in her memoirs, denounced him for drinking too much at the dinner and paying her insufficient attention. But our new policy stuck, and we were able later to extend the list of eligible women to include political aides and party officials. My reward was the pleasure of escorting one of the most popular women in politics at that time, Flora MacDonald — popular, that was, with everyone except Diefenbaker and his cronies who hated her with a passion because she had helped engineer the succession of Stanfield. But as relations between politician and press changed, much of the good humour seemed to evaporate, and the dinner became an on-the-record affair at which journalists appoint themselves critics of the speeches they invited the party leaders to make. My interest soured long before my Gallery membership expired.

I and others engaged in a little more consciousness-raising by picketing the annual National Press Club ball after the members had voted not to admit women. The following day, the president of the club complained that our picketing had embarrassed his wife, and he promised to retaliate by taking the first opportunity to embarrass my wife. Knowing my wife, I told him he was welcome to try. But victory was ours when the press club soon reversed itself. When the report of the Royal Commission on the Status of Women was tabled in the Commons in 1970, I wrote that it was a bomb, primed and ticking and far more explosive than the famous report on Bilingualism and Biculturalism: "It is concerned not merely with relations between French and English, but between man and woman. The history of the problem it describes and seeks to solve is not 100 years of Confederation but the story of mankind." (Note that slip into incorrectness.) It would be implemented, I said, because government was responding to the rising ferment of the women's movement, but the real problem was to change attitudes:

> It will be a bitter struggle, perhaps a civil war, within the family and society as women fight for a place in the power structure controlled by men. The depth of male chauvinism has seldom been more obvious than it was yesterday when the commission chairman (sic), Florence Bird, met we gentlemen of the press

who are not only her friends and acquaintances but supposed to be alert to current trends.

The first question was about the incredible possibility that under the report's proposals women may fly airliners and stewardesses may not all be young and sexy.

The second question was prefaced by the gratuitous comment that the report seemed very logical, as if it were remarkable that a report by women could be logical. The third suggested that women will never play a full role in public life because they hate and refuse to work for each other.

Mine was not a popular attitude in the press gallery, or perhaps among men generally, but it was correct. So while I was far from a model husband, I did skirmish in the gender wars, and on the right side.

I have mentioned that when I went to Ottawa, reporters occasionally had informal access to the prime minister on an off-the-record basis. My first opportunity was when Prime Minister Pearson, shortly after my arrival, took off on a swing across the Prairies, and I went along, with a few other reporters, primarily to make contact with the great man. The Commons was in an uproar over allegations that Liberal aides had been involved in attempts to obtain bail for a Mafia drug dealer in jail in Montreal awaiting deportation to face charges in the United States. Pearson was in more than two minds about going ahead with his trip, but when the Cabinet decided to appoint a judicial inquiry, he thought, foolishly, that the Opposition would let go of a juicy scandal, and that he could safely leave town for a few days. As a new bureau chief covering his first crisis, I too had doubts about leaving Ottawa, but I decided that the opportunity of getting to know Pearson was too good to miss, and that my coverage of him on the road might supplement the work of my colleagues in Ottawa. The trip turned out to be more newsworthy than I had expected and gave me my first opportunity to experiment with a new form of reporting that soon became my trademark in Ottawa.

Facing increasing competition from radio and TV which could report bare facts faster and with more dramatic impact, newspapers were seeking ways to convey the colour and flavor of events, to put facts in context, to explain what the news meant. The division between fact and comment was eroding, and what came to be called the New Journalism was emerging. In Ottawa, Peter C. Newman led the way with columns, articles and books exploring the personalities of those making the news, the drama of politics, and the conspiracies behind the day's events. I developed my version of new reporting not as a columnist or a commentator on a feature page where some latitude had always been allowed, but as a reporter writing in the news columns. It is commonplace now to see news pieces identified as "Analysis," and to read judgmental reporting, but in those days it was revolutionary — and controversial. As a former editorial writer I had fewer inhibitions than most reporters about making judgments, and, equally important, I had a good working relationship with the *Globe's* editor, Dic Doyle, which gave me confidence to experiment. My priority of course was to report the news in the conventional way, but occasionally I could slip off the straitjacket of news writing and prepare a long and, I hoped, insightful account of some complicated event or sprawling situation that orthodox news stories could not properly explain.

Pearson's trip across the Prairies was just such an event. The conventional news was that he was speaking about national unity, and receiving standing ovations from political and non-political audiences that showed little interest in the unfolding scandal in Ottawa. The story behind that story was that he was desperately worried by the political crisis developing in Ottawa but indecisive about whether he should cancel his itinerary and fly home to face the music in the Commons. Much later, I got hold of his diary — how is another story to be told later — in which Pearson described his feelings:

This problem, coupled with the very strenuous and crowded program which I was trying to carry out, gave me two or three of the most difficult days I have ever had. Naturally, I was being criticized strongly in the House of Commons by the Opposition of (sic) running away from what they considered to be my duty; lack of courage etc. This upset me to the point where, on Thursday, I telephoned that I was flying back that night and that I would cancel the engagements in Winnipeg the next day, even though I knew this would cause maximum disappointment there. I felt better having made up my mind, but not for long ... For a couple of days now I had been getting contradictory reports in this connection; some saying, don't come, and others, come. But Thursday night the Cabinet was unanimous in its decision that I should not for a moment consider returning.

The fact that none of we reporters in the party knew what was happening until the Thursday night is a comment on our limitations as journalists. But even if we had known it would not have made much of a conventional news story: There was no single fact or event, and no quotable source; it was a developing situation, and this I was able to describe with illustrative detail, even a touch of drama, in my wrap-up "new journalism" at the end of the trip. I wrote about the constant exchanges with Ottawa, interrupted when we arrived in Portage LaPrairie, Manitoba, because there were no phones in the hotel rooms and the PM's staff had to commandeer the manager's office; Pearson's wandering mind as he spoke that evening to a Chamber of Commerce dinner; the crowded press conference in the Vimy Legion Hall at which he began to hedge on the plan already announced to return, causing I and other reporters to worry about the stories we had filed earlier; Pearson's appeal at a reception to "the British sense of fair play" when considering the allegations in Ottawa; the atmosphere in the plane at 11 p.m. with deadlines passing and it still not sure whether we were going to Ottawa or to Winnipeg; Pearson's press secretary, Dick O'Hagan, running across the wet tarmac from the control tower where he had been on the phone, again, to Ottawa, and bounding aboard to say, "It's Winnipeg." He had been assured that the government would survive a vote in the Commons that night, and the immediate crisis was over. My story raised a lot of conventional eyebrows in the press gallery, but Doyle liked it, which meant that I could experiment some more.

Back then, it was not done to write about the role of journalists in the news — we were just those objective flies on the wall — so there were a couple of incidents on the trip that I did not mention, both concerning the late Norman DePoe, CBC-TV's senior man in Ottawa and one of the best reporters of his time. Norman was often accused by critics of being too kind to the Liberals, but nobody could have made such a charge that night in the Vimy Legion Hall. Pearson was explaining that whether or not he would return to Ottawa would depend on whether the Commons passed the Justice department estimates, on which the critical vote was to be held. Stabbing him in the chest with one forefinger, DePoe thrust his microphone under Pearson's nose and demanded to know whether the real issue was the passing of the estimates or the reputation of Pearson's government. There was no answer from a shaken prime minister. DePoe was worried because he had filed a story for the CBC main newscast based on the announcement that the prime minister was returning, and now there was doubt. I had phoned a similar story to the *Globe*, but knew that with luck there would be an opportunity to change it for a later edition. When we heard in the plane that the plan had changed and we were going to Winnipeg, there was nothing we could do until we got there. As soon as the plane landed DePoe and I leapt off ahead of Pearson, ran for the nearest building, and found two phones: I can still hear in memory, DePoe's anguished cry down the line to Toronto: "The eleven o'clock news was wrong."

But the fact that the trip yielded a good story was a bonus. As I have said, my primary purpose in going on the trip with Pearson had been to get to know him, and that paid off too. Part of our travels were by train, and one night as we rolled across the prairie Pearson invited us to his private coach for a drink and a chat. Somehow we got onto the subject of the Suez crisis in 1956 when Pearson won the Nobel Peace Prize for inventing the idea of a UN peacekeeping force and persuading other countries to adopt it — the initiative, incidentally, from which all subsequent UN peacekeeping operations have flowed. He explained to us that nations formerly opposed to UN peacekeeping changed their minds because the alternative seemed likely to be much worse, a nuclear confrontation between the Soviet Union and the United States. He added that it was only in times of crisis that people and countries could be persuaded to abandon the status quo and try something new. I was intrigued by that insight into his thinking because Pearson and his government were crisis-prone, always stumbling into trouble and then negotiating desperately to find a way out. His reputation was that of a bungler, but I began to wonder if inducing crises was not his way of bringing about change. After all, his friend Bruce Hutchinson, the distinguished journalist and author, had observed that Pearson was never happier than when hanging by his fingernails over some political precipice. I have advanced this theory of change-by-crisis to those who were close to Pearson and been assured that it was not so, but how else can one explain the way in which he secured adoption of a new Canadian flag? First, he invited a few journalists, including my near-namesake Stanley Westall, to 24 Sussex Drive for drinks and suddenly produced a design for a new flag. The stories the next day produced the storm he must surely have anticipated, but he went further and next unveiled his flag to the most hostile audience he could have found, a Canadian Legion convention at which the delegates had fought proudly under the Red Ensign. Flapping a red flag in front of a bull had nothing on it.

Another storm in the Commons followed, but the outcome was a committee to study various flag designs. The committee rejected Pearson's design — Diefenbaker was able to crow that the "Pearson pennant" had been hauled down — but it recommended the flag we now fly. From parliamentary deadlock, Pearson had extracted what he had wanted from the outset, a new national flag adopted by a Parliament in which he had only minority support. If Pearson did not consciously produce crises, he was certainly able sometimes to take advantage of them, using the skills of negotiation and compromise that had made him such a successful diplomat. This helps to explain one of the mysteries of the era: His two minority governments — 1963-65, and 1965-68 — seemed to stagger from one blunder to another, but emerged with an extraordinary record of reform including Medicare, the Canada Pension Plan, the Canada Assistance Plan, and the conception of official bilingualism which transformed the federal civil service.

I went on another trip with Pearson in the summer of 1965 when he was exploring the mood of the country before deciding whether to call a general election. In Vancouver, he announced federal support for a new agriculture building in the grounds of the Pacific National Exhibition. I saw nothing unusual about this, but Jack Cahill, the Ottawa correspondent for *The Vancouver Sun* who was travelling with Pearson, did. He had previously worked in Vancouver and realized that the new building might turn out to be hockey stadium in disguise. When he could not arouse much interest in the story at the *Sun*, he mentioned it to me, and after checking I wrote a piece for the *Globe*. I added that the

Sun must have been aware of the real purpose of the building but had published little about it, and implied with a disapproving sniff that this may have been because the *Sun's* publisher, Stuart Keate, was a friend of Pearson's and had been entertaining him. On the way back to Ottawa, Pearson stopped in Saskatchewan where, out of the blue at a reception, a local businessman mentioned to me that the *Globe* had been sold to FP newspapers, a loose group of half a dozen major papers, including the *Sun*. Much concerned, I hurried to phone Managing Editor Davey who made inquiries and assured me it wasn't true. Back in Ottawa, I heard from Doyle that Keate was complaining about my story, but I brushed that off, saying in effect, "Who cares what Keate thinks." Pretty soon, I cared: Without telling anyone in Toronto, Webster had indeed swapped the *Globe* for a one-third share in FP, and Keate was now a director of the *Globe*. He was, however, a good chap, and I heard no more about my offending story. As he revealed later, he was having his own troubles with FP, which was run by Richard Malone, whose chief claim to fame was that he had been General Montgomery's PR man during the Second World War. He still carried the title of brigadier and talked endlessly of his military experiences. One of his stories concerned the draft of the communique to be issued by Eisenhower announcing the landing in Normandy on D-Day; American and British but not Canadian forces were mentioned although the Canadians of course played an important role. Malone took credit for getting the Canadians included at the last moment. But whatever credit he might have deserved for that, he was a pompous idiot who managed several good papers into terminal decline and succeeded in annoying almost everybody he worked with. They included Keate, who in his book, *Paper Boy* (Clarke Irwin, 1980) wrote: "The roster of FP alumni who tried (to get along with Malone) but gave up in despair, was impressive. Anthony Westell, Jack Cahill and Stan McDowell, all first-rate journalists, went to *The Toronto Star...*"

As it happened, even when he became publisher of the *Globe*, Malone was to me no more than a minor irritation. He even entrusted to me the care of his unfortunate son who was supposed to be learning the business. I went to the *Star* for reasons other than Malone, to be explained later.

My next opportunity to experiment with the new way of reporting came during the 1965 election campaign, an extraordinary event even by the standards of that extraordinary period in politics. A reluctant campaigner at best, Pearson called the election because he was assured by his friend and advisor Walter Gordon that he would win a majority, putting an end to the crises in the Commons. He would also have the satisfaction of finally besting his old foe and tormentor, John Diefenbaker, who would then be replaced as leader of the Conservative Party and of the Opposition. A crushing defeat for the Tories indeed seemed likely, causing a number of leading party members who had deserted Dief in 1963 to return to the aid of their party. Among those were Eddie Goodman, an ebullient Toronto lawyer, known to his annoyance as Fast Eddie, who became campaign manager with few resources but lots of ingenuity. He ran a guerilla war against the Liberals, writing an attractive Conservative manifesto at his kitchen table and fabricating favorable polls, among other tricks. In his stump speech, Pearson was arguing for a majority government on the grounds this was the third election in four years and that if the voters again elected a minority government there would inevitably be another one soon. He made this obvious point for the umpteenth time in Toronto, and a mischievous Canadian Press reporter realized that if Pearson's words were reported straight, without context, it might look as if he were threatening that unless he got a majority he would call another election. A number of Conservative-inclined papers jumped at this story — including the *Globe* which chose to ignore the anguished objections of its own reporter, Geoff Stevens, who knew it was a distortion of what Pearson intended. While this version of events was taking shape in the newsrooms of the nation, Pearson was flying across the country and when he landed at Vancouver he was surprised to be met by a horde of reporters demanding to know why he was threatening the voters. Pearson of course denied having said any such thing, and Goodman, back in Ottawa, saw an opportunity: He patched together on one tape a clip of Pearson in Toronto and then seemingly denying himself in Vancouver, and fed it to radio stations where it became a hot item, helping to bring about the result Pearson had feared, another minority government.

Goodman's goal was not to save Dief but to save the party, and when toward the end of the campaign the Tories were doing much better than expected, he was facing a disaster: He might actually be re-electing Dief, an incompetent prime minister who had split the party over the nuclear issue.

In his cheerful way, Goodman and a few allies agreed that if Dief indeed won the election they would join hands and leap from a high window in the Chateau Laurier Hotel where the Tories were to hold their election night party. When the first results from the Atlantic provinces showed Tories winning, Eddie called ahead to his allies who were already at the Chateau. "Open the window," he said, "I'm coming over." But it was Diefenbaker himself who deserved most of the credit, if that is the word, for doing so well. He was a great campaigner on the hustings, an orator who could play a crowd like a fish on a line. Having made his name as a crusading lawyer, he was in the habit of standing with one hand on his hip, pushing back an imaginary gown, and he would play the fiery attorney at one moment, summing up his charges against the villainous Liberals, a comedian the next delivering political wisecracks with perfect timing, then the prophet pointing the way to the promised land into which his next government would lead the people. It was fascinating to watch him casting lines — a joke, a catchword from his campaign, a fearful warning — before the audience until there was a strike, applause perhaps, or laughter, and then he was away, reeling them in. He had a stock of political anecdotes, many of them about Sir John A. Macdonald, the prime minister he wished to emulate. My favorite story was about Sir John standing at the graveside of a political comrade as the coffin was lowered. An ambitious Tory nobody stepped to his side and whispered, "A great loss, Sir John. A great loss, but I'd like to take his place." Sir John glanced at the little man and down into the grave, and sighed. "How I wish you could." he said, "How I wish you could."

Dief liked to campaign across the Prairies by train, whistle-stopping through the small towns far removed in both distance and spirit from the urban Canada where the Liberals ruled, and where he was still a local hero. This was his country and these were his people, loyal to the old leader, the old flag, the old distrust of Eastern city slickers, and suspicious of the French fact in Canada. It was an education for me, and perhaps for the dozen or so reporters on the train which we called the Diefendeisel — no doubt to the annoyance of Dief who didn't like people taking liberties with his name. We each had a roomette in which to write and sleep, and a shared car in which to eat, drink, argue, and gossip between stops. The musically talented wrote songs about the campaign, which we eventually recorded in a radio studio in Prince Albert,

Dief's riding, with our own musical accompaniment — P.Newman on the drums. They became one side of a privately produced LP record, of which I still have a copy. On the other side were recordings of Dief's speeches and meetings, made by Newman who was pioneering the use of a tape recorder in place of a pen and notebook. At one stop he recorded a town band so awful as to be heart-warming, and if you listen closely you can hear the late Ron Collister, then of the *Toronto Telegram*, telling us in his Liverpool accent that he had been unable to file his copy because the town telegrapher was "playing 'ter drum."

During that campaign, we spent a weekend in Saskatoon, and Dief had the idea of inviting a few of us to join him on a tour of his old familiar places, with his brother Elmer driving. His wife, Olive, advised against it because she thought we reporters ought to have a rest. Dief was concerned that we might write stories mocking his sentimentality, but in fact, although I disliked and distrusted him, I learned a lot that day and wrote a sympathetic piece in my new journalism style:

> He stood ankle-deep in the ploughed-up prairie looking slightly incongruous in his rakish grey homburg, with his topcoat tightly buttoned against the wind that never seems to stop and the clouds of dust blowing before it. But his eyes were misty and his voice was choked as he looked at the decaying shack that he had helped to build as the Diefenbaker homestead on virgin land in 1905.

As I reported, Dief talked almost non-stop for three hours, and it became clear that his early experiences were at the root of many of his policies. Most of the other pioneer families were English and made fun of his German-sounding name — an anglicized version of Diefenbacker, as I learned later. He was made to feel a second-class Canadian, neither English nor French, and out of that came his federal Bill of Rights providing equal rights for all Canadians, of which he was very proud. His antipathy to Bay Street and big business had its roots in his belief that eastern grain dealers had cheated his family out of a fair price for the first, hard-won wheat crop.

But, again, there was that day an incident that told something about the uneasy relationship between Dief and the media. Riding in the front seat of the car with Elmer and Dief was Pierre O'Neil of the nationalist *Le Devoir*, the most influential Quebec journalist in Ottawa, and it seemed to us in the back that he was falling under the spell of Dief's story-telling, even calling him Chief. That would never do, we teased Pierre at one stop; his paper was anti-Dief. Pierre awaited his chance to demonstrate the proper journalistic skepticism, and it seemed to come when Dief was telling us the story Gabriel Dumont, the great Metis buffalo hunter and general in the Northwest Rebellion. He talked in his expansive way of Dumont killing hundreds of buffalo in a day, and Pierre leapt in to point out it would have been impossible to load his gun and fire that many times. "Drove them over a cliff, my boy," said Dief, "Just drove them over a cliff," and swept on with his narrative while Pierre shrank into his seat and we in the back suppressed our chuckles. Dief of course was right, they did slaughter buffalo in that way.

But it was not all fun and games on that swing through the west. The Liberal scandals and misadventures had provided Dief with plenty of ammunition, but the facts were not enough for him. To put it mildly, he was careless with the truth in telling the voters about the Liberal record, and this created a problem for reporters, or at least for me and a few others. Aware of my political values and prejudices, I was determined to be fair, but it seemed to me that simply to report what he said lent credibility to what was untrue as a matter of established fact. For example, he was not above holding up the Hansard record of Parliamentary debates and misquoting. He made great play with what he insisted was a mysterious "hidden report" on fraudulent bankruptcies and associated crimes, but it turned out that the report was far from hidden; it had been published, although in French and in Quebec. He recited a list of names, mostly Italian, of alleged criminals the Liberals were supposed to have admitted to Canada, although the record showed that some at least had entered when he had been in power. Other reporters thought it was our job to report his words, true or false, and for reporters covering Pearson to report any denials he cared to issue. The debate on the train was hot at times, and was subsequently discussed in *The Canadian Annual Review* for 1965, where I discovered that I represented the "social responsibility" school of journalism, deciding what the public ought to know. My opponents represented the libertarian "put the cat among the pigeons" school, holding that simply because Dief made statements they were news to be reported without bothering about whether they were true or false. W.A. (Bill) Wilson of *The Montreal Star* shared my concerns, and a reporter for the Southam chain, caught between the demands of his editors for more of Dief's charges and his own knowledge of the facts, took refuge one night in the bar, where he became so conflicted that he wired his editors to say that as what Dief was saying was untrue, he would not be filing a story. His Tory editors were not amused.

I tried for a time correcting Dief's obvious whoppers by putting the facts in brackets after his wilder misstatements. The *Globe* seemed happy with that, but I was not because I felt as if I were calling the leader of the Opposition a liar, which was not my job. And in truth I didn't think he was a liar in the sense of deliberately saying something he knew to be untrue; I thought him to be an actor playing in a political theatre and able to believe whatever seemed useful at the moment. I decided that the best course was to lay the issue before the public, and with Doyle's consent I left Dief's campaign in Calgary, spent some time in the public library checking my facts, and then flew to Vancouver where the *Globe* had an office in which I could work. The result was a piece in which I introduced the issue by writing:

> At the back of many reporters' minds there was the memory of the McCarthy years in the United States. The press helped to boost McCarthy to power by reporting factually and uncritically his allegations which were known to be untrue. Diefenbaker in his campaign is conducting a witch hunt not for Communists but for criminals in the government. He has solid material on which to work ... but he seldom uses it. Instead he conjures from a mass of nonfacts the image of a government riddled through — as he says — with criminal influence.

I went on to show in detail how he was twisting the truth. But I filed the piece with misgivings. Was this really my role as a reporter? Maybe I should leave it to the columnists or the editorial writers. So I was much relieved to get a congratulatory wire from Doyle, but many of my competitors on the campaign were annoyed that I had made public our private argument. For example, when I rejoined the Diefenbaker campaign later, Don McGillivray, of Southam, became so distracted and frustrated by his argument with me that he sat fuming in his roomette, forgot to get off the train when it reached Union Station in Toronto, and wound up miles away in the shunting yards. He tramped across the tracks and finally caught up with us in Montreal, to where we had flown from Toronto. Dief said merely that I was accusing him of McCarthyism, which of course I wasn't. But he got his own back later when he asked a question in the Commons about a story I had written and referred to "Mr. Weasel — I beg his pardon, Mr. Westell." The *Globe* thought it was hilarious and subsequently printed it in a front page list of his witty remarks. For better or for worse that article did more to establish me as a "new journalist" than anything else I ever wrote. But journalists today would wonder why. It is commonplace now to expose politicians who are careless with the truth. Indeed, it often seems to me that reporters are too eager to make the worst of a slip of the tongue in a media scrum, or of an ambiguous remark. The role of the media as actors in politics, also, is discussed, although journalists remain defensive about their own activities. But everything about the relationship of journalists and politicians has changed. Consider, for example, that in 1965, when the Diefendiesel was making its last stop, we reporters took up a collection and presented Olive Diefenbaker with a pair of gloves. She was all aflutter, or pretended to be, and said we must have noticed that her old gloves were dirty. It's all recorded on that LP record I mentioned earlier. I thought at the time that we were going a bit far, but at least we were not in those days rude cynics about our elected leaders.

Back in Ottawa, I was interviewed about the issues I had raised by a student from the School of Journalism at Carleton University who was writing his honours paper on the coverage of the campaign. His name was Eric Malling, and we became friends, colleagues, and sailing companions. Over my protests, he appointed me his mentor, and when he became the best known investigative reporter in Canada, working both for CTV and the CBC, he insisted on telling audiences that I had invented investigative journalism in Canada in the 1965 campaign. That of course was ridiculous; I had merely checked a few facts and pointed out that Dief had a different version of the truth, but Eric was nothing if not stubborn in his opinions. He took from another mentor, Ron Haggart, his producer at *The Fifth Estate*, the idea that what everybody knows to be true is probably wrong, and delighted in being a contrarian. In the premature and bitter end, that was his undoing, in my opinion: He refused to accept that he had become an alcoholic, and as a result died in a domestic accident. I sometimes think, remorsefully, that I could have done more to help him when he became depressed and turned to the bottle, but probably he was too much of a contrarian to take advice from anyone, even his mentor.

~ *Chapter 9* ~

The Last Days of Pearson and Diefenbaker

D iefenbaker won at least a moral, or perhaps I should say immoral, victory in the 1965 election, but lost the war. Instead of being wiped out, the Conservative party gained two seats — denying Pearson his majority — and Dief returned as leader of the opposition. But he had now lost two elections in a row, and it was time for him to go. A ferocios battle for control of the party ensued, and at one point when Dief and his supporters suffered a setback he used a quotation much favoured by politicians in distress:

Fight on, my merry men all,
I'm a little wounded, but I am not slain;
I will lay me down for to bleed a while,
Then I'll rise and fight with you again.

Writing the story for the *Globe*, I thought readers might like to know the source of those stirring words, and was charmed to be told by Ottawa Public Library researcher that they were attributed to Johnnie Armstrong, a celebrated bandit and cattle rustler on the Scottish border in the 1500s, who was later hanged with his men. It was not I think the message Dief intended to convey, although it turned out to be prophetic if one translates hanged into the political equivalent, kicked out of office.

The anti-Dief forces led by Dalton Camp won control of the party and put in place a review of the leadership, which meant that other candidates could challenge Dief for the leadership. But first came a Thinkers' Conference, at Montmorency Falls in Quebec, in the summer of 1967, designed to modernize policy and broaden the party's appeal. The official theme was Post-Industrial Society, far ahead of its time because few of us had ever heard of the concept. I remember asking in puzzlement at the press conference if it meant there would be no more industries, by which I meant mines and mills and factories, and getting no answer I could understand. But the real issue that emerged at Montmorency was Quebec's place in Confederation: Isn't it always? The political classes in Canada seemed to be moving gradually toward consensus on some form of special status for Quebec, based on the belief that the two founding nations, English and French — Deux Nations — had been equal partners in Confederation and that Quebec, therefore, was not just a province like the others. The New Democratic Party had adopted the principle at its founding conference in 1961, casing the redoubtable constitutional scholar Eugene Forsey to walk out in disgust. It was the official policy of the Quebec Liberal Party, and the Pearson government had edged nervously toward it in practice. Under Diefenbaker, the Tories had stood instead for One Nation — to be interpreted as one wished — which made them unpopular in Quebec. But at Montmorency, after a fierce debate, the delegates voted for the Deux Nations concept. Just what that implied for Tories was not clear. Some thought it no more than a gesture of goodwill to French-speaking Canadians, others that it meant special constitutional status for Quebec, but it was certainly a major move in mindset. The resolution went forward to the national leadership convention in the dusty old Maple Leaf Gardens in Toronto.

Geoff Stevens and I went to Toronto to cover the convention, and were assigned the help of a promising young reporter called Michael Enright, now of course a national figure as a CBC radio host, and better known than either of us. Geoff had a taste for dry martinis and stocked his hotel room with gin and vermouth. When we retired to plan our coverage out of sight of wandering editors, I too acquired the taste, and enjoy it to this day, which I consider one of the fringe benefits of that great political story. The first big event was on the Friday night when the leadership candidates spoke, and the question was whether Dief would withdraw or stand in the following day's ballot. When he got up to speak it was getting dangerosly close to deadline for a major edition of the *Globe* and it was clear I would have to file before he finished. He was in fine form, marching to the podium behind twelve pipers, with Olive at his side. The crowd of eight thousand was friendly and emotional, believing that it was probably hearing for the last time from the old Chief who had led them to victory in three elections. He was sentimental about his years in the party, inspirational in urging young people into public service, and passionate in his rejection of Deux Nations — a policy borrowed from Liberalism, he said, his favourite insult. I listened as long as I could and then went to the press room where there were TV monitors I could watch while dictating my story. Dief went on and on and, typically, finished without making clear his intentions. I worked into my story crowd colour, background on the Deux Nations issue and the implications for the party, quotes from Dief, and reaction by Camp and others provided by Stevens and Enright who were working the crowd. When I had finished I knew I had written a good story about a great political event. I had had a lot of experience composing on the phone back in Britain, and when it went well a dictated story took on the immediacy of a conversation with a friend. But for me, this was the old journalism, not the new, and I was surprised that Managing Editor Davey was so enthusiastic that night, and amazed later when he entered the story for a National Newspaper Award, saying:

> Although Mr. Diefenbaker spoke without a text, Mr. Westell had finished dictating his story to the desk before the ovation for the Old Chieftain had faded away. Working against a copy deadline of 11.00 p.m., Mr. Westell dictated the early takes of the story from notes as he simultaneously monitored the end of the speech on a television set in the Maple Leaf Gardens press room. For later editions the story was fleshed out with reaction quotes, but the basic structure of an eminently readable account was just as Mr. Westell dictated it to the rewrite desk. It is an outstanding example of a professional being up for a big test.

What had seemed to me a routine piece of reporting actually won in the Spot News category. I'm sure it was the first time that merely reporting a political speech had won a NNA, and it was probably the last. In those days competition for the awards — it was my second — was less intense than it is now. To round out this story, I should say that Dief withdrew from the leadership contest the next day after doing poorly in the second ballot. The premier of Nova Scotia, Robert Stanfield, became the new Tory leader, and quietly shelved Deux Nations. Pierre Trudeau, the emerging Liberal star, trumped everybody with his slogan: One Nation, Two Languages. And Dief, instead of retiring from the Commons to give his successor a free hand, remained to harass Stanfield, and to keep planning and replanning his own state funeral until he died in 1979.

Not so Pearson. Late in 1967 I wrote an analytical story on the decay of the Liberal government. The occasion was the second anniversary of its return to office, if not exactly to power, in 1965, but the purpose was to draw attention to the disarray in a Cabinet overwhelmed by problems, discouraged by criticism, and waiting for the prime minister to make known his retirement plans. It was new journalism in the sense that it dealt with a situation rather than a news event. The day it was published I met Walter Gordon in the parliamentary dining room, and he remarked that I had ruffled some feathers. I had no idea how many feathers until 1973 when Denis Smith published a biography of Gordon, *Gentle Patriot* (Hurtig Publishers, Edmonton). Smith described my piece as a "devastating essay," and disclosed that Gordon had taken it as his text when he went to see Pearson that afternoon. Gordon wrote in his notes:

> I had a straight talk with Mike (Pearson's friend called him Mike) in his office after the Orders of the Day (Question Period in the Commons). He was flushed, tired and unhappy. I said I had not felt like telling him at lunch on Saturday what was in my mind but wished to cover the following points:
>
> (a) I said the Westell article in *The Globe and Mail* this morning is a fair reflection of the situation in my opinion — and the views expressed by Members. Mike agreed.
>
> (b) I said that six weeks ago I had given him a memo suggesting he stay on to try to resolve the constitutional issue — but it assumed a major reorganization of the government. Mike admitted he is not up to this.
>
> (c) In that event I urged him to get out as quickly as possible ...

Six days later Pearson announced his intention to retire. Gordon, in his notes, only part of which I have quoted, suggested that Pearson had been reluctant to retire, and implied that he, with a little help from me, influenced the decision. But Pearson, in his own autobiography, said he had long planned to announce his resignation at that time, just before Parliament adjourned for Christmas. So I cannot claim to have persuaded him out of office, but I may have nudged him. I was, however, to have another remarkable encounter with Pearson, and I'll tell that story here although it does not fit comfortably into the chronological order of my narrative.

In February of 1969, after Pearson had retired — and I had moved from the *Globe* to *The Toronto Star* to become national affairs columnist — I thought it would be interesting to take him to lunch to see what he might have to say, and invited my friend Bill Wilson, of the *Montreal Star*, to join us. We three were chatting around our table at the Rideau Club, across the road from Parliament Hill, when Pearson said he was unhappy about the shadow cast on his reputation by two recent books, Judy LaMarsh's memoir titled *A Bird in a Gilded Cage*, and Peter Newman's account of the Pearson years, *The Distemper of Our Times*. As Pearson put it later in a note to Wilson and to me, "I am anxious to remove the impression that I sacrificed (Guy) Favreau and (Lucien) Cardin for my own selfish purposes and that they felt that this was being done; that I was throwing them to the wolves to protect myself." Both men had held the important job of justice minister, honourably if not always wisely, and had resigned after being involved in a scandal for which Pearson held some responsibility.

I have described earlier how Pearson went on a trip across the Prairies while a scandal over a Mafia drug dealer was developing in the Commons, leaving Favreau to face the storm. Worse than that, before going west Pearson had said in the Commons that he had known nothing about the affair until a few days before it broke. The clear implication was that Favreau had failed to inform him. It was an understandable slip of memory — Favreau had in fact mentioned it to him during a brief conversation on plane journey months earlier when Pearson was preoccupied with constitutional problems — but when he realized he was wrong Pearson hesitated for days before admitting the error in the

Commons, hanging Favreau out to dry, as it were. A subsequent judicial inquiry cleared Favreau of any wrongdoing beyond an administrative foul-up, but he had to resign from the Justice department. Pearson's second concern was a much more serious affair involving Cardin, but to explain that I have to go back a few years. On a Saturday morning in May 1965, the External Affairs department issued a statement describing two cases of Soviet spying in Canada. The timing itself was curious, but even more so was the fact that the statement went on for several hundred words to describe the two incidents when normally such matters were dealt with as briefly as possible. As we learned later, Pearson, when he saw the draft, objected that the language was "lurid," but was told that was deliberate because the RCMP wanted to call attention to the danger of espionage. So we heard about what came to be called the Good Spy and the Bay Spy. The Good Spy was a naturalized Canadian who had been approached by a Soviet agent and told that unless he cooperated his relatives behind the Iron Curtain would suffer. He thought about it for several days and then took his problem to the RCMP who told him to pretend to go along with the Soviets but to report to them. For three years he was a double agent, and a model the government wished others to follow. What happened to his relatives was not disclosed. The Bad Spy, on the other hand, was said to be a junior civil servant who, before he was caught, had been paid thosands of dollars by the Soviets to help them with economic and other forms of espionage.

The statement was so unusual as to prompt questions, in the Commons and in the country, which the government stonewalled, pleading national security. A week or so later, Pearson was visiting his riding of Algoma East, strung out along the north shore of Lake Huron. His main purpose was to reassure the voters in Elliot Lake that there would soon be booming new markets for the uranium they were mining, or if that failed, as it did, their town would become a cultural centre like Banff, which it never did. I was one of the half-dozen reporters on that trip which looked as if it would be of little news interest but offered another opportunity to get to know the prime minister. We stayed at an old hotel in Sault Ste. Marie which proved to have an unusual feature. Pearson was on the top floor and when he invited us up for a drink the creaky elevator delivered us into another world, a penthouse suite with picture windows overlooking the rapids. Pearson explained that when Sir James Dunn, the financier, gained control of Algoma Steel in the 1930s he created the suite in order to have suitable living accommodation when he was in town. No doubt it was occupied also by his secretary-confidant-business associate and finally his third wife, Marcia Christoforides, known as Christofor, a half-Greek beauty who made her own fortune with the help of wealthy men. After Dunn died, she became the second Lady Beaverbrook, who joked that he married her for her money.

But, again, I digress. Pearson was relaxed and began to talk about the spies case, dribbling out scraps of information, including the fact that the Soviets were using Canada as a base in which to train spies before sending them into the United States. As Pearson gossiped, his press secretary, Dick O'Hagan, was fidgeting nervously in the background. At the first opportunity, he jumped in to say, "Prime minister, this is all off the record, of course." But Pearson said casually that we could use it as long as it was not attributed to him and not filed until we got back to Ottawa. That gave me, and others, a front page story, attributed to "security sources," and the result of course was renewed interest and more questions in the Commons. It became part of a trail of evidence that led Vancouver journalist Tom Hazlitt, who had good contacts in the RCMP, to identify the Bad Spy as George Victor Spencer, a postal worker. One of his tasks had been to prowl cemeteries to collect names and dates of dead persons which could be used to fabricate identities for Soviet spies. To prosecute Spencer would have meant revealing security information in court, and so he had been quietly fired from his job and denied a pension. Anyway, his doctors said he would soon die of cancer. Not much might have come of that had not Cardin agreed to be interviewed on the CBC-TV show "This Hour Has Seven Days," which specialized in putting unwary politicians in what it called its Hot Seat and extracting embarrassing statements. Trying to excuse the fact that Spencer had not been prosecuted, Cardin blurted that he would be under RCMP surveillance for the rest of his life. That was untrue — the RCMP had no such plans — but it gave the opposition parties a new opening, and they attacked on two fronts. Diefenbaker and the Tories charged mishandling of a security case, while the NDP argued that with no opportunity to defend himself a civil servant had been fired, deprived of his pension, and was now to be watched by the police until he died.

There was an additional factor at work. Cardin, usually polite and inoffensive, had once attacked Dief in the House, and nobody could carry a grudge like Dief, who now set out to destroy Cardin, and succeeded. He was relentless in his questioning, and Cardin, who never knew when to keep his mouth shut, was goaded to shout back one day that, given his own handling of the "Monseignor case," Dief was the last person to give lectures on security. The blackest of cats leapt from that bag. The case concerned a German-born prostitute living and working in Montreal, Gerda Munsinger — Cardin got the name wrong, which indicated how little he really knew — who had connections with organized crime. The RCMP had somehow discovered that she had a liaison with Pierre Sevigny, associate minister of defence in Dief's Cabinet, and when they checked on her background in East Germany it turned out she had been involved in a small way with the security service. Alarm bells rang and they reported to Dief who, instead of firing Sevigny, or at least removing him from a sensitive department, merely warned him off.

The RCMP found that unsatisfactory, in part perhaps because they knew that a second minister had had some contact with Munsinger, although it is not clear that they ever told Dief. But they did not hesitate to tell Pearson when he, mired in the Spencer affair, inquired about any other scandals which had involved MPs in the past ten years. When he was later accused of rummaging through security files in search of information damaging to his critics, he claimed that he had merely become concerned about the reputation of Parliament and was happy to have found nothing of substance except the Munsinger affair. With explosive charges flying, the Commons had some of the worst days in its history, and behind the scenes both Pearson and Dief behaved disgracefully. Pearson wrote to Dief, hinting that he would expose the Munsinger case unless he laid off Cardin. In return, Dief threatened to make public old American rumours that Pearson had been a source of information for Communist spies in Washington. Cardin had insisted throughout that there would be no inquiry into the Spencer case, and Pearson had backed him until the issue became Spencer's civil rights. He then decided to compromise by agreeing to a limited inquiry in private. Reversed by his prime minister, Cardin decided to resign which, following Favreau, would have made him the

second federal justice minister from Quebec to fall. The Quebec
Liberal caucus was in an uproar, and there were threats that if Cardin
quit, others would follow. We did not fully realize it at the time, but the
government was on the edge of disaster, and in fact it was only when
Cardin was made to realize this that he agreed to remain in office.

Pearson, as I have said, was much concerned about allegations that
he betrayed both Favreau and Cardin. I suggested to him that day in the
Rideau Club that the solution was to tell his side of the story in his
memoirs. He said that would take too long, so I made another suggestion: Any magazine writer in Canada would be happy to tell his story.
"Why not you two?" replied Pearson. Wilson and I were, of course,
excited by the prospect, but we put on our most responsible faces and
said that we were reporters; we would not wish to be merely his mouth-
piece, and that if we were to write his story we would need supporting
evidence from his private files. Pearson hesitated, but then agreed that
we would meet at his house, look through his papers, and decide what
we would need to use to show that he was not merely putting a
favourable spin on his conduct of affairs. In fact, Bill and I borrowed a
mass of his papers — which I promptly photocopied — decided what
we wanted to use, and then negotiated with Pearson before returning
the originals. We each wrote a series of articles. I called mine "The
Pearson Papers," and *Star* syndicated it to major newspapers across the
country. What I had not expected was that the *Montreal Star* would syndicate Bill's version to almost every other paper, so that between us we
blanketed Canada. We told Pearson's story with extracts from the diary
he kept intermittently, records prepared at the time by his staff, and letters and memos from Favreau, Cardin, and others proving beyond a reasonable doubt that they at least had not blamed Pearson for their misadventures, and had continued to hold him in high regard. I hope I can
say without boasting that it was an extraordinary journalistic coup — as
witness to which were the anguished cries of foul from other Ottawa
reporters and columnists. My answer was that we had had the enterprise
— I might have said luck — to take Pearson to lunch, while they had
not. It was the first time a former prime minister had opened to journalists his files about the most sensational political events of the time,
and probably the last. Incidentally, Pearson did publish two volumes of

his memoirs and was working on the third, covering the period of the scandals, when he died. When two historians who had been assisting him, John Munro and Alex Inglis, were authorized to compile the third volume by editing such records as he had left, I was able to help by providing copies of Pearson's papers and my interpretation of them, and was pleased to have my aid acknowledged in the volume.

Thus ended my coverage of Pearson, on a high note. I liked and admired him. Occasionally under pressure he said and did things that were foolish and not worthy of him, but he was an honourable man and politician. What follows is my last word on Diefenbaker, on a distinctly low note. It is Pearson's record of what George Hees told him at the height of the Munsinger uproar in the Commons. It may well include exaggeration by one or both, but I have no doubt it is grounded on truth. Hees, it may be remembered from the previous chapter, had led the Cabinet revolt against Prime Minister Diefenbaker before the 1963 election. When that failed he decided to leave the Commons, but then returned in 1965. I found Pearson's note among his papers but could not have published it at the time because it concerned a conversation between two members of the Privy Council bound by an oath of secrecy. Both are now dead and it becomes a footnote to history and an insight into Dief. It is dated March 22 (1966) and timed 9 a.m., the morning after the meeting:

Mr. Hees phoned Sunday to ask if he could see me personally and confidentially on Monday evening at Sussex Street. I told him we had a Cabinet meeting that evening but he asked if he could drop in after the meeting as he wished to discuss with me, as a matter of urgency and on a personal and private basis, some matters arising out of the Munsinger case.

So when I arrived back at the house last evening at 10:20, there was George Hees in the library, waiting; genial and unconcerned, at least on the surface, as ever.

He began by expressing his disgust and abhorrence at what had happened in Parliament in this last two weeks. He blamed it all on Diefenbaker, who had begun well this session and had made Hees happy to be back in Parliament. But then he had returned to his normal form — in the House and in their Caucus — over the Spencer case, bankruptcy and in his transparent determination to destroy Cardin because of a personal vendetta. Hees then described his Chief in terms of criticism and dislike quite as strongly as he had ever used to me before he rejoined the Party (before the 1965 election) — a "menace," cruel, vicious, cowardly, deceiving, etc.

Hees said that he and some of his friends had rejoined the Party before the recent election to save it from Diefenbaker domination and, as he candidly and disarmingly admitted, to win for himself the leadership after Diefenbaker had gone. Once back in the fold, both during and after the election, he had acted as a good Party man and had naturally given no indication whatever of his private feelings, of any "alarm and despondency" over Diefenbaker's "decline and fall" during the session. He blamed everything on him, not on Cardin, who, he admitted, had been "goaded beyond endurance" and he felt things might now go from bad to worse. The question was now above politics. It was "How to save Parliament," how to get rid of Diefenbaker and, I gathered, how to prevent Diefenbaker getting rid of Hees via Munsinger! George says Diefenbaker is quite happy to use Munsinger to pay off old scores against disloyal followers and doesn't seem to feel he is in any danger himself.

I said little but told Hees that Diefenbaker was deceiving himself if he thought he was in no danger from "mishandling" a security case. This cheered Hees up but not as much as when I told him that, though I had not seen the full police reports, the "brief" from the RCMP did not mention him or any of his colleagues by name — except Sevigny. I could give no information on the full report which I had not seen, only on the "brief," so that is why we could not give any specific clearance to anyone once Cardin — unfortunately — had talked about "Ministers" being involved.

Hees told me the story of his brief and innocent encounters with Munsinger, whom he described as an extraordinarily attractive woman, and swore vehemently that this was his only contact with her.

I expressed the hope that the Judge (the Commissioner appointed to inquire into the affair) would clear up this aspect of the matter, as it was the mishandling of a security problem that was the issue, and this only. Here it was a Prime Minister and Minister of Justice who were "involved."

I then told Hees that, if he were really concerned with getting rid of Diefenbaker for the good of the country, of Parliament and of Hees, he and his Tory friends, who felt that way, should be ready to act quickly when the Commissioner's report was made.

He agreed that this was their responsibility and this time they would discharge it effectively. Meanwhile, he would have to live as best he could with the unhappy Munsinger publicity he had received until the Judge cleared the matter up.

By the end of our talk, he was a much less exuberant person; a much more serious one. I know he has personal and political interests in the affair but I think that he also retains his fear and disgust with Diefenbaker as a menace to all decency in politics and would like to see him destroyed not only for selfish reasons.

He gave me a lurid story about the sadistic persecution of Sevigny by Diefenbaker once the latter had discovered his association with Munsinger. The Prime Minister called Sevigny into his office, gave him a tongue lashing and then played back to him a recording — obtained by the police — of a "meeting" with Munsinger. He used to repeat this at intervals and Sevigny, said Hees, told him he had gone through hell; that the PM would neither fire him nor forgive him but kept on torturing him!

What a revelation about those who claimed that morality and integrity in Government were the real issues facing Canada and one which the Liberals had betrayed and disgraced!

It was a revealing hour and a half and left me rather uncertain what it all may mean.

Hees was called as a witness before the Munsinger inquiry, which Stevens and I covered at length for the *Globe*, but the nature of his relationship with her remained unclear. He ran for the leadership when Diefenbaker was removed the following year, but lost.

~ *Chapter 10* ~

Trudeau and Transition

When I arrived in Ottawa in 1964, the Quiet Revolution in Quebec was still gathering force, but nobody was talking seriously about separation. René Lévesque was still a Liberal Cabinet minister in Quebec and the federal government was focused on completing the welfare state; never mind that social policy was a provincial jurisdiction; ways around that irritating anomaly would be found. The Royal Commission on Bilingualism and Biculturalism was accused of gross exaggeration when it rushed out an interim report in 1965 to warn that Canada was passing unaware through the greatest crisis in its history because Quebec was challenging the very basis of Confederation. But when Daniel Johnson led the nationalist Union Nationale to victory in Quebec in 1966, some people in the rest of Canada began to worry. One of those was Premier John Robarts in Ontario, who had formed a friendship with Johnson when both were young lawyers and had come to realize that when Johnson said the choice for Quebec was "Equality or Independence" he probably meant it. Pearson was hesitating to call a constitutional conference, and his new justice minister, Pierre Trudeau, warned that to do so would be to open a Pandora's box. But Robarts went around them by convening in 1967 a conference of the provinces on "Confederation for Tomorrow." It was held on the top floor of the Toronto-Dominion Centre — the first of the skyscraper bank towers in Toronto and uncompleted — so that the premiers of the less fortunate provinces could look out across the promised land of urban growth and prosperity and be impressed. Ottawa sent observers and Pearson, realizing that the constitutional

ball was now in play and that he would have to pick it up or be out
of the game, called a full-fledged federal-provincial conference for
February 1968.

I had already decided that if constitutional reform was going to
become a big story I had better learn something about it. I believed, wrongly as it turned out, that my colleagues and competitors who had been educated in Canada would know all about Confederation and the British
North America Act, and thought I could catch up by skimming a few
books — a typical journalistic conceit. I read among others Donald
Creighton's splendid two-volume biography of John A. Macdonald for his
conservative account of the negotiation and achievement of Confederation;
J.M.S Careless' two-volume biography of George Brown, who not only
founded the *Globe* but also led the opposition Reform party in that period; and *The Confederation Debates*, an edited version of the key speeches
made when the parliament of the old Province of Canada, in which Canada
West (Ontario) and Canada East (Quebec) had equal representation, debated and approved the Confederation plan. With what seems in hindsight to
be staggering presumption, I drew two conclusions from this little knowledge, and began to write about them. In that centenary year of 1967
Macdonald was endlessly celebrated as the Father of Confederation, and
one of my ideas was that the title properly belonged to Brown. With the
Province of Canada hopelessly deadlocked — there had been three governments in twelve months — and party politics bitterly divisive, it was
Brown who had put aside personal animosity and political ambition by
offering to serve under his rival Macdonald in a Great Coalition if it would
attempt to break out of the impasse by negotiating some form of
Confederation. Without that statesmanlike initiative, who knows what
would have happened, but probably not much. With it, Macdonald seized
the moment and brought about the union of the British colonies in North
America, becoming in my view the Midwife rather than the Father of
Confederation. The *Globe* was of course happy to run my tribute to its
founder in its weekend magazine and I waited for the rebuttals from the
historians and from Macdonald's fan club. There were none. My reading of
history was not original but it was certainly an unconventional wisdom, and
nobody seemed to care. Perhaps the Canadian way of dealing with a down-
grading of one of the country's few political heroes was simply to ignore it.

The second conclusion I drew from my cram course in history was more important and should have been even more controversial. I decided that the BNA Act was a hopelessly flawed constitution, and that we should go back and renegotiate Confederation. I laid out the argument in a major article in *The Globe Magazine*, again in 1967. The title was "Reconfederation," a word Robarts had used but, as it proved, didn't really mean. Like the other premiers, he was prepared at most to tinker with the constitution. I argued that tinkering would not work because the 1867 deal had two fatal flaws. One flaw was that BNA Act purported to establish a federal form of government allowing substantial autonomy to the provinces, but in reality the Fathers had set up something close to a unitary system in which overriding powers were held by the national government, enabling it to interfere in provincial jurisdictions whenever it wished. That flaw had compounded as the role of government had changed in a century since Confederation. Originally, Ottawa had been awarded overriding taxing powers because it was expected to handle all the important matters of state. The provinces were limited to direct taxation, which in those days meant property taxes, because their responsibilities were local. But over the century everything had changed. Local services such as education, health, and social and cultural development which had been allocated to the provinces had become the major concerns of government. Direct taxes originally allocated to the provinces had become, in the form of the income tax, the major source of revenue, and had been seized in part by Ottawa. The result was — and still is — constant competition and bickering between the two levels of government. I proposed that we should do again what the Fathers had done in 1864-67; abandon the existing form of government and negotiate a new deal with a better balance of responsibilities and resources.

Again, there was no response. I should add that, presumptuous as my analysis may have been, I have never had reason to change my mind. Even when I appeared by invitation before a Senate-Commons committee to explain my views, the most severe dissent was a muttered comment — "Rubbish" — by Eugene Forsey, by then a senator and a noted authority on the constitution. He did not elaborate, and that was surprising because he could be explosive in his criticisms. He was also a wit and a famous letter writer. He once mistook me on a crowded bus for another journalist, and I did not bother to correct him. Later he realized his mistake and sent me a note of apology, explaining "I am becoming old and infernal." A lovely man, but wrong in his defence of the constitutional stats quo, and, yes, I know that is heresy.

But back to chronology. In Ottawa, Pearson and his new Quebec advisers, including Trudeau, seemed to think that guaranteeing French language rights across Canada would solve the unity problem. Conveniently in 1967 the B and B Commission produced the first volume of its final report laying out a plan under which living in French would be made possible in every part of Canada in which there was a viable community of French-speaking people. But buried in the report was a disclaimer, pointed out to me by Pierre O'Neil, of *Le Devoir*, when we journalists were studying advance copies of the report:

> The Commission does not take the position that in dealing with the problem of language it has reached the causes of division between Canadians. In certain respects the problem of cultural duality is even deeper, and the political question has many components besides linguistic difficulties.

This warning that language rights would not alone be the solution was largely ignored, at least outside Quebec. Bilingualism was the catchword of the time and that shadowy consensus that had been building around the idea that Quebec was not a province like the others and should have special stats within Confederation was dissipating.

Pearson had already announced his intention to retire when the federal-provincial summit convened early in 1968. It was his swan song, and in his opening statement, in the gold-and-glitz Confederation Room on Parliament Hill, he sounded as if he was ready at last for decisive action:

> There are times in the life of a country when the assurance of good intentions, the discharge of normal duty and acceptance of routine responsibility are not enough. What such times demand is the exercise of courage and decision that go far beyond the needs of the moment. I believe that this is such a time for Canada.

Here the road forks. If we have the resolution and the wisdom to choose now the right course and to follow it steadfastly, I can see few limits to what we may achieve together as a people. But if we lack the courage to choose, or if we choose wrongly, we will leave to our children a country in fragments, and we ourselves would have become the failures of Confederation.

Sitting beside Pearson was Justice Minister Trudeau and he took the fork in the road leading to One Nation with two official languages. He envisaged a Canada in which French and English language rights would be guaranteed wherever there was a sufficient demand, ensuring that French Canadians could move out of Quebec and appreciate the rest of Canada without losing language or culture. Government services, education, TV, and more would be available in French — and of course in English in Quebec. The premiers of the English-speaking provinces were ready to agree, at least in principle, although Ernest Manning of Alberta — father of Preston — grumbled about a "Munich," meaning appeasement of Quebec. I promptly labeled him The Abominable No Man, a title invented originally for Soviet Foreign Minister Molotov.

Quebec Premier Johnson chose the other fork, leading to a partnership of Two Nations. He was gratified by the acceptance of French language rights — he called it a breakthrough — but said bluntly it was not enough. If Quebec were to be able to protect and develop its role as the homeland of one of the two founding nations, it would need more powers, particularly control of social programs which Ottawa had surped. A lively ninety-minute debate followed. It was mostly in French and not easy for me to follow, even with simultaneous translation, but I knew that this was an historic occasion. Two articulate Quebeckers were laying out opposing views on the future of their province, and thus of Canada, each claiming to be the true spokesman for French Canadians. Here at last was the great debate in sharp political focus, presented with wit and subtle insults. Attempting to dismiss Trudeau, Johnson said, "Although the adamant few still refuse to admit it, we all know Canada is made up of two nations." Trudeau rejected as impracticable the idea that Quebec could have special status, enjoying more powers than other provinces. If, for example, social policy were to be made for Quebec in Quebec City and for the rest of the country in Ottawa, what role would Quebec MPs play in Ottawa? Johnson referred to Trudeau as "the member for Mount Royal," omitting the customary ministerial "honourable." Trudeau in turn referred to the premier as "the deputy from Bagot" — and for good measure jibed that Johnson was an Irishmen. The debate ended inconclusively and my French-speaking colleague Lewis Seale and I pieced togther a lead story for the next day's front page. The conference itself ended with a tenuous agreement on language rights and plans to meet again, but the most important result was that the televised debate had given Trudeau the momentum to win the Liberal leadership, and the prime ministership, a few months later.

And so the country took the road supposed to lead to a Canada that would be bilingual for official purposes in which French Canadian discontents would disappear — a road, incidentally, already opened by Pearson although Trudeau often gets the sole credit for official bilingualism. Equally important, it closed the road to special status for Quebec in a Two Nation Canada. In hindsight, my earlier analysis — that the BNA Act was fatally flawed — should have shown me that Trudeau's fork was the wrong one, and experience has confirmed that view. His vision of a Canada in which Québécois could feel at home outside their province never took shape, and the country has been wracked for more than thirty years — continues to be wracked — by the issue of Quebec's place in Confederation. Even when Trudeau forced through his grand design for a Charter of Rights, including language rights, Quebec refused to sign on. There are today still Two Nations, and the forces for separation are far stronger than they were in 1968. Given my view at the time that we should renegotiate Confederation, even if that meant that Canada would become two associated states, I should have realized that Johnson was closer to wisdom than was Trudeau. Also, my own experience and those of many others in Ottawa should have warned that popular bilingualism was not a realistic vision.

Despite my abject failure with French while at school, I decided in the spirit of the 1960s to take the French course offered by the government to members of the press gallery. That involved spending our weekends immersed in French at a school in Quebec, across the river from Ottawa, learning from experiences of the Thibault family in Paris. The audio/visual program had been invented by the French government for new citizens who needed to learn fast how to conduct their everyday lives in French, so it was not ideal for our purposes. We were not likely, for example, to need to know, with Madame Thibault, how to arrange linen in the closet, or to deal with the French cops, and most of us soon became fed up with the whole family. But that was not the reason I gave up after a few months, having learned only a few useful phrases. One reason was that my family objected that in addition to working long hours during the week I was now disappearing on the weekends. Another reason was that I came to realize that to achieve a useful degree of bilingualism would take years. That was not only because my ear for French was still made of tin; I noticed that the few senior civil servants I knew who became fluent did so only after months of total immersion in Quebec or France, and I did not have that sort of time to spare. Nor of course did the vast majority of Canadians. Public services in their own language seemed to me simple justice for minority communities. The dream that all of Canada could become home to French-speaking Canadians was far out of reach.

Although for these reasons my sympathies should have been with Johnson, I was drawn to Trudeau. He was a captivating figure in that shining year of 1968, arguably the high point of the century for Canada. It was Expo-Plus-One and the old politicians, Pearson and Diefenbaker, were going at last, taking with them, or so it seemed, the old politics. Onto the national stage, seeking and winning the Liberal succession to Pearson, stepped Trudeau, the perfect Canadian, fluently bilingual, internationally educated, athletic, sexy, relaxed, and informal. He even wore sandals and a cravat in the House of Commons, shocking Diefenbaker, which was always to be commended. A new man for a new age. By contrast, the United States was slipping into chaos, popular leaders assassinated, cities burning, rebellious students taking to the streets and a few entering the terrorist underground. Maybe the twentieth century would, after all, turn out to belong to Canada. I wanted Trudeau to be the next prime minister, even if I was skeptical about his vision of a bilingual Canada. I didn't recognize it at the time, but I was encountering the contradiction between Trudeau's style, which was new and radical, and his content, which was pragmatic and cautious. He appeared to represent change but in fact spoke for continuity. Of course, it was the style which caught public attention and won him, narrowly, the Liberal leadership. Geoff Stevens and I led the coverage of the leadership convention for the *Globe*, but this time managing editor Davey, a former Ottawa correspondent and still a political junky, announced that he would come to Ottawa to help out. This threatened our operating procedure of having a private place in which to talk, and so — unknown to Davey but at the *Globe's* expense — I rented a trailer, had it parked outside the hall, and stocked it with martini makings, plus typewriters. Alas, even the best laid plans go awry, and the weather turned so chilly that Geoff and I could not survive in the unheated trailer and had to return to the press room and to our managing editor. I don't mean to imply that Davey was an ogre; he was helpful and supportive. It was just that Geoff and I had a writing partnership that needed no third party. But all good things come to an end, and with Trudeau's victory at the convention, a new era was dawning, both in politics and, as it turned out, for me personally.

Trudeau did not hesitate for long before calling a national election. The Liberal campaign was brilliantly conceived and conducted — and lucky. While Conservative Robert Stanfield and New Democrat Tommy Douglas ran conventional campaigns, speaking every night to the party faithful in town halls and church basements, Trudeau hurtled across the country by jet, appearing in shopping plazas and public parks where the uncommitted people were. There was no need for the news media to invent Trudeaumania, as is sometimes charged. The adoring crowds appeared, we reported on the phenomenon, and by doing so we encouraged bigger and more excited crowds at the next campaign stop. I remember in particular one glorious evening when thousands of people gathered on a green hill outside Victoria, with views across the blue waters of the Straits of Juan de Fuca to snow-capped mountains. From high in the sky and far away came the chopping beat of a helicopter and Trudeau landed among the multitude like a god. And like a god, at that stage of the campaign, he was not so much making political speeches as preaching sermons. His staff produced detailed policy documents and he did make a few major policy speeches, but he warned that leaders were driven not by campaign promises but by circumstances they could not foresee. In the United States, he pointed out, President Lyndon Johnson had promised a Great Society but had bogged down in a war in Vietnam, and in Britain Prime Minister Harold Wilson had promised a white hot technological revolution, only to face a run on Sterling which forced him to appeal to the International Monetary Fund for a humiliating bail out. Look at the man and his approach to solving problems, said Trudeau, not at his specific promises. But people heard what they wanted to hear, and Trudeau was going to bring about the Just Society.

Even when things might have gone disastrously wrong they turned to his advantage. People still remember, and journalists still write about, that day when he went swimming in a motel pool west of Toronto during a campaign lunch break. A photographer caught him in a graceful dive and the picture became the graphic image of his campaign. It was all a lucky accident, as I discovered later. Trudeau was becoming increasingly tired and irritable as the campaign wore on and local Liberals kept adding engagements to his schedule. To relax him, his chief of staff, Bill Lee — yes, the same Bill Lee who had been active as an RCAF public relations man in the nuclear weapons crisis in 1963 that brought down Diefenbaker — sent someone out to buy a pair of swimming trunks so that Trudeau could cool off in the pool. The tactic didn't work because, while he made the famous dive, Trudeau emerged from the pool to tell his staff flatly that he was going to cancel the planned swing through the West which would launch the last phase of the campaign. He needed to rest and restore himself, he said, and if that meant he would lose the election, so be it. The staff were appalled and appealed to Senator John Nicol, the campaign chairman in Ottawa, to intervene. That night Nicol drove his own small car to Ottawa airport to meet Trudeau and they were still arguing fiercely when they arrived at 24 Sussex Drive. So fiercely, in fact, that the Mountie on guard outside the front door was hovering nervously and wondering when it would his duty to intervene to protect the prime minister. Finally, Trudeau agreed to go west, and the rest, as they say, is history. What remained in the Canadian memory was the prime minister diving.

In the midst of all the campaign excitement, Trudeau was more realistic than his admirers and knew that the magic would not last. In the closing days of the campaign, when his victory was assured, he invited me to breakfast on his plane. I asked him what he thought would be his major problem when he formed his government, expecting him to say inflation, which was emerging as a problem, or something like that. He had a much wiser one-word reply: "Expectations." He knew that disillusionment would soon follow adoration. When in office he proved to be slow to deliver the Just Society — he spent part of his first year reorganizing the government's decision- making process — the reaction set in, encouraged of course by journalists. This process was well described long ago by American writer, Leo Rosten, in his book *The Washington Correspondents* (Harcourt Brace, 1937):

> Newspapermen greet (a newly elected leader) with the hope that here at last is the great man incarnate. The great man's talents are sung, oversung, in the struggle for journalistic existence. Then "incidents" occur, a political compromise of not admirable hue, a political setback, attacks come from the Opposition, the newspapermen begin to see the feet of clay. They have been taken in, their faith has been outraged. How did they ever "fall for that stuff"?... Other newsmen, columnists, publishers cry that the press corps has been hamstrung by phrases. The correspondents are hurt. They are irritated. And they feel guilty. The breaking of the myth begins by the very men who erected it.

As I have said, I don't think the media created the Trudeau myth, but we certainly did little to calm the public hysteria. And when hysteria began to sour into, in some cases, downright hatred, the media did little to calm that either. In part, that was because Trudeau was not an easy politician to report. He seldom provided conventional news leads for the papers or sound-bites for radio and TV. He also frustrated reporters by replying to a question with another question, a technique which we learned to call a Socratic dialogue. It was intended to lead to a deeper understanding of the issue, but it didn't make news — and, worse, it seemed sometimes that he was toying with ignorant journalists, "dissing" them in today's slang. He used the same rhetorical technique in speeches, asking questions that sometimes got him into trouble. An infamous example occurred when he asked a Western audience anxious about foreign markets for wheat, "Why should I sell your wheat?" The quote was used for years by critics to prove his disregard for Western concerns, and still is. What they didn't say, or perhaps know, was that in his speech he went on to answer the question in a reasoned discussion of relations between government and farmers. But, again, that didn't make news.

Was he contemptuous of journalists, as has often been said? I never found him so, but he did like to put down journalistic pretensions. To cite one example, when I was teaching at Carleton University — about which more later — I asked if he would be willing to meet my students. The answer from his office was a tentative yes, with the date to be fixed later. The end of the academic year passed, and then came a call: You and your students may come to 24 Sussex Drive on such and such a Wednesday. Thanks, I replied, but there are no students; they've all left. Consternation, and then the solution: Well, the lunch is booked, so you come and we'll invite a few other journalists. On the appointed day, I joined half a dozen of the most senior journalists in the press gallery on the back lawn at 24 Sussex and sipped drinks until Trudeau came bouncing out of the house, remarking, "You're only here because Tony's students couldn't come." Still, it proved to a pleasant lunch. (It would have been even better if he had said correctly, "You're here only because... etc.")

With Trudeau firmly installed as prime minister, Ottawa settled down after six tumultuous years. But change came for me early in 1969 when I got a call at home from Peter Newman. He told me he was moving to Toronto to become editor in chief at the *Star,* and asked if I would be interested in taking over his column. Newman and I were acquaintances, not friends, and the invitation was a surprise, but flattering and welcome. I was tired of chasing the daily news for the *Globe* and the idea of having to write only three columns a week struck me as luxury. Plus Newman had built a large following for his column which was syndicated across Canada. I flew to Toronto to discuss terms with publisher Beland Honderich, and readily accepted his offer of $20,000 a year, plus 50 percent of the net proceeds of syndication. I asked for guarantees that my copy would not be changed without my consent, and at Honderich's invitation I sat at his secretary's desk to put my conditions in writing, which he then accepted with his signature. I didn't know then that trying to impose conditions on the newsroom bureaucracy of the *Star* was about as useful as negotiating with an ocean liner at full speed. On the other hand, the *Star's* bureaucracy could be useful. The syndication deal was more generous than I had expected, and the explanation, I discovered later, was that at some time in the past there had been a writer who had asked for a lower salary and a bigger cut on syndication because he was paying alimony based on salary. In time, the *Star* forgot this was a special deal and I, and I suppose others, inherited the 50 percent rate. In some months, syndication paid me as much as salary, and for the first time in my life I felt rich — well, comfortable.

But the *Star* wanted value for its money, not thumb-sucking opinion pieces but news, or at least a new slant on current events. Newman had broken many important stories and I was expected to follow suit. I started with a bang with an exclusive and controversial interview with Trudeau and thereafter enjoyed some successes, but I can see now that my interests were already turning away from news. I was keenly aware that most of the people with whom I was associating had a university education, and when I discovered that there was at the journalism school at Carleton a one-year program for students who already had a degree in another discipline I got the idea that if I could teach them journalism maybe some of their other learning would rub off on me. The director of the J-school at that time was Joe Scanlon, a former *Star* reporter whom I had known briefly at City Hall in Toronto — before he went off to Queen's University to obtain a graduate degree, no less. Of course, I didn't have much time to spare from my column so Joe kindly agreed to hire me to help teach a half-course in which students studied books on social, political, and economic ideas, with the odd bit of philosophy and psychology thrown in.

At first as an assistant to an experienced teacher and then on my own, I participated in the weekly seminars at which we discussed the ideas and then related them to journalism, in theory and practice. It was a perfect fit for me, and I went on teaching that course for years. I soon discovered that possession of an undergraduate degree did not mean the students had much to teach me, but I was forced to become sufficiently familiar with the assigned books to debate them with young and lively minds. However, I was never more, and sometimes less, than an adequate teacher. Before the university introduced a process by which students rated teachers and courses, I distributed my own evaluation form, and usually came up with a grade in the B range. In the first year the main complaint was that I was intimidating, so I went out of my way in the second year to be, I hoped, friendly and informal. We gave student parties at home, but the complaint remained that I was intimidating. So I concluded that I was who I was, and we would all have to live with me. In part, I suppose, the fact that I was a nationally known columnist intimidated the fledgling journalists so doubtful of their own abilities and prospects — some of whom now hold jobs that no doubt intimidate today's students. But, in another part, I always expected more than was reasonable from students and so was a too-tough editor and marker. No doubt, also, the students perceived that while I was intrigued by the radical politics of the era, in my own life I was conservative to a fault. I wanted no part of any drug, having grown up with the idea, probably gained from lurid thrillers about Victorian London, that to touch any narcotic meant waking up addicted in an opium den in Limehouse, the Chinese quarter of London, or even in Shanghai. At one seminar in which we were discussing the drug culture, or something similar, a student lit up a marijuana cigarette, took a deep drag, and began to circulate it around the seminar group. My instinct was to leap for the alarm bell, but I realized that the students were all watching to see what would happen when the joint reached me: I passed it on unsmoked, said nothing, and the seminar continued. Pretty cool for a straight guy like me.

While on the subject of smoking, I can add smugly that around that time I gave up smoking tobacco, after more than twenty years. Indoctrinated at school, our kids told me that by smoking I was endangering my life and, therefore, their welfare. I waited until we went on holiday in a cottage by a lake, breaking my usual routine, took some drugstore tablets that were supposed to reduce the craving for nicotine, and simply stopped. By the time our holiday ended I felt I had broken the habit. But when I returned to work and sat down at the typewriter, I reached automatically for a cigarette. The habit was obviously related to the routine of work, and it was a little harder to break that, but I did. A few years later, of course, the kids began to smoke, and one still does, despite my reminders that she is endangering her health and therefore my welfare. I reflected at the time on a notion that still intrigues me. If one cigarette will not cause cancer but a million probably will, there must be a point between at which one lights the fatal smoke, even takes the fatal drag. To put it another way, if one did not take that drag, one would remain cancer free; take it, and the result is cancer. The same idea is true of course in many other aspects of life, the seemingly insignificant decision that has enormous consequences.

To return to my story, when I moved from the *Globe* offices to the *Star*, next door on the top floor of the National Press Building, I had friends waiting. Jack Cahill, whom I had known when he was Ottawa correspondent for *The Vancouver Sun*, had subsequently moved to the *Star* in Toronto, but was now back in Ottawa as bureau chief. One of his reporters was Eric Malling, whom I had met when he was a student at Carleton. While working in Toronto, Jack had decided to take up sailing, and with Aussie boldness bought a boat and launched his family onto the unpredictable waters of Lake Ontario, teaching himself seamanship. When he was assigned to Ottawa he took the boat with him, an O'Day Tempest, about twenty-three feet, with a large cockpit and a two-berth cabin, which he named *Binalong*, an Australian aboriginal word meaning something like On the Way to Dreamy Places. The name was appropriate for what was then a quiet, twenty-mile stretch of the Ottawa River west of Ottawa on which he could sail. He soon invited me to join him and we spent many happy weekends dodging log booms, weathering thunder storms raging down the valley, and finding some secluded spot in which to anchor for the night. Malling, too, had taken up sailing while in Toronto, bought a boat and launched himself onto Toronto Harbour with a young woman reporter as his crew. He intended to sail across to the exclusive Royal Canadian Yacht Club on the Toronto Islands and apply for membership. Sailing in a stiff breeze proved more difficult than he, a Prairie boy, had expected, but he eventually blew ashore at the club where he used his leg as a fender between the dock and the bouncing boat. He despatched the crew to the club office to apply for membership, but the official in charge took one look at the hapless Eric and decided he would not be a suitable member for the RCYC. When the *Star* posted Jack to Hong Kong, Eric and I bought *Binalong*, and subsequently moved it to Toronto and sailed on the lake before he developed a passion for "killing fish," as he put it, and bought a motor cruiser on Georgian Bay. While in Hong Kong Jack bought a British-built thirty-footer, sailed her in the South China Sea, and had it freighted back to Canada on his return. The *Star,* usually generous with expenses, paid the bill, so Jack was not required to resort to the ingenious accounting of an American TV correspondent in Hong Kong who bought a sailing junk and obtained permission from his unwary company to ship home "household goods and junk." Jack and I resumed sailing, this time on Lake Ontario, visiting more than once most harbors on both Canadian and U.S. sides, and in all sorts of weather. One reason I enjoyed sailing was that it is one of the few activities in modern life in which, when things turn rough, say a sudden thunder storm, you can't just pack up and go home; you have to deal with the conditions and overcome the danger.

To return to less serious matters, I have already mentioned that among Trudeau's first projects was reorganization of the central command of the federal government. That involved, among other things, enlarging the political staff in the Prime Minister's Office, and constructing an elaborate system of Cabinet committees, which had the effect of increasing the influence of the Cabinet secretariat in the Privy Council Office because it controlled the agenda. These changes were fiercely criticized on the grounds that Trudeau was centralizing power in his own hands, and before long Quebec and other provinces were accusing him of being a federal centralist. This myth is now part of his accepted image, but any examination of the record proves the opposite. He was much more careful than most previous prime ministers to stay out of provincial jurisdictions, and in fact he handed over to the provinces a large chunk of the federal revenues, to the point at which the provinces collectively spent more than Ottawa. The legitimate criticism of the new Cabinet system emerged only much later: the machinery was so elaborate that ministers spent endless hours in committee meetings instead of in their departments, and rather than speeding decision-making, it slowed it down. Trudeau also set out on a controversial reform of the rules of the Hose of Commons, which he finally achieved with the consent of the Tory Opposition — to which he provided a handsome budget. I tried to make sense out of all this in a series which the *Star* headed "How We Are Governed." Again to my surprise, this worthy but unexciting series won, in 1970, a National Newspaper Award, this time for Staff Corresponding, my third and last. I was told that I was the first person to win awards in three different categories, but that record I'm sure has been surpassed in far more competitive circumstances.

Another aspect of Trudeau, and I think another misunderstanding of the man, came with the October Crisis of 1970 when a small group of terrorists calling themselves the Front de Libération du Québec (FLQ) kidnapped the British trade commissioner in Montreal, James Cross, and then kidnapped and murdered a Quebec Cabinet minister, Pierre Laporte. It was the most dramatic story of my years in Ottawa, a watershed in Trudeau's career, and perhaps also in the history of Canada. It dragged us from the age of comparative innocence into the age of political violence and the consequent growth of security consciousness. During the crisis politicians and public opinion were swept up in a mood bordering on panic, encouraged by the news media which, as always, tended to dramatize and exaggerate events and opinions. I tried to be skeptical in reporting and balanced in commentary as the crisis unfolded, which pleased nobody. Journalists and others accused me of being an apologist for Trudeau, but the NDP published some of my columns as a pamphlet, and a radical magazine of the era, *The Last Post*, published in Montreal, used my reporting as a basic source of information for its own analysis. A few months after it was all over, I went back to the story and eventually developed a unique interpretation of what had happened. Trudeau was widely seen then, and is still remembered, as a resolute, even authoritarian, leader ready to go to any lengths to preserve law and order: the man who called out the army to guard the homes of prominent politicians in Ottawa and to aid the police in Montreal, and who proclaimed the draconian War Measures Act to give the police power to round up supects in Quebec. This image is captured in the TV picture of him outside Parliament being interviewed by a reporter who asks how far he is prepared to go: "Just watch me," he replies, and for good measure dismisses liberal bleeding hearts. A few days later, Trudeau activated the War Measures Act, imposing something close to martial law. That outraged many liberals who had believed him a champion of civil rights and now saw him as a ruthless law-and-order conservative. It also raised the suspicion that he was taking advantage of the crisis to intimidate Quebec nationalists and separatists, some of whom were arrested for no good reason.

That conspiracy theory persists, particularly in Quebec, despite the evidence of those who were insiders at the time. The most recent of those is Gordon Robertson, then the Cabinet secretary, who relates in his *Memoirs of a Very Civil Servant* (UofT Press, 2000) how he took the phone call at home from the Quebec Cabinet secretary asking for the imposition of the WMA as an aid to the police. Robertson replied that there was no chance of that unless Premier Robert Bourassa could convince Trudeau it was necessary, which he did. Trudeau, in his *Memoirs* (McClelland and Stewart, 1993) says Bourassa asked for both troops and the WMA. He agreed to the troops, indeed, had no choice under the National Defence Act which provides for a province to receive military support for the civil power on request. But he insisted on waiting to see how matters developed before invoking the WMA, which he did several days later, reluctantly, at the urging of Bourassa, the mayor of Montreal and others. I saw Trudeau as neither strong man nor conspirator. He appeared to me to be the head of a government caught flat-footed and uncertain how to respond to an act of terrorism that should have been predictable. There had already been several bombings in Montreal and much talk of revolution. In his *Memoirs* he confirmed my analysis to some extent, saying he had been concerned about political violence in Quebec and had urged the RCMP to greater efforts, but:

> That being said, I have to confess that we were completely stunned by the kidnaping in Montreal of the British diplomat James Cross, and his detention as a hostage by a cell of the FLQ. Nothing like it had ever happened in Canadian history, and the sheer senselessness of it caught us off guard, which meant that we were badly equipped to deal with it.

Although the Cabinet quickly decided in private not to give in to the FLQ's demand for release of terrorists already in jail, there were different opinions on how serious the crisis was, and about how to defuse it. To buy time for the police, there was at least the appearance of negotiation. The kidnappers were offered free passage to Cuba if they would release the hostages, and their revolutionary manifesto was read on TV. The FLQ fed inflammatory communiques to the radio stations, and their negotiators and sympathizers operated openly in Montreal. In the absence of much real intelligence from government, newspaper headlines grew bigger and blacker, and students at the University of

Montreal and elsewhere planned demonstrations to support the terrorists. In this mood of excited uncertainty in Quebec opposition politicians, labour leaders, and influential media commentators began to
question the ability of the Liberal government to lead the province
through the crisis. This became exaggerated by the Ottawa gossips into
the threat of a coup to install a new provisional government in place of
the Liberals. The story showed up in the *Star* without a byline, but written, I believe, by the editor, Peter Newman, without the knowledge of
his Ottawa staff. The likely source was Bryce Mackasey, a Cabinet minister but also a notoriously unreliable gossip. It pumped excitement and
speculation even higher. Larry Zolf, of the CBC, with whom I was
exchanging notes at the time, had close contacts among Trudeau's staff
and told me they were drawing parallels with France in the 1930s when
the Third Republic collapsed. Trudeau had never concealed his belief
that democracy was a tender flower in Quebec; after all, the Duplessis
regime against which he had fought for years was far from a model
democracy. When he was being questioned in the Commons about his
reasons for imposing the War Measures Act, he snapped in irritation, "I
acted on the information I have been accumulating since I was three
years old." Although he never spoke of it publicly, he had had a call from
elderly friends in Quebec saying they were afraid to go out of their
home, and driving down to Ottawa from his official country place on
Harrington Lake in the Gatineau Hills, he had noticed parents anxiously escorting their children to school. But he was also aware of the
danger of being provoked by the FLQ into harsh measures that would
unite liberals against him. He referred in the Commons to Sophocles'
play in which Antigone defies a harsh order by the ruler, Creon, who
orders her entombed, making her a symbol of the individual's right to
resist the unjust state. Trudeau was determined to defend the legitima-
cy of the Canadian state against all challenges, but did not want to be a
Creon. For that reason he was reluctant to invoke the WMA on the
grounds of "apprehended insurrection." But in fact it was not unreasonable to fear an insurrection in the form of student riots and demonstrations leading to clashes with the police and, if there were armed terrorists or panicky police around, the bodies of martyrs in the streets. The
WMA was the only form of emergency power available, and it is to

Trudeau's credit that he soon added a less draconian Public Order Act. But, in the event, the imposition of the WMA and the presence of soldiers in the streets did restore confidence almost overnight. When the terrorists responded to the WMA by cold-bloodedly murdering Laporte Quebeckers came face to sobering face with the meaning of revolution, and support for the FLQ drained away. So I saw Trudeau in that crisis as neither hero nor villain, but as an unprepared leader responding to an unprecedented challenge, and in the end making the best of a bad job.

But if the October crisis separated many intellectuals from Trudeau, it also divided friends, or at least acquaintances. A few months after the crisis, Newman left the *Star* to become editor of *Maclean's*, with a mandate to transform it into a newsweekly. I wrote to congratulate him on the improvements he had made at the *Star*, and to wish him well. But in one of his early issues on *Maclean's* he wrote what seemed to me a dangerously wrong-headed column about the FLQ crisis in which he said that the country had been divided by a wall of bayonets. This myth, in which English Canadians had been on one side and French Canadians on the other, seemed to me to play into the hands of separatists who were encouraging the idea that Trudeau had sent soldiers into Quebec to crush a popular revolt. I wrote a column criticizing Newman's piece and pointing out that Trudeau's actions in the crisis had been overwhelmingly supported both inside and outside Quebec.

But before it was published someone at the *Star* told Newman it was in the works and he called to ask me to withdraw it. He was under the impression that I was out to damage him as he was starting a new job, and when I declined to cancel the column, he said something to the effect of, "My turn will come," and hung up. I wrote him again to make the case that journalists should be able to disagree without taking personal offense; he did not reply and we have not spoken since. Highly talented people, I suppose, are often highly sensitive — which causes me to reflect on the fact that criticism seldom bothers me. Untalented or insensitive? If I am to keep the chronology reasonably straight, I have to interrupt this discussion of Trudeau to explain a change in my own career in 1971. After only two years writing the column, I had come to realize that I wasn't doing a wonderful job. There were no complaints from the *Star*, but papers on the syndicate were using me less frequently. There were a couple of hints that because I sometimes said kind things about the New Democrats, Brigadier Malone had "suggested" to editors of his FP papers that they consider using material from the group's Ottawa bureau in place of my column, but probably the explanation was simpler. As I wrote to my editor, Marty Goodman, I have come to the conclusion that I am not a good columnist. This is not false modesty; I still think I'm a pretty good political reporter and analyst. But I do not write well enough to be worth reading on that score alone, and I am not enough of an extrovert to impose my personality on the facts.

I can see now the underlying truth that the interests that had prompted me to jump from the *Globe* to the *Star* were still not satisfied. Daily politics still seemed trivial, and daily journalism unable to address the ideas and forces transforming Canadian society and the world. I was more interested in analysis than in reporting, and I was concerned also by a style of journalism becoming adversarial and destructive rather than supportive of democratic institutions. We seemed to be exercising power without responsibility, as Stanley Baldwin had put it. I wanted to take a couple of years at Carleton to work out my ideas, and maybe write a book about Trudeau's first term. The *Star* in its agreeable way not only granted me leave but also invited me to supplement my income as a part-time professor by writing a weekly column on the editorial page, and occasional editorials. The publisher, Beland Honderich, also asked me to report to him on any conclusions I might reach about journalism and futures.

I did in fact write a paper, "The Future of Newspapers," which had consequences for me and for the *Star*, and I'll say more about that later. But first, I had to write the book to try to make sense of Trudeau's first four years. That too was in part a reaction to daily journalism that seemed to me to focus on the personal and the one-day wonder while ignoring the changing context in which government had to work. My theme was Trudeau as a paradox, using the dictionary definition: a statement or proposition seemingly self-contradictory or absurd but in reality expressing a possible truth. As I pointed out, he was loved and hated more than most politicians, praised and damned, denounced as a playboy and as a constipated constitutionalist, a leftist and a rightist, and that he himself had said that the only constant in his thinking was opposition to accepted opinion. So I called the book *Paradox: Trudeau as Prime Minister* (Prentice-Hall of Canada, 1972) — the French edition became *Trudeau, Le Paradoxe* (Les Editions de L'Homme, Montreal, 1972) — and set out to contribute to the national debate by examining precisely what he had done in four years. Somewhat to the disappointment of my publisher, I refused to say anything about Trudeau's private life, or to try to find explanations for his actions in his education or upbringing. In other words, I was at my detached best, or worst, depending on your point of view. I was able to write it in seven weeks because I had done the research and worked out my analyses in two years' worth of columns. It was reasonably well received and sold a few thousand copies. Walter Stewart, a radical journalist, had already published a polemical attack on Trudeau, titling it *Shrug*. That prompted Zolf, the wit, to call my book *Plug*, but that wasn't fair. Rather, as one reviewer said, it was a balanced summing up for the jury of voters about to go into the election of 1972. Balanced books, of course, fail to please partisans on every side and therefore seldom become bestsellers. The upside was that sometime after publication Jeannie found *Paradox* remaindered for nineteen cents a copy and bought a bundle, which I signed and generously gave away when inquiries about the book trickled in over the years.

The enormous popularity Trudeau enjoyed during the October Crisis quickly evaporated in the face of rising unemployment, and he did not improve matters when he conducted the 1972 election campaign as a tutorial for the electorate, under the vacuous slogan of "The Land is Strong." He announced that rather than engage his opponents he would hold a dialogue with the people, and went about the country talking quietly about the choices that had to be made — for example, between rapid economic growth and conservation of the environment. It was noble in concept, putting into practice his motto, "Reason over Passion," but dreadful politics. The audiences I saw appeared genuinely interested in what he had to say, but it made no headlines for frustrated reporters looking for news. Conservative leader Robert Stanfield, meanwhile, was flailing away at unemployment, and NDP leader David Lewis attacked what he called the corporate welfare bums who were avoiding taxes and growing fat on government subsidies of one sort and another. The Liberals were fortunate to scrape to victory with 39 percent of the vote and a two-seat margin. The experience transformed Trudeau more than has been generally recognized. In Zolf's witty phrase, he went from Philosopher King to Mackenzie King — that is, a wily politician. I discussed this with Trudeau some months after the election, and he was frank:

> During the last Parliament, and certainly up to the election, I tried to talk in terms of reason, long-term issues, rational approach to problems, not campaigning against the oppositions, but just explaining the future of our country as seen by the liberal man and woman, and obviously I have had to have second thoughts about that type of approach to politics because of the results ...
>
> There is no doubt that since the last election, not only in our approach to government, but even in, say, the choice of some of my cabinet ministers I felt I had to lean a little more on the side of emotional involvement than rational involvement.

I asked him if he now accepted that the sort of "new politics" he had preached in 1968 was not viable, and he replied:

> Unfortunately, yes, I do. I'm probably a bit sad about it. I have always thought, and certainly it was my approach ... that if you talked honestly and sensibly to people they would respect you for it. But during the campaign, and indeed every day in the House of Commons, I see people trying to create prejudices based on people's emotions.

It is the theatrical, post-1972 Trudeau who has lingered in the public memory, but the real Trudeau, at least in politics, was the rational philosopher of 1968-72.

Of course, it was not only the near-death experience of the election that changed him. He had also run into economic problems that all his famous reason could not solve and which did more than any other issue to tarnish his reputation. It was partly bad luck. When he took office in 1968 inflation was becoming an unfamiliar problem. Nobody realized it at the time, but the postwar years of guaranteed growth were coming to an end and, even more seriously, so was the ability of national governments to manage their economies by adjusting fiscal and monetary policies to regulate supply and demand, and so to ensure growth without inflation. Around the democratic world, governments were struggling and mostly failing to regain control of their economies, which were behaving in ways not predicted by Keynesian theory. When they tried to control inflation by reducing demand, they wound up with stagnant economies in which unemployment rose along with prices — the new phenomenon of stagfla-tion. Canada, like the United States and Britain, experimented with wage and price controls, but with only limited success, and when unemploy-ment rose governments were driven by public expectations into deficit budgeting in an attempt to stimulate activity. It has often been said that Trudeau was so fixated on Quebec and the constitution that he ignored economic policy, but that is not correct. He had been trained in econom-ic theory but the problem was that the theory no longer worked, and he was left to flounder, as the following story illustrates.

When he announced in December 1975 that he would be address-ing the nation on TV, Bruce Phillips, the CTV bureau chief in Ottawa, asked me to join him at the network's local affiliate, CJOH, to listen to what the prime minister had to say and then to comment. Trudeau's text was issued to the media shortly before broadcast time and Phillips arrived at the station with a copy. He gave it to me to read, saying that there was interesting stuff at the end about "a new society." In fact, after talking about the recently introduced income and price controls, Trudeau said:

I will be speaking to you again in the coming months about the new kind of society we will need to create in response to the new economic circumstances in which we are living, here in Canada and throughout the world.

In our comments, Phillips and I drew attention to these intriguing words, and a CTV producer suggested we might follow up with an item on the Sunday night program, "W5." Most ministers are eager to appear on TV whenever they can, and Phillips had no difficulty in lining up Finance Minister Donald Macdonald and Treasury Board President Jean Chrétien for the program. We all met at CJOH on the Sunday afternoon to record the item, and when Chrétien twigged that we were going to raise the question of the new society he suggested to Macdonald that they should walk out rather than seek to interpret the prime minister. It was apparent that neither had any idea what Trudeau had been talking about, but somehow we stumbled through the program. Shortly thereafter, Phillips was preparing for his annual New Year's Eve interview with the PM, and we discussed how he might pursue Trudeau's elusive vision of a new society in a new economy. I had been reading Daniel Bell on *The Coming of Post-Industrial Society* (Basic Books, 1973) — that is to say, an economy in which service industries outstrip the old heavy and manufacturing industries — and Samuel Huntington and others on *The Crisis of Democracy* (New York University Press, 1975), by which they meant the unsustainable demands voters were making on governments. So I was full of ideas on what Trudeau might have in mind. But it turned out in the interview that he had very little in mind about a new society, beyond some vague and contradictory ideas on what might be happening in the global economy. The broadcast interview might have passed unnoticed but for an accident of the news business: CTV deposited the transcript in the press gallery in the dead period between Christmas and New Year when Canadian Press, the national news service, had only a junior on duty, and he, following the conventions of journalism, chose to highlight the most exciting quotes that could be read to make it appear that Trudeau was announcing the end of capitalism and the birth of some new form of regulated economy. To those who had always suspected that Trudeau was a Red preparing to march us all off to Siberia, this was the final proof, and the business community erupted in outrage. Trudeau soon made a speech in which he attempted to explain what he had meant, which was not much at all, but the damage was done, and he never recaptured the neutrality, let alone the goodwill, of Bay Street.

He did, however, go on to his greatest triumph, the patriation of the Constitution and the inclusion of the Charter of Rights and Freedoms. I say that was a triumph because that is how it has come to be regarded by most Canadians, but I have reservations because the outcome has been to change very substantially our parliamentary system of government. By guaranteeing rights, the charter puts them beyond the reach of Parliament and into the hands of the courts for interpretation. The inevitable result is to politicize the courts, as we have seen in the United States where great issues of public policy — abortion for example — may depend on the political leanings of the justices of the Supreme Court. People who support a right to abortion will tend to vote for a president who will nominate judges whose legal record leans in that direction. Those who oppose will campaign for a president likely to nominate judges who lean in the opposite direction. So the issue returns to politics through a backdoor, but it is decided without debates and votes in the Congress. That is already beginning to happen in Canada where there is agitation for some procedure that will allow parliamentarians to question persons nominated to the Supreme Court in order to determine their legal philosophy. Trudeau grew up in Quebec opposing the Duplessis regime and its attacks on civil liberties, so it is not surprising that he favoured a bill of rights to protect citizens from the excesses of their governments. But I was surprised at the enthusiasm for the project in the rest of Canada, where we have always seen government not as a threat but as the agency through which we build our society.

I was in the middle of writing this chapter when Trudeau died, and I was again surprised at the extent of public mourning. Many of the mourners I saw on TV had been children or teenagers when Trudeau was prime minister, and much of the media commentary seemed to be about a man unlike the Trudeau I observed and with whom I had a slight acquaintance. I never thought him a heroic figure — a Northern Magus as my friend Richard Gwyn called him. Nor was he as wildly popular as now seems to be imagined. In his best election, in 1968, his Liberal party won forty-five percent of the vote — and less than that outside Quebec. John Diefenbaker in 1958 and Brian Mulroney in 1984 both did better. In my view, the media and the political elites have created a myth to take the place of the real Trudeau, an exceptional personality and political leader, but at best only a modest success as head of government at a difficult time when all the verities were changing. At worst, history may show that he took the wrong fork at that constitutional conference in 1968 and, as Pearson warned might happen, became a failure of Confederation who left the country more fragile than he had found it. Or, to be charitable, it may have been that the forces of global change driving Canada were such that no prime minister could have done better.

While still on the *Globe* I had written a magazine article on the young MPs who might become prime ministers, and one of them was Jean Chrétien. It took no great foresight because it was obvious that Prime Minister Pearson was grooming him for the major league. For example, it was customary for French Canadian ministers to be appointed to a professional department such as justice, leaving the business departments like finance and trade to supposedly hard-headed Anglo-Saxon businessmen. But Pearson sent Chrétien to understudy Mitchell Sharp in finance, and in due time he did in fact become finance minister, although not a very good one. But his first job in the Trudeau cabinet was as Minister of Indian Affairs and Northern Development, and he invited me to join him and his party — his wife and small daughter, a couple of civil servants, and his political aide, John Rae — on a visit to the Arctic.

We travelled most of the way by float plane, and our first adventure was in the Belcher Islands in Hudson Bay. The locals insisted that the great minister had to hop into a canoe with a large outboard motor to go and shoot seals. That was not something Chrétien was supposed to do — I forget exactly why, perhaps he wasn't a licensed hunter, or it was out of season — but rather than offend his hosts he agreed to go if I would join him: Perhaps he wanted to make sure that as a journalist I would be a partner in whatever crime was to be committed, and thus unable to write about it. With Chrétien in the bow nervously holding a rifle, we set off into the calm waters between the islands, but there were no seals to be found. Suddenly, our guide revved the motor and we shot out into the rougher waters on the great bay, and soon there were seals popping up to look at us. With the guide pointing to the round heads in the water and shouting excited encouragement, Chrétien rose unsteadily to his feet in the bouncy bows of the boat and began to swing the rifle from side to side, seeking to fix on a target. It was immediately apparent that I, sitting amidships, was in greater danger than the seals, and I fell to my knees in the bottom of the boat, out of the line of fire, I hoped. Chrétien did fire one shot, but from that sporting expedition we all returned safely, including the seals. High up on Baffin Island we visited a small camp for fishermen tourists, and Chrétien had to try the waters for Arctic char. Large rods were produced and — reluctantly because I had no interest in killing fish — I allowed myself to be instructed in baiting and casting from a black sand beach. The inevitable happened; almost with my first cast I got a bite and reeled in the biggest fish of the day. For years afterwards, whenever we met, Chrétien would recall the story of my prowess as a fisherman. On that trip we went also to Grise Fiord, on Ellesmere Island, the northernmost Innuit community in Canada; it was summer, the ocean blue with white iceflows, the frozen land was coming to life, and I thought it enchanting. But unlike many people who fall in love with the Arctic, I had no desire to return, and never have.

But the story I most enjoyed doing as I was winding up that period of my work at the *Star*, before moving to Carleton, had nothing to do with current politics, but a lot to do with the history of politics. I got a call in March from Mel Hurtig, the Edmonton publisher/politician/campaigner for economic nationalism. I had been covering some of his activities and maybe his call to me was his way of saying thanks. He told me that he had in the basement of his house twenty-six cardboard boxes, of the sort used by movers to pack books and china, which he thought would be worth exploring. The strange story was that an American sociologist teaching at Edmonton had been prowling a sales room in Scottsdale, near Pheonix, Arizona, and found forty of the sealed boxes being auctioned to cover unpaid storage charges. He pried up the a corner one box and saw inside a folded Union Jack, a black hat, and a mass of papers. That was enough to pique his curiosity and he managed to buy twenty-six boxes for a few dollars each before others started to bid and pushed the price higher than he was willing to pay. Back in Edmonton, Hurtig heard the story and bought the boxes from the sociologist. They seemed to contain, he told me, the papers and possessions of René Beaudoin, a former Speaker of the House of Commons. I knew enough of the Beaudoin story to agree at once to fly out to Edmonton. He had been the most popular Speaker of the Commons in history, with friends and supporters in all parties, a self-made lawyer and politician from Montreal, both an authority on parliamentary procedure and the host of swinging parties on the Hill — at one of which he introduced rock and roll to MPs and senators. Then came the infamous Pipeline Debate in 1956 which raged for weeks, outraged public opinion, and set in train the defeat of the Liberal government in 1957 and the rise of John Diefenbaker. If Beaudoin's papers could shed new light on what happened on Black Friday, as it was called in the media, it would be a contribution to Canadian history. Hurtig welcomed me to his home, showed me the pile of boxes, and left for his office.

I soon discovered that Beaudoin had been the type of person to keep every scrap of paper that crossed his desk, but what was important to me was his account of the Pipeline Debate. If correct, it showed that the crisis need never have occurred. The Commons debate had been about the government's decision to lend $80 million to U.S.-controlled Trans-Canada Pipelines Ltd. to start building a billion-dollar line to carry Alberta natural gas to Toronto and Montreal. The bill authorizing the loan had to be passed by June 7, but the Conservatives and the CCF (Co-operative Commonwealth Federation, forerunner of the NDP) denounced it as a sell-out to Americans, and set out to block it in the Commons, using every procedural delaying tactic they could find. In response, and to be sure of meeting its deadline, the government decided to use the closure procedure under which debate could be limited and votes forced. Closure was seldom used, and normally only when there had been a lengthy filibuster, but this time the Cabinet made the fateful decision to impose it from the beginning of the debate at every stage of the bill. This was widely seen as a threat to parliamentary democracy, but the government hung tough through weeks of uproar, forcing the bill through stage by stage. At the end of May, with the June 7 deadline approaching, the government, citing a dubious precedent, imposed the final closure to force through all the remaining clauses of the bill. The opposition parties objected bitterly but fought on, and thought they had won when on the night of May 31 Speaker Beaudoin accepted for debate a CCF question of privilege. Privilege was not covered by closure and might be debated for days, but when the Commons met the next day — Black Friday — Beaudoin announced he had made a mistake in accepting the question of privilege and that debate would resume on the pipeline bill. It was known that two Liberal ministers had called separately on the Speaker, and widely assumed they had pressured him into to changing his ruling. Again the House erupted. At one point, the dignified leader of the CCF, M.J. Coldwell, advanced on the Speaker shaking his fist. Newspapers wrote their fiercest editorials, angry letters and wires poured into the Speaker's office, and Beaudoin, sitting white-faced and unmoving in his chair, was denounced as "the rapist of Parliament." The government won the battle of the bill but lost the election war the following year.

In the unsigned and undated document I found among his papers, Beaudoin claimed he had been misunderstood, and had acted only in the best interests of Parliament. As one would expect from a former Speaker and authority on procedure, much of the account was a discussion of the often arcane rules of the Commons. But, in essence, he claimed that on the evening of May 27 he had invited to dinner the CCF's Stanley Knowles, already then an authority on procedure, and they discussed the tactics of all the parties. He told Knowles he thought that government's final closure motion was not justified by precedent and wanted to find a way to rule it out of order, which would make the question of privilege irrelevant. That was exactly what the opposition parties wanted, and Knowles told him the Tories were working on a way to give him that opportunity. Beaudoin said he himself then bent the rules to throw out of the question of privilege and give the Tory House leader a chance to make his case that the closure motion was out of order. But it was too late, and when he announced his change of mind a on privilege, order and procedure disappeared. The time for reasoned discussion, if indeed there had ever been such a time in this affair, was over. In short, it was all a horrible misunderstanding. When I read this account I suspected it was an excuse made up long after the event, but that was not so. Among his private letters written at the time of the crisis I found several in which Beaudoin used the same reasoning to explain and justify himself. Before writing the story, I checked with Knowles, the one person around who might confirm or deny Beaudoin's story. He remembered the dinner but denied that the conversation that night could explain Beaudoin's action in the House. However, that may have been part of the misunderstanding.

There was also a human and rather sad side to the story. Rows in the House quickly blow over and Beaudoin survived as Speaker and resumed cordial relations with members of all parties. But his creditors were pressing and his marriage was in trouble, and although he was re-elected as an MP in 1957 he was no longer Speaker. The following year he ran away to Pheonix, Arizona with a twenty-three-year-old blonde

Ottawa socialite, and married her after getting a Reno divorce. But life cannot have gone well. Among a packet of photographs I found was a picture of a barroom in Scotsdale: two men are drinking beer and behind the bar stands a man in shirt sleeves, René Beaudoin. He eventually returned to Canada and even talked of resuming a political career, but died in a taxi with $3 in his pocket. His first wife with whom he shared his glory days as Speaker was found working as a sales clerk in Eaton's in Montreal. His second wife remarried in the United States. And Hurtig sold the Beaudoin papers to the National Archives for $5,000, where, I suppose, they await a parliamentary historian.

I wrote the story of the Beaudoin papers as a long feature. It attracted great interest in Ottawa, less elsewhere. The fact that I so much enjoyed writing a story unrelated to current affairs was another indication of what was happening in my career as I prepared to take my leave of absence from the *Star* at Carleton.

A.K.A.
AN ACADEMIC

~ *Chapter 11* ~

Sideways to a New Career

I was forty-five in 1971 when I moved to Carleton as a temporary, part-time visiting professor of journalism. Having left school at fifteen and never since brightened the door of an educational establishment, I still entered in the middle rank of the professorate as associate professor. This was justified, I suppose, by the fact that the J-school was regarded as a professional school and I had experience in the "profession" — which is in fact a craft rather than a profession because there are no recognized qualifications for admission and no peer regulation. The journalism program included both craft and theory courses. The craft I knew about, but I was not even aware that there were critical theories of journalism, and was as intrigued as any student to discover them. More intrigued in fact, because most students wanted to learn only the basics of the craft in order to get a job, the sooner the better, while I had been a reporter and was interested to discover what crimes against humanity I might be thought by critics to have committed.

I feared my comfortable arrival in the university might be resented by real academics who had spent years acquiring PhDs, but quite the contrary: I was accepted with respect as someone who had succeeded in "the real world." But I have never lost my respect for scholars and when, at retirement, I was asked if I would like to be proposed for an honourary degree, I declined. Handing out the honourary title of doctor may occasionally be justified when the person to be honoured has made a significant contribution to knowledge outside academe, which I had not. To hand out the title to persons who merely give money to the university, or in the hope that they will give money, is to sell it, and so tarnish it for those who have earned a doctorate by scholarship. When appointed at

Carleton, on two years' part-time leave from the *Star*, I was edging toward a new career, although I didn't fully realize that at the time. Perhaps I was experiencing a mild mid-life crisis, but more likely I was prompted by the same restlessness that had driven me to make a risky change in career by moving from Britain to Canada. I was becoming bored and seeking a new challenge. But whatever my motive, I enjoyed and profited from those two years at Carleton. For the first time in a quarter-century I was blessedly free from deadlines and, even better, I was being paid to read, think, and argue with bright students. I seldom lectured, at which I feared I would be boring, preferring the seminar format in which a student presented an analysis of the book we were studying and I began the discussion by attempting a Socratic dialogue.

The weekly column for the *Star* was more of a problem. Peter Desbarats had taken over the regular national affairs column and I didn't want to trespass on his turf, so I took advantage of my spot on the editorial page and my roost in a university to bring a more scholarly approach to my commentary, discussing the news in the context of books and ideas with which most busy journalists would not be familiar. It seemed to work. Editor Goodman told me that while I did not have a lot of readers, those I did have were in a class the mass circulation *Star* wanted to attract. The other task of writing a couple of editorials a week was routine for an old hand at the game like me.

I had previously spent a few weeks as holiday replacement for the editorial page editor and knew how the system worked. The *Star* was an afternoon paper in those days, and the first edition was printed in the early morning, so most of the editorials had to be written the day before. As editor responsible for the page, I went in at about six in the morning to make any necessary updates, and sometimes to write a new leader on any important overnight development. Publisher Honderich arrived early also and would read through the proofs of the editorials while I watched anxiously to see how many would survive. It was essential to have a reserve because on occasion he would reject half the pieces we had prepared so carefully the day before. "Why are we saying this?" he would ask. I would explain our reasoning. Infuriatingly, he would answer, "You haven't persuaded me," and the proof would flutter into the wastepaper basket, with only an hour or two to press time.

He had risen through the newsroom — in fact, he was the founding chairman in Toronto of the journalists' union, the Newspaper Guild — and was a first class journalist. He was also a successful but difficult manager with a style to match his Germanic name. It looked to me as if he deliberately appointed editors with overlapping responsibilities and watched them fight it out. The turnover of editors was remarkable, and among the many rather bitter newsroom jokes about Honderich was the answer to the question of why the *Star* moved to a new headquarters on the Toronto waterfront: "So that Bee can park his U-boat." He insisted that editorials, like news stories, should get right to the point. On one occasion I was writing a new leader as deadline approached and sending it down to the composing room a "take," or paragraph, at a time. Honderich wandered in and began to read the carbon copies as I continued to write, with one eye on him and the other on the clock. "When you get to the point I think I'm going to agree with you," he said, and ambled out. And he was right; I had been groping toward a conclusion. But he was always more than fair to me and I came to like and respect him, and later introduced him when he received an honourary degree at Carleton for his services to journalism — one of those honourary degrees I thought well earned.

During my time as columnist, he became convinced, like many others in the media, that Ottawa was squandering money on a program to provide summer work for young people called Opportunities for Youth. The youngsters were invited to propose social and cultural development projects on which they would work, and news reports, inevitably, exposed a few that were scams. Honderich asked me to go across the country and do a comprehensive exposé. I agreed to go, but without preconceptions, and in fact I returned with a series about how well the program was working. To his credit, Honderich swallowed hard and ordered that the series be given front page treatment. However, I always said no when he pressed me to move to Toronto to become an editor. I would object, "There are lots of issues on which we don't agree." He would promise, "We'll work it out." But I knew he would always win the argument. I saw editors come and go, and was wise, I'm sure, to remain in Ottawa, if only because I retained his respect.

Between Carleton and the *Star* I was kept busy in those two years, but found the time in 1972 to go on a national tour to promote *Paradox*, my book on Trudeau's first term. Flying from city to city to be interviewed on radio and TV, mostly by people who had not read the book, was tedious, and I found it hard to believe that what I had to say would prompt anyone to rush out and buy a copy. But the publisher's reps assured me the exposure did promote sales. The fun part of all that was in Montreal when the French edition was launched. The publisher's party was considered a great success because two celebrities attended: Claude Ryan, the high-minded editor of *Le Devoir* and the main interpreter of Quebec nationalism to the rest of Canada, and the first woman to have appeared nude in a Quebec film, who was by then mistress to some important person. I narrowly escaped disaster born of vanity, realizing only at the last moment that it would be folly to attempt any sort of French-language interview on the radio.

Then, in 1973, before returning to the *Star*, came the task of writing that paper I had promised on the future of newspapers. I had done some reading and thinking on the subject and rattled off my ideas in a day or two, attaching no great importance to the task. But it caused a stir at the *Star*, and a version was later published in *Content*, a magazine for journalists, long since defunct. Looking at it now, I can persuade myself I was wrong in some details but right on the general thrust. My thesis was:

> The industrial revolution produced the mass society of readers and consumers. The mass circulation newspaper grew up to serve that society as an educator and a distributor of goods. But we are now moving from the industrial to the post-industrial society ... The post-industrial society is a highly decentralized society. That is already apparent in many areas of life. There is a wider and wider choice in everything from education to autos. Among the media, mass circulation magazines are collapsing while special-interest magazines are springing up and flourishing. It is a similar story with books; there are more and more specialized book clubs addressed to particular interest groups.
>
> Is the mass circulation paper an exception to the rule of fragmentation? No. The number of such papers is steadily declining, while the number of limited or local circulation journals directed to special markets is rising ... The mass market for

the mass paper will obviously exist for some time. But perhaps for a shorter span than we can now guess ... The first generation of the post-industrial society is now emerging from the universities to become citizen-consumers. The price of survival will be to meet the needs of this market of specialists.

I went on to argue that when newspapers tried to make a general appeal to every type of reader they were not good enough in any area for the reader with a special interest. To compete in the new society they would have to be as good in specialized fields as the specialist publications. This would require specialized journalism free from the homogenizing instinct of a central news desk that wanted every story to be simplified and told in terms understandable to every reader. In other words, I was advocating decentralization in the newsroom to empower writers at the expense of editors — the opposite of the *Star's* operating principles. I addressed also the new challenge presented to the conventional paper by TV and radio:

What is the role of the newspaper when the city worker hears three radio newscasts as he drives home from his office, turns on the 6 p.m. TV news as he has a drink before dinner — and then picks up his afternoon paper ? Newspapers have been able to present more news and more varied news than TV. But that is a declining asset in the age of specialization. Further, there will be more and more news on TV as channels multiply and satellites relay the world to the world. The TV mass market is already fragmenting and as it divides into smaller sections broadcasters will become increasingly specialized. Movies on one channel. News on another channel, 24 hours a day. And already much of the commentary and analysis on TV is equal to that in the newspapers. The fact that mass newspapers still have a mass audience may mean no more than that the TV generation is only jst growing to maturity.

As the Star had recently gobbled its old rival, the *Telegram*, it was fat and complacent, and to shake things up I finished my paper — or "Notes" as I called it— with a cautionary tale:

Buckminster Fuller, in one of his visionary books on change and
the need to adapt, writes of a type of sea bird which stood in
tidal waters in prehistoric times and made its living scooping up
small fish. Through centuries of evolution it became more efficient by growing a larger beak which enabled it to catch more
fish which made it fat and happy — rather as mass circulation
newspapers have devised new ways to catch every little reader
and advertiser and have become rich in the process.

But then, says Fuller, there came a shift in the ecology, and the
little fish began to move away to new waters. The birds wanted to
follow them but they could not fly: Their efficient beaks were too
heavy. As the fish left the birds grew thinner and eventually died
— victims of change to which they could not adapt.

Whether it was that parable or simply the logic of my argument that
caught Honderich's interest, I don't know, but his reaction surprised and
somewhat alarmed me. He proposed to lay my "Notes" before the *Star's*
board of directors, and I could see myself defending my ideas before a
bunch of business moguls who knew a great deal more about the business of publishing newspapers than I did. So I hastened to point out that
I was just one journalistic voice, and that perhaps it would be advisable to
circulate the paper to his senior editors and writers, invite their comments, and then have a discussion. So it happened, and the *Star's* senior
journalists agreed almost unanimously that I was not only wrong, but perhaps a little crazy. My only support came from the late Sandy Ross, then
a thoughtful columnist, and the market researchers who feared there
might be a little something in my ideas.

Experience has shown, I think, that indeed I was on to something.
Newspapers had always striven to differentiate themselves in the market-
place, usually by backing different political parties. But they had all competed for the same readers by covering the same type of news. Now they were
moving to much sharper marketing to different segments of the mass market. The *Star*, like most afternoon papers, switched to morning publication
where the competition with TV is less intense, and has survived as a general interest paper, so I was wrong to suggest it might be in imminent danger.
But the secret of its survival may be that it is the last paper in the market spe-

cializing in Toronto. The former *Telegram* journalists who bravely launched the tabloid *Sun* specialized in sensational design — frozen TV, as I wish I had called it — lots of young flesh, and right wing commentary. One columnist suspected Trudeau of being a Commie. *The Globe and Mail* ceased to be mainly a Toronto or even an Ontario paper, claiming instead a national audience, and it has become increasingly a business paper. Its "Report on Business" section now spins off ever more specialized supplements dealing with management, technology and so on. *The National Post*, when it appeared, branded itself as the voice of the right in Canada, specializing in conservative comment and angled political reporting — something like the party organs of long ago. So these papers are segmenting the market, as I had thought they would, because they can't compete with radio for speed in covering the news, or with TV for graphic presentation.

But if Honderich was reassured by the meeting with the editors and their rejection of me in the role of Cassandra, he did not forget about my ideas. With Goodman, he asked me if I could see some way, when I left Carleton, to experiment with my ideas about specialized journalism. I replied with a memo describing what seemed to me to be an ideal Ottawa bureau, including a splendid job for an Ottawa editor — which I intended for myself. I proposed to increase the size of the bureau from seven to ten, and to transfer some authority from the editors in Toronto to the Ottawa editor, who would have the rank of a deputy managing editor. In fine bravura style I wrote:

> There should be as little interference — rewriting, second-guessing, arbitrary editing — as possible with the daily file from the bureau ... senior editors up to an including the Publisher should hesitate to make changes .... Within the bureau, specialist reporters should be given considerable freedom to work their own beats and develop and write stories as they see them, rather than conform to the conventional judgement of what makes a news story.

The high-minded idea was to dig much deeper into the processes of government than had been customary, and to provide ongoing information on policy development long before the topics reached the normal news agenda. In fact, the bureau would treat much of the routine daily news, including question period in the Commons, with the respect it deserved by leaving it to the Canadian Press news service. As all this was almost the reverse of the *Star's* operating methods, I expected my ideas to be acknowledged and ignored, and I was contemplating a future at Carleton. But Honderich and Goodman at once accepted my plan, gave me an official job description and a budget, and told me to get on with it.

One task was to recruit a national affairs columnist, Desbarats having left for a job in TV. There was a rising star in Vancouver, Allan Fotheringham, who was writing a much admired column of investigative reporting and comment for *The Vancouver Sun*, precisely the sort of journalism the *Star* most admired. He and I talked about it, but he eventually said no, probably wisely because he went on to fame and fortune as columnist, correspondent and TV personality. I then approached Ron Collister, a CBC-TV correspondent at the time with many years of experience in Ottawa. But journalists are terrible gossips and when I talked to him he already knew Fotheringham had turned me down, and he was offended to be my second choice. So no sale there either. Then, one day, I met Richard Gwyn in the bar of the National Press Club; I had known and admired his work as political reporter for several news organizations, including *Time* Magazine, and as an author. I was intrigued by the fact that he had since worked on the other side of the street, as it were, as a political aide to a controversial Quebec Liberal, Eric Kierans, and then as a federal civil servant in Kieran's communications ministry in Ottawa. I thought he might bring a new and better informed perspective to political reporting, and Richard jumped at the idea of returning to journalism as the *Star's* columnist. We flew to Toronto to see Honderich, and Richard was appointed. Some thirty years later he is still writing a distinguished column, and recruiting him was probably the best day's work I ever did for the *Star*. To be bureau chief in charge of daily operations, I recruited Carl Mollins, whose work at Canadian Press had made him a role model for many younger journalists, and we added a mix of experienced reporters and talented youngsters.

And away we went on our bold experiment in a different sort of journalism. It attracted much attention in both the journalistic and political communities, but soon proved to be all a mistake. In my idealism I probably overrated the public interest in serious journalism, and there is absolutely no doubt that I vastly overrated the *Star's* interest. Mollins and

I soon discovered that despite our mandate the news editors in Toronto were not prepared to surrender to us their authority to decide what we should be reporting and how we should write it. They were happy with any exclusives we could provide, but their first priority was to match whatever was on the CP news wire, on the CBC-TV news, or in early editions of the *Globe*. If we did not provide the necessary matching story because we thought it wrong or trivial, they simply rewrote our copy or used a CP story. In short, there was to be no change: the Ottawa bureau would remain the agent of the national editor in Toronto.

Mollins and I kept flying to Toronto to complain, and the inquests of course made things worse rather than better. The crisis came during the 1974 election. Edwin (Ted) Bolwell, a former colleague at the *Globe*, had become managing editor, enjoying his fifteen minutes in the revolving door, and was dissatisfied with the low key coverage of the early days of the campaign which, by design, we were providing. He decided to liven things up by replacing members of my bureau with "stars" from Toronto, notably my old friend Val Sears. Sears combined an acid wit with a colourful writing style. He had been the *Star's* Ottawa bureau chief during the 1962 election and was best known for his remark as reporters boarded Prime Minister John Diefenbaker's campaign plane, "Come gentlemen, we have a government to overthrow." But when he replaced my bureau reporter on the campaign, it was obvious to all that our experiment was failing, and bureau morale sank. To try to improve things, Mollins moved to Toronto to handle election coverage copy, but soon found he was being overruled or ignored. He and I met in his hotel room in Toronto, reviewed our frustrations and decided the time had come to give up. He posted his resignation on the newsroom notice board. I sat down in the newsroom and typed a memo to Bolwell:

> As you may have guessed, I have become increasingly frustrated in recent months. I have not been able to achieve what I hoped to achieve when I took over the Ottawa bureau a year ago ... So this is to let you know that I have decided to leave the *Star* .....
>
> In retrospect, I think the agreement— about the status of the Ottawa bureau — under which I returned to the *Star* was unrealistic. This has been the root of my problem and I see no

way to resolve it. So I am not blaming anyone but myself for my frustration. But I should be less than frank if I did not say that the *Star* is quite the most extraordinary and infuriating place in which to work. It seems to me to be designed to reduce good journalists to burnt-out deadbeats. I hope it doesn't happen to you. I'm not going to let it happen to me.

A year or two later when it was Bolwell's turn to quit he told me he had remembered my warning. But back to my resignation: Bolwell tried to persuade me to stay, but I agreed to remain only until the election was over. I had realized that I might have been wrong in my original criticism of mass appeal journalism, and the editors right in insisting that the average reader wanted the daily news in dramatic or entertaining stories, perhaps to be backgrounded with weekend features. I no longer enjoyed that style of journalism, and there was my problem. Honderich and Goodman both believed it was necessary for the *Star* to attract a large audience before it could deliver its serious message on social reform — banging the drum to get the people into the tent to hear the sermon, as Goodman put it. My reply was that if the paper had to behave like an entertainer to attract an audience, why should it expect the readers to take seriously what it had to say about the state of the world? I thought my rude resignation would be the end of my association with the *Star*, but not at all. Both Goodman and Bolwell apparently assumed that my resignation was mere petulance and that when the election ended all problems would be worked out. When I finally made clear to Goodman that I had no intention of spending years, perhaps the rest of my career, fighting for change at the *Star*, he was amazed: Hadn't I realized, he asked, that it would take years of patient effort to turn around an institution like the *Star*? He suggested that I could quit as Ottawa editor and take some other position at the *Star*. I replied that I thought it best to make a clean break, but he and Bolwell took me to lunch and suggested I become a once-a-week columnist for the editorial page. I was about to say no thanks when he mentioned the pay, $20,000 a year, a heap of money at that time, and in fact what I had been earning for three columns when I was the full-time national affairs columnist. It was an offer I was too greedy to refuse, and I continued to write happily for the *Star* for twelve more years —

although the pay was eventually halved to a more reasonable $10,000 during an economy drive. All that remains today of my misguided experiment in journalism are questions I raised in the original "Notes" on newspapers:

> Is the mass circulation paper really an efficient way to deliver information to a fragmenting audience? To put it another way, how long will it seem sensible to deliver a 200-page paper to a reader who is interested in 20 pages?
>
> How long before conservationists and perhaps governments object to the fact that six million trees have to be cut each year to make paper on which to print *The New York Times*, most of which is discarded unread?

Even better questions now that most newspapers publish also on the Internet.

~ *Chapter 12* ~

News versus Truth

With the prospect of returning to Carleton and spending the rest of my career in academia, I decided with appropriate modesty that perhaps I should try to acquire some academic credentials. But, immodestly, I had seen enough of undergraduate studies to want to skip them, if at all possible. My good luck struck again when I met Davidson Dunton, then director of the graduate Institute of Canadian Studies, in the elevator of what was then called the Arts Tower and is now the Dunton Tower, renamed in memory of that remarkable man. He had started working life as a reporter in Montreal, became an editor, chairman of the CBC, co-chair of the historic B and B Commission, and president of Carleton, before retiring to the institute. In that elevator conversation, I asked him if I could be admitted to Canadian studies without an undergraduate degree. After consulting the dean of graduate studies, he returned with his answer, "Yes, it's possible, but why not come and teach instead?" I didn't know it at the time, but while he had a bagful of honourary degrees and had studied at universities in Europe and Canada, he had never earned a degree in the usual way, which probably made him sympathetic to my request. So I became in 1974 a part-time visiting fellow in Canadian studies. As I have mentioned in the introduction, there was another new fellow that year, David Lewis, who had lost his seat in the Commons and so ended his career as leader of the New Democratic Party. I had known him in politics and our relationship had developed despite a rocky start: Years before, when I was an editorial writer, he had made some accusation against *The Globe and Mail* which enraged the publisher, Dalgleish, who instructed me to write a one-paragraph editorial saying that Mr. Lewis had lied, and knew that he had lied — in effect, a challenge to sue us. Wisely, Lewis declined the provocation, but he was still smarting when I was posted to Ottawa, met him at lunch in the parliamentary restaurant, and felt obliged to confess that I had written the offending editorial. He got some of his own back when, at Carleton, we were presiding at a seminar in which the subject of modern art came up. In art, I know what I like and it does not include much modern art, much of which strikes me as a conspiracy between artists, galleries, and art snobs to pass off non-art as works of merit and value — value in dollars, that is. I had begun my comments to the seminar by saying, "I don't know whether I'm a philistine or the last honest man ..." when David, a wicked debater, stopped me dead by interjecting, "The former." Even I had to smile, but with difficulty. Presiding with Dunton and Lewis at weekly seminars at which students presented their research was my principal duty at the institute, and I learned, from the research papers and from my two eminent colleagues, at least as much as I would have as a student. So I continued for two more years as a volunteer, as it were, at the seminars, and even became in time a member of the institute's committee of management, which rejoiced in its acronym of COMICS.

Academics are expected to publish as well as to teach — "Publish or perish," was the threat, more imagined than real at Carleton — which suited me because I already had a book, my second, in mind. In *The New Society* (McClelland and Stewart, 1977), I drew together the ideas I had been developing in my columns and articles on trends in post-industrial society in Canada. This involved trespassing in many disciplines, and I was aware that John Porter, the distinguished sociologist and senior academic at Carleton, had observed about journalists, "Perhaps no other occupational group in modern society appropriates to itself a role which requires all-seeing wisdom in so many spheres." Journalists, he also remarked, seemed prepared to write about anything. I replied to that put-down by suggesting that somebody ought to try to bring together and weave into a pattern the many strands of expert knowledge and opinion, and asked, "If not brash journalists, who will?" After all, I had no scholarly reputation to lose, which proved to be an asset later when I was asked to be a guinea pig in an experiment to see if anyone teaching journalism could advance to the rank of full professor. My academic colleagues were reluctant to allow their names to be put forward because they might be found wanting in the lengthy peer reviews to which promotions were subject. I had nothing to lose, and as it happened my professional reputation was accepted as sufficient grounds for promotion. With that ice broken, several others in the journalism school followed.

Writing *The New Society*, I was selecting and interpreting evidence for my arguments, so I thought it time to declare my political leanings, something I could not have done as a reporter:

Journalists are not objective. We are conditioned by upbringing, education, and experience, and the best we can do is to strive to be fair. But I should point out the perspective from which I approach this book. From the age of about twenty, I have thought of myself as a socialist, although I have tried not to let that influence my reporting of politics and government. I hope that this declaration will not prejudice the reader because for me socialism is an end, not a means. I seek equality and fraternity in liberty by a process of evolution rather than revolution, by improving the existing social and economic order rather than by demolishing capitalism to build a new Jerusalem on the rubble. Some of the means to the end are suggested in this book and the reader may conclude that I am better described as a social democrat then as a socialist — but so, I think, are the great majority of modern "socialists" who have had to revise their ideas about the virtues of public ownership, the evils of private profit, and the perfectibility of man. It will take a little longer than once we thought.

Looking back on it now, I see that the major failure of the book was not to foresee the emergence of neo-conservatism, then only a couple of years away. My opening premise was that the trend to collectivism — that is to say, a society in which the state plays a central role in planning the economy and setting social priorities — would continue in Canada, and in all other developed social democracies. The choice, I said, quoting Michael Harrington, the American socialist theorist, would be between totalitarian, bureaucratic, and democratic collectivism. I opted of course for the democratic model and a good part of the book was about strengthening democracy in Canada by reforming the political system. It did not occur to me that there might be a corporate collectivism, a system in which huge business enterprises dominate the society, including politics — making government, in Marx's phrase, the executive committee of the bourgeois classes. That is what many observers think has happened, but I am not convinced. Much has been made of the so-called triumph of neo-conservative capitalism and the defeat of social democracy, but in the two decades since Margaret Thatcher in Britain and Ronald Reagan in the United States took office, I don't see much evidence for the claim. It's true that governments of all persuasions have thought it wise to restrain growth in the public sector, but in most cases the "savage cuts" we hear so much about merely returned public spending to where it had been a few years earlier. Spending is now again on the rise as voters in most democracies, including Canada, continue to demand more and better public services in preference to tax cuts. Governments have also deregulated some industries and privatized some functions, but they continue to be held accountable by the voters for management of the economy and the health of society.

In my view, the neocon resurgence has been much overrated, and the capitalism we now enjoy bears little or no resemblance to the laissez-faire monster of earlier times. So while I was certainly shortsighted when I wrote *The New Society* I am not convinced that I was wrong in the long view. In fact, I was spectacularly right in describing the emergence of "International Society" and its implications for Canada, but I'll have more to say about that in the next chapter. *The New Society* was published by McClelland and Stewart, and chosen to be one of the books to be promoted as a possible bestseller. So I was invited to address the sales force, only to discover that the publishing date had been delayed. I asked Jack McClelland why it took so long to publish a book, pointing out that the *Star* managed to publish every day the equivalent of short book. He found that an interesting observation, but had no answer. When eventually I did set out on the cross-country promotional tour I soon discovered that the book had not yet reached the stores. I deceive myself by thinking that is the reason it never became a bestseller.

When I received my part-time appointment in Canadian studies, I was also given a part-time appointment in the School of Journalism, which became full-time in 1975. My speciality, naturally, was political reporting. I had been interested for some years in polling which seemed to me to be a new and better way of discovering and reporting the concerns and opinions of the public, particularly during elections. We political reporters of the time attempted to discover shifts in opinion by knocking on doors like a candidate for election, or phoning a handful of trusted sources across the country, or even by swapping impressions with colleagues and competitors in the press bar. Then we wrote weighty articles on how the people felt and were likely to vote. It seemed obvious to me that it would be more reliable to interview, say, a thousand people across the country, chosen at random to represent the entire population, asking standardized questions. But political polling was still in its infancy in Canada, dominated by the Gallup organization, and few journalists had much idea how it was done, or what questions to ask the pollsters when they announced their findings as if they were the revealed truth.

So I decided in 1975 to organize a telephone survey — not strictly a poll — as a classroom exercise and learning experience. With the help of Pat Nagle, a veteran Vancouver journalist who was spending a year at the school, we got hold of a list of the delegates to a forthcoming national Liberal conference at which they were to vote on Trudeau's leadership, designed a questionnaire, and set students to telephoning as many delegates as they could reach. One day when Nagle, I and the students were struggling to make sense of hundreds of answer sheets, a new member of the faculty, Alan Frizzell, happened by and pointed out that by feeding the answers into the university's computer system he could do a faster and better job. For example, the computer could in a flash break down answers by gender, region, age, education, and more. Alan had a degree in statistics from Strathclyde University in Scotland and studied for a doctorate in political science from Queen's in Kingston, and so had the expertise I lacked. He was also, and still is, one of the smartest people I have ever met. His range of knowledge in a variety of disciplines is extraordinary. He and I became polling partners in what we called the Carleton Journalism Poll, and also friends. Our goal was to provide survey data to the news media at cost, as an alternative to Gallup. We resolved never to do market research for commercial companies, but we did on occasion work for public bodies. I never did understand how to program a computer, and had only the slimmest grasp on the statistical theory and methods behind the science of polling. But I had the writing skills to help construct a value-free questionnaire, and the credibility in the media to give our poll results authority. Alan organized and trained the student interviewers; with input from clients we constructed questionnaires; Alan entered the data into the computer; and together we analyzed and wrote up the results, which I was available to announce and discuss with journalists, on and off the air.

From our insignificant beginnings, we rapidly progressed to becoming the CBC's pollsters in the 1979 and 1980 elections. Like most of the news media at that time, the CBC was making its first nervous ventures into polling as a form of news, and the journalists with whom we worked were always afraid we were going to make some ghastly mistake for which they would be held responsible — particularly when our numbers varied significantly from those of the great Gallup. In truth, Alan and I were hardly less nervous, but we soon learned that a pollster has to have faith in the numbers, even when they are at odds with a gut feeling about the public mood. The results of our poll in the 1979 campaign were a challenge both for the CBC, and for us, because they showed the Conservatives to be ahead of the Liberals but by a margin so narrow as to be statistically insignificant. Knowlton Nash, who presided over the National News, was dismayed when I told him that we could not realistically say which party was ahead. Having spent all that money — well, enough to pay for our phone calls across the country — he had no news to trumpet. Fortunately, our figures showed the Conservatives ahead in Ontario, which suggested they were going to win nationally, but by a narrow margin. I went out on a thin limb and agreed that Nash could start his report by saying, "Tories take the lead," which I qualified later in the news to suggest that it would probably mean a Conservative minority government — which, of course, it did. Nationally, the Liberals finished with forty percent of the vote, and the PCs with thirty-six percent, but in Ontario the Liberals won 32 seats, and the PCs 57 which enabled them to form a government. There was no such difficulty in 1980 when Prime Minister Joe Clark's miscalculation brought about the defeat of his government in the Commons, and another election. It was clear from the beginning of the campaign that the Liberals were going to win handily.

But our successes and exposure in the media had a result we had not foreseen. Commercial pollsters realized that if they got into the election business, even if it meant working at a loss, they could get priceless exposure on television and so attract commercial clients. We could not operate at a loss, and in any event the CBC had always been worried about working with an outfit that could easily be dismissed by the party we showed to be losing as "just a bunch of students." The commercial pollsters had more impressive credentials, and so we eventually lost the CBC as a client for election polling. However, in 1983 when I was in New York on six months' research leave from Carleton, Alan accepted a CBC contract to poll Canadians on their sexual habits. The first I knew about it was when the director of the J-school, Stuart Adam, called to ask what I thought about this project. I told him I thought it was a thoroughly bad idea; the president of the university, and probably the chancellor and the entire board of governors, would be less than pleased to hear complaints from across Canada about students calling at dinner time to ask intimate questions. Alan had no qualms, and anyway the contract had been signed, and so the interviewing went ahead, with interesting results. Peter Mansbridge, looking pink, announced the results on a CBC-TV special, and remarked that he didn't know how our interviewers had had the nerve to put the questions. But there was a problem unforeseen by anyone. Alan had underestimated the costs of the survey because the people interviewed not only answered the questions, but insisted on talking at length about their sex lives, pushing the telephone charges far above budget. Make of that what you will, taking into account that there were no complaints from anyone, as far as I know, about the survey.

The 1984 election was our last big election success. We were hired by Southam News, the national news service for the Southam chain of papers, and that led to a hair-raising experience. One of the givens in election reporting at that time was that the Liberals would win Quebec — they almost always had — so Alan and I were shocked to find that our poll was showing the Conservatives ahead in Quebec. There had to be an error somewhere, so we checked the random sample in Quebec to make sure it was reasonably representative of the population in age, gender, language, education, income etc. No problem there, so we ran the numbers again, making slight adjustments to ensure the sample was exact, and still the implausible Tories were on top. We were still fretting over the numbers when we jumped into a cab to go to the Southam offices and reveal our findings to the assembled Ottawa bureau journalists. As we feared, they jeered at our report. The Tories winning Quebec? Nonsense, and that's what came of hiring a bunch of students instead of serious pollsters. But then Southam's Quebec City correspondent spoke up: "Those numbers sound about right to me," he said quietly. He had sensed that the vote was shifting, partly because the new Tory leader, Brian Mulroney, was from Quebec. In our poll, we had stumbled upon the big news of the election, and Southam News was among the first, if not in fact the first, with the news that the Conservatives were carrying Quebec and probably the election.

But that was the end of our few years of fame as election pollsters. The commercial big names took over. Alan continued polling for public institutions, and created the Carleton University Survey Centre which became the Canadian partner in the thirty-country International Social Survey Programme. But the achievement of which I remain proud is that together we launched in 1984 the Canadian General Election series of books. Until then, curious as it may seem, the only lasting account of what happened in Canadian elections had been produced by American scholars. Alan and I recruited scholars and journalists to contribute chapters on various aspects of the campaign and assembled them into a book, *The Canadian General Election of 1984: Politicians, Parties, Press and Polls* (Carleton University Press, 1985). The fifth in this series of election studies, and the first in which Alan and I have had no part, is in production as I write. If I have done nothing else for Canada, I have made that contribution to political history.

By 1984, when I passed my peak — perhaps foothill — as a pollster, I was already engaged in another project. I have always been interested in the theory and practice of democracy, and at that time there was discussion among political scientists about whether in the developed countries the democratic systems were approaching a crisis. The prosperity of the postwar years had given rise to enormous public expectations, and to the dangerous belief that governments could do everything for everybody. If they didn't deliver, it was because they were incompetent, or worse, biased against the deserving classes. For these reasons the intractable economic problems that had appeared in the 1970s did little to diminish public expectations. To win an election, a political party had to engage in a bidding war with its rivals — and in that process were the roots of the inflation of the money supply, years of deficit budgets, and the national debts we are now struggling to pay down. The essential question was whether government in a democracy could be tough enough to force down voter expectations before the country, in effect, went bankrupt. The director of the J-school at the time was my friend Stuart Adam, a journalist and also a political scientist. We interested Patrick Watson, the TV journalist and documentary-maker, in the possibility of a TV series on the "Crisis of Democracy," and after an exchange of ideas he invited us and others to a planning meeting in Toronto. It soon became apparent to me that Watson was more inclined to do a series on the history of democracy than on what I saw as its current crisis, and eventually he paid me $2,500 for my idea, and got on with his own. So I was not disturbed when, by some series of accidents, as he explained, my name disappeared from both the TV series — "The Struggle for Democracy" — and the accompanying book. But when the advertising sponsors, Petro-Canada, threw a glittering launch party at the National Gallery in Ottawa in 1988 I was invited and Watson picked me out in the crowd and publicly identified me as "the Godfather." It was gratifying, but on reflection, I think I would have preferred grandfather. In a letter, he said the work of production had been "harder and more unremitting than I ever imagined, damn you for suggesting it, and in the end probably the most worthwhile thing I have ever done, bless you for suggesting it." In truth, as an admirer of his work, I thought the series far from his best, but no doubt I was biased.

My happiest memory of the whole affair is of an incident when Adam was driving another political scientist and me to Toronto for our first planning meeting. We were bowling down Highway 401 when, suddenly, the car engine died and we coasted onto the verge. Now, as anyone in my family will be eager to tell you, I am no handyman. I can't manage chopsticks, or even turn pasta neatly around a fork. So when Adam and his colleague opened the hood to peer knowledgeably at the engine, I stood discreetly silent. But when they could not figure what was wrong and were sadly discussing in which way to walk to find help, I did the only thing I could think of, pushing the leads firmly onto each plug. I thought as I did so that they felt loose, and so advised in my best imitation of a motor mechanic, "Give 'er a go now. " Stuart turned the key, the engine fired, and I rode all the way to Toronto feeling as Walter Mitty would have felt had one of his imagined triumphs come true. And democracy survived, so all ended well.

Polling and TV documentaries, however, engaging as they were, were not my principal business in a school of journalism. Teaching was the first job, and if I wanted to go beyond craft skills I had to read what others had said about the role of journalism in society, stir in my own experiences, and develop an overview I could present to students. This of course was no burden because one of the reasons I had gone to Carleton was my concern about the way journalism was developing. The new, more interpretive and analytical reporting I had helped to introduce in the 1960s seemed to me in the 1970s to be degenerating into adversarial comment. As the American intellectual Norman Podhoretz put it in a 1971 article in *Commentary*, journalists were failing — I might say unwilling — to distinguish between:

> ... the impulse to expose dishonesty or error or corruption on the one side and the impulse to discredit through the tendentious manipulation of evidence on the other; between the wish to keep the officials who conduct the public business honest in every sense, and the wish to prove a case against the entire set of arrangements through which the public business is conducted in a polity like our own; between in short (to borrow from the late Richard Hofstader), the realm of "socially responsible criticism" and the realm of the adversary culture.

I presented my criticism in class, of course, but also in a paper for a conference at Simon Fraser University on legislative studies, and it was subsequently published in a book, *Parliament, Policy and Representation* (Methuen, 1980). I argued that the concept of the press as a natural adversary of government was associated with the United States and reflected the history and liberal philosophy of that country. The press had been a leader in the revolution against arbitrary government and thought it should continue to view all governments with suspicion. As the U.S. constitution made no provision for an official opposition, the press often saw itself in that role and claimed it was for that reason that its independence had been guaranteed in the constitution. In Canada, the press had a different history and had tended to reflect a different set of political values. While often ferocious critics of government in a partisan way, journalists had usually been respectful of public authority and the established institutions. But now, I wrote, the press was adopting the American adversarial attitude. I was not of course saying that journalists should never be adversaries. A reporter would often have an interest directly opposed to the interest of a source — say for example, a Cabinet minister — when seeking to discover and publish information the source wished to conceal. But I was saying that journalists, and indeed the news media as an institution, should not think of themselves as adversaries of democratic authority which it was in their interests to uphold. I acknowledged, and still do, that the new journalism was in some ways superior to the old. This is certainly the case when, for example, it goes behind the stage sets of the political theatre to expose the real workings of the system; when it relates today's events to the great tides of social and economic change; or when it encourages journalists to rise above the conventions of their craft to become literary artists, even social scientists. But what troubled me then, and troubles me still, is that journalism no longer does the basic work of reporting without which a democracy cannot flourish.

I found the key to my understanding of what was wrong with the new journalism in an old book, *Public Opinion*, written in 1921 by Walter Lippmann, one of the great journalists of the last century. He said there was a difference between news and truth, an idea that would still shock most journalists who conceive themselves to be finders and recorders of truth. News, said Lippmann, concerns an event. As many of the events of public interest are the work of public institutions — governments and their agencies, courts, the police, hospitals, and so on — much journalism is, or should be, a record of what those institutions do. Institutions need to have a reliable channel of communication with the public, and the public has to have the information if it is to oversee the institutions. But who now covers a debate in the House of Commons? Instead we have "scrums" in which reporters joust with politicians. Who takes the trouble, and the space, to tell us what a politician actually said in a public speech? Instead we get an opinion on whether or not the speech was a political success. Where do you find the details of a new piece of legislation, instead of a knowing assessment of the political motivation and an estimate of how popular it is likely to be? Modern journalists are too busy seeking to reveal the truth about events to bother with the simple facts, but truth, as Lippmann wrote, is mostly a matter of opinion in which the journalist's judgement is no better than that of anyone else:

> There is no discipline in applied psychology, as there is a discipline in medicine, engineering, or even law, which has authority to direct the journalist's mind when he passes from the news to the vague realm of truth. There are no canons to direct his own mind, and no canons that coerce the reader's judgment or the publisher's. His version of the truth is only his version.

I must add that Lippmann thought that truth would become more accessible as institutions became more transparent and open to independent audit. He urged the creation of "intelligence" bureaus within institutions to help provide a reliable version of the facts on which people could act a steady beam of enlightenment, rather than the roving searchlight of the news media flicking from one event to another. Today we have many auditors and analysts, some official such as the auditor general, and some private such as think-tanks and advocacy organizations. And there's the rub; there are now so many "intelligence" bureaus that the journalist can pick among many versions of the truth to choose that which best accords with his or her opinion, and truth remains elusive. Consider that in the legal process lawyers can compel testimony under oath, summon and cross examine expert witnesses, and offer competing versions of the truth to impartial judges and disinterested juries, and still the courts can arrive at the wrong conclusion. So what chance do mere reporters have? Lippmann was essentially right when he said there is a difference between news and truth, and it seems to me we have increasingly lost sight of that fact. Good as much of the new journalism is, it should supplement rather than replace the old task of reporting the daily work of institutions.

The institutions themselves are, of course, in trouble. Every time a poll seeks to measure public regards for the various professions, politicians are close to the bottom, and government as a whole is in low repute. Adversarial reporting and cynical commentary cannot escape their share of the blame for this unhappy situation, nor for the fact that journalism now competes with politicians for the contempt of the public. To think that the media can replace institutions by serving as a daily forum for debate, a daily referendum that can reveal the popular will better than elected politicians in parliament is a fallacy born of vanity.

Lippmann again:

(The press) is too frail to carry the whole burden of popular sovereignty, to supply spontaneously the truth which democrats hoped was inborn. And when we expect it to supply such a body of truth we employ a misleading standard of judgment. We misunderstand the limited nature of news, the illimitable complexity of society; we overestimate our own endurance, public spirit, and all-round competence.

One obvious explanation for the change in the style of Canadian journalism was Watergate. The role played by the investigative reporters at *The Washington Post* has, I think, been misunderstood: Their coverage was crucial in bringing the scandal to public attention, but they did not uncover it, and their sources were mainly in the official investigative bodies, the FBI, prosecutors, and courts, which alone had the power to summon witnesses and compel testimony. Nevertheless, Canadian journalists suffered an acute attack of Watergate-envy, and students entering Carleton in that period were gung-ho to investigate and overthrow somebody, anybody, but preferably a politician. Ironically, many thought that by challenging the political establishment they were advancing the radical left whereas, in reality, by discrediting government, they were opening the way to the neo-right.

Another factor in changing the style of journalism was the rapid growth of television, which soon became the principal source of news. TV required a more personal kind of reporting, with the journalist as actor packaging the news in dramatic and often judgmental mini-dramas — reporting not only on who, what, where, and when, but also on why and who was right. The newspapers sought to compete by offering journalism that extended the news instead of merely reporting it, by columnists and analysts, and with reporters who interpreted the news and predicted the consequences. Increasingly, newspapers have become viewspapers, with opinions on everything from the important to the trivial, from politics to private love lives.

The ownership of the press also was changing. What had been local, provincial, or even regional papers with deep roots in their communities were gathered into national chains. Publishers and editors rotated through the papers without much opportunity to acquire local knowledge and sympathies. Instead of having in Ottawa their own reporters with local knowledge, chain papers were often required to carry the work of a central news bureau, including opinion pieces by columnists who also appeared regularly on TV and radio, increasing their incomes, influence and sense of importance. Some commentators with personality and theatrical talent became national celebrities. *The Globe and Mail* became a national paper, often setting the agenda for TV and for lesser papers. In short, the daily press became more national and less local. Reinforcing this trend, *Maclean's* became a national weekly news magazine. Concern about the concentration in the ownership of the press sparked two major inquiries, the 1969-70 Special Senate Committee on Mass Media, chaired by Keith Davey, and the 1980-81 Royal Commission on Newspapers, chaired by Tom Kent, a former newspaper editor and adviser to Prime Minister Pearson. No action followed either report, in my view for two good reasons: there was no persuasive evidence at the time that chain-owned papers were of poorer quality than those independently owned, and the fact that the chain owners seemed to be interested primarily in profit rather than in advancing any political party or ideology. There was also the difficulty of proposing action by government that would not be more dangerous than the disease in the sense that the freedom of the press would be endangered.

That did not deter me from arguing in *The New Society* that if the trend to monopoly in the market in news and opinion continued, it might make sense to treat news as a public resource rather than private property by vesting ownership of newspapers in public corporations legally at arms length from government. But by the time I appeared before the Kent commission, as an invited witness, I had retreated to the idea that a national newspaper produced by a "print CBC" would help to keep the privately-owned press honest. After all, the publicly-owned CBC-TV and radio provided the best national and international news service available to Canadians. My opinion changed again, some years later, when Conrad Black bought the Southam chain and launched a new national daily, the *National Post*, giving him almost 50 percent of daily newspaper readership. He did what chains had not done before, by making his papers the voices of neo-conservative ideology, and he abruptly sacked long-serving journalists if he considered them too liberal in outlook. But that was not his first assault on Canadian journalism. As a privileged but aimless young man of twenty-two, in 1966, he wandered into the newspaper business by investing $500 in two rural Quebec weeklies owned by his friend Peter White. White apparently thought that the papers could help him begin a political career with the Union Nationale, the conservative and nationalist party destined soon to disappear as Quebec emerged into the modern world. Three years later, in 1969, the partners bought a local daily, *The Sherbrooke Record*, and in those modest pages Black aired his views on the war in Vietnam, which he supported, and other international issues of the day. Black then felt qualified to tell the Davey committee on mass media:

> My experience with journalists authorizes me to record that a very large number of them are ignorant, lazy, opinionated, intellectually dishonest and inadequately supervised. The profession is heavily cluttered with abrasive youngsters who substitute "commitment" for insight, and to a lesser extent, with aged hacks toiling through a miasma of mounting decrepitude. Alcoholism is endemic in both groups.

He also deplored the fact, as he saw it, that the Southam management had yielded control of the contents of their papers to reporters. If it was not clear then, it became clear later that he felt himself much better qualified than any journalist to edit a newspaper. One might be inclined to write off such arrogance to the mischievous high spirits of a juvenile seeking attention, but years later, in his autobiography, *A Life in Progress* (Key Porter Books, 1993) he looked back with satisfaction on his performance before the Davey committee, quoting his criticisms of journalists in general, and adding, "... they have never been and, at the time they were made, could not be authoritatively refuted." If nobody bothered to refute his allegations, it was probably because he had never bothered to substantiate them. They were simply a contemptuous sneer. In any event, I was less than complacent when Black became the dominant press owner in Canada, and I suggested in an article in the *Globe* — I had by then retired from the *Star* and was freelancing — that in order to ensure competition in the market for news and opinion, and of course for journalists, the government would be justified in legislating to provide that no person or corporation could own more than one daily paper in each province or, alternatively, control more than 20 percent of total circulation in Canada. I hoped to provoke discussion, and succeeded to some extent. Several journalists called to approve my suggestion, but with Black as the dominant employer no one wanted to go on the record. I was further dismayed when Black was elected to the Canadian News Hall of Fame. It was not uncommon to elect prominent publishers to the hall, but most if not all had given long service to the industry, and were not in the habit of publicly insulting journalists. Having previously been elected to the hall, to my own surprise, I was on the committee to select new members. When Black was chosen over my objection, I resigned from the committee, and also from its sponsor, the Toronto Press Club. At the time, I kept the matter private because a relative was working for one of Black's papers and while I did not believe that Black would be so petty as to take revenge on him I had no such confidence in Black's minions. As it turned out, Black soon sold most of his papers in Canada, including his share in the *National Post*, and renounced his Canadian citizenship so that he might become a Peer of the Realm in Britain. This leaves the press club and the hall of fame in what one might call an interesting position, honouring a Canadian newspaperman who promptly sold his newspapers and left the country. I also wrote a piece for the *Globe* happily waving him goodbye, which prompted one of his featured reporters in the *Post* to write, twice, that she would like to cut my heart out. That's what is known, I suppose, as the new, more personal journalism.

Black sold the papers to Can-West Global, a television company which thereby became a media giant. More convergence in the industry followed, so that while there are now more media of news and opinion there is also greater concentration of media ownership. It can be argued that with the arrival of twenty-four-hour TV news channels and the Internet, ownership of the older media is no longer important. CNN in the United States and, to a lesser extent, CBC Newsworld in Canada, have become the journalism of record, offering live coverage of the most important news events for those with time to watch. And the Internet does indeed provide access to almost limitless resources of news and opinion — for those with a computer, a modem and the patience to search what amounts to a vast library for the information they require. But let's not forget that the new media giants sell access to the internet through their portals — BCE owns *The Globe and Mail*, CTV and also Sympatico, the largest Canadian access company — and provide news and opinion as content for the net. I do not say the media owners are misusing their power, but the potential for misuse exists, and that is not a healthy situation in a democracy. It is time, I believe, to look again at the idea, expressed by the Davey committee, that news should be regarded as a public resource rather than as property to be bought and sold. Any such notion shocks the conventional wisdom that a free press is necessarily a privately-owned press. But experience suggests a different wisdom: The publicly-owned CBC provides the best new service in Canada, and the publicly owned PBS-TV and National Public Radio in the United States offer the most thoughtful news and comment on the continent. To adapt a famous remark by C.P. Scott, a great editor of *The Manchester Guardian*, facts should be a sacred trust, opinion as free as possible.

~ Chapter 13 ~

The Rise and Fall
of Canadian Nationalism

Another great adventure began in 1979 with an out-of-the-blue — or rather, out-of-New York — call at home from the secretary of the Carnegie Endowment for International Peace. He explained that one of the endowment's activities was to bring foreign journalists to New York to spend six months or a year researching and writing about a foreign policy issue of interest to the United States. The endowment had decided that maybe it was time to include a Canadian journalist in the program. Might I be interested? Indeed, I replied, trying not to sound too eager. But what issue would I want to write about? Canada-United States economic relations, said I at once. But, said he, puzzled, that's not a problem, is it? It might not be a problem in the United States, I explained, but it was *the* problem in Canada. The secretary, I think, was not wholly convinced, but he said the endowment's president, Tom Hughes, would be in Ottawa to talk to me and perhaps others. (Incidentally, I soon discovered that to be president of the endowment was a prestigious position. Hughes had been a top official in the state department, but among his predecessors at Carnegie had been another state department luminary, Alger Hiss, denounced as a Soviet spy and eventually sent to jail for perjury.) Soon after the phone call, I was invited to breakfast with Hughes at an Ottawa hotel, and we discussed terms. He asked how much I would expect to be paid for a year, and I said as I was making about $50,000 in Ottawa I would expect the same in New York. He hesitated at that, but eventually agreed that I would spend the calendar year of 1980 with the endowment.

There was more good news: the endowment offices were on the fifty-fourth floor of the Rockefeller Center — the tower with the skating rink in front and the famous Diego Rivera murals in the lobby. And more, I would be provided with a researcher, a secretary, and help with finding a suitable home. Jeannie of course was delighted; New York had always been one of the cities she wished to experience, and she still remembered her disappointment when Beaverbrook had turned me down for a New York posting a quarter-century earlier. Now, here was the second coming, and a huge change in life. Our children had left home, and our old dog was dead; we could not have gone to New York if he had still been alive and dependent on us. But we did ask our son to take our two cats to Toronto, where one soon fell ill and died, and the other disappeared. I still feel guilty about that; did she perhaps set out to return to her home in Ottawa and die on the way? I arranged for a year's leave of absence from Carleton and, after a short previously-arranged research visit to Britain, we began the task of dismantling the home in which the family had been happy for fifteen years.

Denis Harvey, then the editor-in-chief at the *Star*, had agreed to allow me a year's leave of absence from my weekly column, so I was surprised to get a call from him one evening, just before we were due to leave, to say that as the regular columnist, Gwyn, was out of town, would I please go to the Commons to write, if necessary, on the defeat of Joe Clark's minority Conservative government on a crucial vote. Waste of time, said I; if the Tories count heads and find they are short of a majority they'll simply postpone the vote. Go anyway, said Harvey, and I went, thinking that at least it would be an opportunity to say goodbye to friends. Then I watched in disbelief as the government walked straight into defeat, forcing an election. I had been no fan of Clark or his government, but I thought they deserved more time — and that the Liberals needed more time out of office in which to renew themselves. But I didn't realize the significance for me until two months later, when Trudeau trounced Clark in the election and returned to power on a mildly nationalist platform, causing Canada-United States relations to take another twist.

We put the house up for sale, and left for a short visit to New York to find an apartment. That night, as we were going to sleep in our hotel, the agent called with an offer which we thought pretty good and snapped up. The Glebe district in Ottawa had been nondescript when we bought in 1964, but became fashionable in the 1980s and 1990s when prices soared far beyond anything we had imagined possible, by which time of course we had sold. But we did make money, or at least save it, by selling our car when we left for New York. Who would need a car in Manhattan? We have never since owned one, a huge economy. Public transport, an occasional taxi, and, very rarely, a rented car, have served our needs because we are downtown people, living as close to the heart of a city as we can. In New York, we got lucky and found a modern one-bedroom apartment on the twenty-third floor on West 57th Street — with a view across Central Park to the Metropolitan Museum. The sun shining on the glass roof at the Met would sometimes reflect back into our bedroom. Our block of 57th Street, between 8th and 9th Avenues, was a few hundred yards from Broadway, Carnegie Hall, and the Russian Tea Room in one direction, and the Lincoln Center in another. But in the curious way in which cities develop, it was on the frontier of redevelopment, and while our building had doormen dressed like musical comedy officers, our neighbours were seedy bars, greasy restaurants, and odd stores. One store sold pet supplies and called itself, deliciously, The Canine Castle and Feline Fortress. That's why, I suppose, we paid only $600 a month for our apartment. I could walk to work at 50th Street, and jog in Central Park. To say I was a runner would be a gross exaggeration, but I was a slow jogger for years, and in all the best districts: the Canal path in Ottawa, Kensington Gardens in London, the Bois de Boulogne in Paris, and along the Charles River in Boston. But my best ever effort was clear around the perimeter of Central Park one Sunday morning, about six miles. We grew to love the park, a wonderfully designed space of changing moods and vistas, in which strollers, skaters by road and by ice, runners, cyclists, horse-riders, buskers, baseball players, even lawn bowlers, add the human comedy.

But then, we loved almost everything about the city, or more accurately, Manhattan. As a vast city, New York at that time had among the best and worst of almost every aspect of urban living, and we enjoyed the best. Even the people pleased us, despite their reputation for rudeness. The only thing I ever wrote in *The New York Times* was a letter to the editor in which I quoted my wife: "It may be a jungle out there, but the natives are friendly." When we bought a small, round dining table in a shop on Broadway, I was wondering how to get it home until the storekeeper advised, "Call a Checker cab." So I manhandled the table onto the sidewalk and hailed the first large cab that came along. The little old driver raised no objections so we manoeuvred the table into the back and climbed in after it. "You new to New York?" he asked. Yes, we said. "Doing the galleries yet?" No. "Well, take my advice," he said. "Start with Frick on Fifth; it's reasonable size, not one of those great places where you don't know what to see." And then, he added, "Of course, I'm into postmodernism myself."

Although we had no car we decided to apply for New York driving licences, in case we decided to rent, and went downtown to line up with the motley crowd of every size, shape and colour on the same mission. We filled out the forms and shuffled in the queue toward the counter where it was discovered that Jeannie had not completed one form and would have to go back and start again. Having completed the form she dutifully took her place once again at the back of the line. But she was spotted by the clerk at the far-away counter who shouted "Hey Jeannie, you don't have to wait, you come right up here," which she did, eyed suspiciously by those fearsome characters in the queue. The eye test consisted of reading a sign hanging behind the clerk. I failed and meekly agreed to have my licence endorsed. Jeannie, made of sterner stuff, argued that the sign had been swinging so that it was not a fair test, and got her licence unendorsed. As it happened, that was the day it was revealed that the Canadian Embassy in Teheran had hidden U.S. diplomats from the mob. In the cab going uptown after receiving our licences, the driver asked where we were from, and when we said Canada he insisted on pulling over to the curb so that he could turn around and shake out hands.

Maybe I had seen too many TV shows, but New York cops always looked frightening to me, so my one brief encounter was surprising. There was a transit strike while we were in the city and on every corner there was a cop directing the increased flow of private buses, cars, trucks, cyclists, pedestrians, even horses. I hardly noticed because I walked to work, always lost in thought. At 50th Street I had to cross 6th Avenue — the proper but pretentious name is the Avenue of the Americas — and I stepped off the curb before six lanes of waiting traffic. I was about a third of the way across when the cop swung around and beckoned on the traffic, which began to advance toward me. Suddenly awakening to the perilous situation, I turned to flee back to the curb, but the cop spotted me out of the corner of his eye, blew a mighty blast on his whistle, and flung up both arms to halt the oncoming traffic. Then he turned to me and, in a voice dripping with sarcasm, said, "Not you sir. You keep walking." And so I made my solitary way across while 6th Avenue waited.

At the foundation offices, my window looked south to the tip of Manhattan, the Statue of Liberty and beyond to the ocean. The view was so entrancing that I turned the desk around so that my back was to the window and I could concentrate on my work. My secretary had an MA in international affairs and my research assistant was a prize-winning graduate student. My fellow senior associates, as we were called, were journalists from England, Northern Ireland, Switzerland, and Americans who were pursuing some special foreign policy interest. And soon I was joined by another Canadian, Lise Bissonnette, from *Le Devoir*, the small but influential nationalist daily in Montreal where she subsequently became editor-in-chief and publisher, before launching with equal success into writing novels. She was a separatist, I was not, but in the Canadian fashion that did not prevent us from becoming, and remaining, friends. As a joint project, we decided to invite New Brunswick Premier Richard Hatfield, whom we both knew, to speak at Carnegie. The English-speaking leader of a bilingual province, he was a significant player in the constitutional games. But he was also a colourful and engaging personality who spent a surprising amount of time in New York because — so it was said — he could meet his friends in the gay community safely out of sight of his conservative constituents. Our plan was to take him to dinner when he arrived in his official plane, but he swept that aside by insisting on taking us to a fashionable floating restaurant on the East River near the Brooklyn Bridge. Our doubts about finding a table disappeared when the maitre d' rushed forward to welcome "prime minister" — a promotion from premier — and arrange waterside seating. It was apparent that Hatfield was a frequent and valued customer, doubtless at considerable expense to the voters at home. But he gave an excellent seminar the following day.

My first work was to review the recent history of Canada-United States economic relations which I had been covering as a journalist for years. It is hard to believe now, in our era of free trade and global culture, that only thirty years ago economic and cultural nationalism was a powerful force in Canada. Now it hardly registers on the political agendas of the major parties, although it is attempting a comeback in the form of populist demonstrations against the power that multinational corporations are said to wield under free trade. Anti-Americanism flares from time to time, but it is no longer a popular cause. In fact, it is now possible to discuss the possibility that Canada's future may lie in some sort of union with the United States without being tarred and feathered in the media. All this represents a huge change in political attitudes, and I claim to have had a role in bringing it about. When I arrived in 1956 concern about the level of American investment in Canada was rising and politicians were responding. In the 1957 election, the new Conservative leader, John Diefenbaker, promised to divert 15 percent of Canadian trade from the United States to Britain, but quickly backed off when Britain called his bluff by proposing free trade.

Walter Gordon, then a Toronto accountant and member of the Bay Street business elite, chaired, in 1955-57, a Royal Commission on Canada's Economic Prospects and became alarmed by the rising tide of American investment, which he saw as a threat to Canada's ability to sustain a separate economy and political independence. He led the reconstruction of the Liberal Party after its defeats in 1957 and 1958, and persuaded the leader, his friend Lester Pearson, to endorse economic nationalism as part of the Liberal program. When the Liberals won power as a minority government in 1963, Gordon became finance minister, recruited three advisers from Bay Street, and quickly — too quickly — introduced a budget. His first mistake was to use outside advisers in what was supposed to be a secret process, and that gave the opposition parties an opening to raise suspicions of wrongdoing although there was never any evidence that secrets had been leaked. More seriously, the taxes he proposed as a way of discouraging the foreign take-over of Canadian companies were found to be impracticable. There were cries of outrage from the business community, and Eric Kierans, the president of the Montreal Stock Exchange at the time, warned that if the taxes were imposed there would be a huge sell-off of Canadian stocks. Gordon resented the warning, which he read correctly as a threat, but was forced into a humiliating withdrawal. Liberal confidence was shaken, and the opposition parties, so recently defeated, now felt they had a vulnerable government on the ropes. Gordon offered to resign, Pearson refused, and the government staggered on with none of the high morale and momentum that a new administration usually enjoys.

As previously recounted, Gordon made another bad mistake in 1965 when, as chairman of the party, he advised Pearson to call an election with the assurance that he would win a majority and subdue the opposition parties. Instead, after a gruelling campaign described in an earlier chapter, the government barely won another minority mandate. Again Gordon offered to resign from the Cabinet, and seemed to feel hard done by when Pearson this time accepted. In retrospect, it is clear that Gordon was a political disaster, but he remained a respected and influential public figure, a leader of the nationalist movement and of the Liberal "left." In fact, to appease that wing of the party, Pearson brought him back into the Cabinet with a mandate to inquire further into foreign investment, which led to the appointment of a task force of economists chaired by Melville Watkins, a former Liberal moving rapidly to the left in step with the mood of the time. The report of the task force, in 1968, became known as the Watkins report and launched him into politics, about which more below. In the popular mythology of the times the report became a radical nationalist charter, but in fact it was balanced, recognizing that foreign investment brought both costs and benefits in the form of technology, management, and products.

Another reason for Gordon's continuing influence was that he was a director of *The Toronto Star* which provided him with a bully pulpit from which to preach his gospel. The *Star* had campaigned for decades for the Welfare State, and as it took shape — and not always with the hoped for results — Beland Honderich, the publisher, needed a new cause. He found it in Canadian nationalism, and his staff, always more pious than the priest, gave front page prominence to every Gordon pronouncement, no matter how trivial. When Peter Newman, one of the best-known journalists in the country, became the editor-in-chief in 1969, and he and Gordon soon launched The Committee for an Independent Canada as a lobby to press for policies of economic and cultural nationalism. As the war in Vietnam made the United States more and more unpopular in Canada, many of the country's leading intellectuals signed up in the nationalist case. The philosopher George Grant had published, *Lament for a Nation: The Defeat of Canadian Nationalism* (McClelland and Stewart, 1965) which became, curiously, the bible of the nationalist movement which chose to regard it as a call to arms rather than as an obituary for Canada, which in some ways it was. Grant, a Tory, spent the first half of the book in a polemic accusing the Liberals of selling out Canada to the Americans, and the second half in explaining why Canada was a lost cause anyway. Canada, he argued, was supposed to be a conservative society, more ordered and restrained than the liberal United States, but technology was accelerating the rate of change and:

> The impossibility of conservatism in our era is the impossibility of Canada. As Canadians we attempted a ridiculous task of trying to build a conservative nation in the age of progress, on a continent we shared with the most dynamic nation on earth... It was not conceivable that industrial society would be organized along essentially different principles from those to the south.

This was the fundamental problem for Gordon and Liberal nationalists who had no intention of replacing capitalism. But for the left it was confirmation of the idea that to secure its independence Canada would have to replace capitalism with socialism. Within the NDP, a faction or caucus emerged in 1969 to press this argument. It called itself the Waffle apparently because one of the original members, Ed Broadbent, remarked that if they were going to waffle on policy, he would prefer to waffle to the left. But the real leaders were two university professors, Watkins and Jim Laxer. In some ways, the Waffle was the Canadian counterpart of the New Left in the United States, against the war in Vietnam, for feminism, suspicious of American professors in Canadian universities, and militantly socialist. The movement issued a "Manifesto for a Socialist Canada" and seemed likely to win control of the NDP until the old guard of the party fought back, causing the Waffle to disintegrate, as such populist movements often do.

The National Gallery in Ottawa, in 1971, put on an exhibition by Joyce Weiland entitled "True Patriot Love." The *Canadian Forum* magazine, then the journal of nationalist intellectuals, described the exhibition as a "cathedral hymn to Canada," and declared Weiland to be the laureate of Canadian nationalism. I dissented in a *Star* column, pointing out that the political message was explicit in the caption on a cartoon in which fair Canada was being raped by an American who had a machine tool in place of the normal male equipment, and with the caption, "Death to U.S. technological imperialism." There was also a quilt with the motto, "Passion Over Reason," reversing Trudeau's plea for reason over passion.

When Trudeau won the Liberal leadership and formed his government in 1968 it was widely thought to be bad news for the nationalists because he had been a fierce opponent of nationalism in Quebec. But his opposition was to nationalism based on race or ethnicity rather than nationhood, and he allowed ministers to engage in various Canadian nationalist enterprises without being himself much involved. When he ordered a thorough review of foreign policy, the resulting booklets discussed almost everything except relations with the United States, which nationalists saw as the one great problem. But Herb Gray, then a junior minister without portfolio, headed another and more thorough study of foreign investment and ownership, and produced in 1972 another pro-and-con report. However, the government did establish the Foreign Investment Review Agency, which did a lot of reviewing but not much agenting, and the Canada Development Corporation and Petro-Canada which made public investments to replace foreign capital.

President Richard Nixon had proclaimed a "New Economic Policy" that threatened Canadian exports, and he followed through in 1972 when he visited Ottawa and told Parliament that the "special relationship" was no more: "Mature partners must have autonomous, independent policies." Canadian nationalists welcomed it as a promise that the United States would not object to Canadian nationalist policies, but the government was concerned and decided that it was time to reduce dependence on the American market. This decision was, in effect, leaked in a curious manner during the 1972 election campaign. A special edition of *International Perspectives*, a journal published by the External Affairs department, was distributed in the press gallery. I knew it was special because the name of the editor, my friend and former colleague, Murray Goldblatt, did not appear on the masthead. Murray had been promised independence as editor so when the External Affairs Minister Mitchell Sharp took over the edition to publish a long article under his own name (although in fact it had been written by an official) Murray withdrew his name as a protest. Sharp had long been identified as an opponent in the government of Gordon's nationalism, and had defeated him in a policy debate at a national Liberal party convention, so the contents of the article were somewhat surprising. It discussed relations with the United States and set out three options:

Canada can seek to maintain more or less its present relationship with the United States with a minimum of policy adjustments;

Canada can move deliberately toward closer integration with the United States;

Canada can pursue a comprehensive, long-term strategy to develop and strengthen the Canadian economy and other aspects of its national life and in the process to reduce the present Canadian vulnerability.

The article, and therefore Sharp who had signed it, opted for what became known as the Third Option, a strategy eagerly embraced by nationalists. It was not clear at the time if the cabinet had adopted this strategy, but in his memoir *Which Reminds Me...* (University of Toronto Press, 1994) Sharp said it had been discussed and approved, with the active support of Trudeau who wanted to give evidence of "the determination of the government to maintain Canadian independence." Trudeau, in his *Memoirs,* goes further and claims: "Enormous political will was needed to reverse the growing American ownership of the Canadian economy .... But our measures worked." The mystery remains as to why what is now said to have been a major policy initiative was published as an article in an obscure journal instead of in a *White Paper* or a speech by the prime minister. Sharp evades the question, saying "Whatever the purpose of this subtle differentiation may have been, the Third Option came to be accepted as government policy." The most likely explanation is that during an election campaign Trudeau wanted to have the best of both sides in the debate over nationalism: His minister endorsed a nationalist strategy but the government was not seen to do so. This left Sharp in an unfortunate position. He wrote in his memoir, "Moreover, the Third Option came to be invoked enthusiastically by the government and by others to support policies that were far more nationalistic than my paper had proposed, a consequence that I deplored." As I will explain below, I entered this debate some years later, becoming, as it were, the prophet of free trade, with interesting results.

In the 1960s and 1970s, as a political reporter and columnist, I covered the rise of Canadian nationalism as an important story, and was even identified by Watkins at a public meeting as the journalist who had legitimized the Waffle by writing about its activities. I remember in particular a two-day teach-in, as they were called in those days, at the University of Alberta at Edmonton, now of course the capital of the most right-wing province in Canada. Some sixteen hundred people, mostly students, attended a panel discussion on whether Canada was a satellite within the American empire. When the moderator asked for a show of hands on major issues about fifty voted for Canada to remain in NATO, a dozen supported Canadian participation in the North American Air Defence Command, no more than six agreed that Canada should have nuclear weapons, and just one brave soul voted for research on chemical and biological weapons. The following evening even more people attended a discussion on American investment in Canada. Gordon advanced his familiar ideas on taxes to discourage foreign ownership, and the only mildly critical question was about why he would want to transfer control from American to Canadian capitalists instead of going all the way to public ownership. He had no real answer. However, public ownership was part of the Waffle program, and Watkins drew eight hundred students to a lunch meeting. I was impressed by the whole teach-in, and amused by an incident when Watkins, Laxer and I had dinner at the faculty club. Naturally, we were discussing politics in Alberta, and I said I had never been able to understand what had been economically wrong with Social Credit policy of issuing scrip, a sort of Alberta currency, to relieve hardship in the 1930s depression. Was it not just a way of pumping spending power into the economy? Not at all, said the two eminent academics; the fallacy became apparent in a simple theorem taught to first-year students of economics. Taking pencil in hand, Laxer began to write the theorem on the tablecloth, but then looked to Watkins for help. It turned out that neither could remember how to prove their simple proposition, but no doubt they were correct, and only the tablecloth suffered.

But while I was reporting the rise of nationalism, my own view of how the world was developing and what would be best for Canada was moving in the opposite direction. As I have already written, during the Second World War American troops arrived in Britain as saviours, and that reinforced for me the message of the movies, which usually presented the United States as the land of limitless opportunity. While in the Royal Navy, I had seen something of the U.S. forces at war in the Pacific, and been astonished by the way in which they deployed enormous resources. If we lost so much as a sack of flour it was a serious matter, but I watched as American sailors somehow dumped a whole cargo net full of supplies into the sea and carried on as if nothing had happened. When I saw the U.S. fleet assembling for operations, I realized, and it was a shock, that the Royal Navy was no longer the greatest in the world. But quite apart from those impressions formed in my youth, I had come to admire the United States, despite all its flaws, as a vigorous democracy, an extraordinary economic and cultural powerhouse, with New York as the closest thing to a world capital. Like all great powers in history, it was sometimes arrogant, but its treatment of Canada as a weaker neighbour was exemplary. Canadians who complain that American presidents are occasionally rude to our prime ministers, or worse, inattentive, ought to read a little history and discover what has usually happened to weak neighbours of great powers. The American intervention in Vietnam, for me, was a shocking mistake rather than imperialism, and what made it unusual in history was that American public opinion forced withdrawal. Living in Canada, I considered myself a patriot standing on guard for the country even if was not my native land. But Canadian nationalism, like all nationalisms, frightened me. History shows that nationalism explodes all too easily into chauvinism, directing anger against "outsiders." As a colleague at Carleton put it, rather neatly, "Nationalists start wars, patriots fight them."

I began to lay out in my 1977 book, *The New Society*, my ideas on why nationalism was the wrong way to go, in a section I titled "The International Society." While I do not claim that my ideas were original, they were ahead of their time in Canada, and against the mainstream. That was one of the reasons I always declined to move to a job on the *Star* in Toronto; I knew that if I did Honderich and I would soon lock horns, and he was the bigger and stronger moose. I began by pointing out that, since the arrival of the Europeans, the history of North America had been the consolidation of small units— native nations, colonies, newly explored and settled territories — into larger states. At every stage there had been strong resistance by those who wished to preserve their existing states and cultures. Even those who had brought about change had often been reluctant revolutionaries driven by new technologies that altered patterns of trade, means of communication, and the necessities of military defence. Far from being over, these forces of consolidation had become stronger than ever:

> We share a way of life and a set of values with people in the United States and Western Europe and other countries at a similar stage of development. We read the same books and magazines, watch the same television and movies, listen to the same modern music and absorb the same messages from the lyrics, live in similar houses in similar suburbs or in almost identical apartment buildings, drive the same cars and obey the same traffic signs, eat the same foods and drink the same drinks, pop the same tranquilizers, work for the same corporations, enjoy the same sports, direct dial across oceans, or travel casually at jet speed across mountain barriers that historically divided nations to stay in identical hotels. We are also part of a supranational economy in which capital, managers, technicians, and scientific know-how move easily across borders organizing economic activity on a world scale. Our politics tend to become more and more like the politics of other countries at a similar stage of development because we share the same goals of peace, prosperity, and freedom, and the same problems of inflation, unemployment, pollution, and relations with the Communist countries and the Third World of developing states.

The growth of this supranational system severely limited the freedom of national governments to pursue independent policies. For example, "A country that gets too far out of line on tax or monetary or tariff policies will find capital and knowledge and even skilled labour moving to more hospitable countries within the system." (And that seems to be a lesson that we are still learning.) The choice for Canadians was between exhausting ourselves in a struggle for the impossible dream of national independence or embracing supranationalism and playing a leading role in designing new supranational institutions to control the multinational corporations.

My argument that nation states were becoming irrelevant provoked angry denials. The publisher sent my manscript to several readers for their opinions on whether it merited publication. Walter Gordon, of course, dismissed it out of hand. Abraham Rotstein, a respected political scientist at the University of Toronto and a nationalist, was generally favourable, but added "I think he's nuts in his ideas about the nation-state." The most explosive reaction came from Eric Kierans, who had led the charge against the Gordon budget in 1963 but later changed his mind and became a nationalist — and a minister in the first Trudeau government, when we became acquainted. *The Montreal Gazette* asked him to review my book, and when they received his copy, the editor, Mark Harrison, a former colleague at the *Star*, felt compelled to call me with a warning. Kierans liked nothing about the book, but what really annoyed him was the idea of supranational government:

> The world will share 'an economy and a culture'? Via the global corporation? This is blubbering nonsense ... Somewhere along the line, people are going to react and that is called 'politics,' strange word to mandarins in and out of government. When voters get around to deciding what their priorities, objectives and even prejudices are, they will have no time for Westell's supranational economy that may know how to accumulate wealth, but will leave people gasping for freedom and a decent standard of living.

Maybe his time has come because, as I write, thousands of people are demonstrating against free trade and globalism while the Summit of the Americas meets in Quebec City to discuss a free trade zone for the entire hemisphere. But I don't believe it. The forces driving national economies toward ever greater integration are probably more powerful than they have ever been. Like too many social democrats, Kierans was unwilling to accept that the world within which he planned to reform Canada was changing, and changing Canada with it.

When I was writing *The New Society* in 1977, the rise of the multinational corporation seemed to me to be changing all the rules of trade and politics. I had another opportunity to study and write about the phenomenon when I was invited, in 1978, to contribute to a new publication with a grandiloquent title, *The WorldPaper*. In reality, it was a small operation, based in Boston with an international board of investors, mostly Americans but including Conrad Black. The founders felt that the foreign news Americans were getting in their newspapers was too often written by American journalists and with an American slant on events, rather than by journalists who were native to the countries in which the events were occurring. So the *WP* vision was to assemble a team of associate editors from around the world, including the Communist world, who would write on global issues in a newspaper — first published quarterly, later monthly — which American and foreign newspapers would print and carry as a supplement to their own coverage. As the editor, a Bostonian with the wonderfully New England name of Crocker Snow Jr., and the first managing editor were both Americans, it was thought that the associate for North America ought to be a Canadian. I was recommended to Snow by an acquaintance who worked for a foreign aid nongovernmental organization (NGO) in Ottawa and was keen to see the *WP* succeed. I was happy to accept the post in such an interesting experiment in journalism.

The plan was that the Boston editors and the far-flung associates would meet from time to time in some interesting part of the world to decide on topics to be covered, and then one of the associates would fly to Boston to supervise each issue. We had our first meeting in London in 1978, and I met my colleagues from around the world. They included remarkable people who became, over the years, comrades rather colleagues. One was a delightful old Marxist from Eastern Europe who would bring us up to date on the mood in Moscow by telling us the latest joke — jokes, he said, being the safest way in the Soviet Union to comment on events. Many of his jokes were in the form of a question-and-answer show broadcast on an imaginary Soviet radio station. Here's an example: Caller: "What were the last words of our famous Soviet poet Igor Stravisnky (or some such name)?" Answer: "The last words of our famous poet were, 'Don't shoot, comrades.'" Another associate had been a crusading editor driven out of Sri Lanka by an oppressive government, and who by then was working for the United Nations. He had a valid UN passport, but liked to travel on a document which he had had printed and bound showing him to be a citizen of the Republic of Amnesia. It worked surprisingly well. The associate from China was a senior journalist enjoying rehabilitation after having been humiliated

My earliest family photo. The very Victorian marriage on July 1, 1886, probably at Woodford, London, of my maternal grandparents, Catherine Blanche Woodroffe and George Smedley of Sheffield, England. The top-hatted gent on the right in the back row is the father of the bride, William Woodroffe. The gent on the left holding his topper is the father of the groom, also called George Smedley, and he also had married into the Woodroffe family, which may help explain a strain of eccentricity in my genes. Note the two maids in the door.

Sitting on my mother's lap, circa 1928 when I would have been two, at our summer cabin. On the right is my maternal grandmother — the young bride in the earlier picture — and behind is her second daughter, my formidable aunty Babs — who seems to have a cigarette in her hand, no doubt the working man's Woodbine she favoured.

With my older brother John and our two grandmothers, circa 1930. On the right is my mother's mother, smiling, with her arm around me. She died in 1930. On the left is my father's mother, Alice Westell, all in black probably because she was in still mourning for her husband. When my mother died in 1932 it was the widow in black who took charge of our household.

Sailing my first boat, on the estuary of the River Exe in Devon, England, about 1938 when I was aged twelve. It was the first boat designed and built by my brother John who became a well known professional designer and builder. We hand-cut and stitched the sail from heavy canvas.

Me at the helm while ferrying a sail boat through the Trent-Severn Waterway, the system of rivers, lakes, canals, and locks that connects Lake Huron to Lake Ontario. My friend and former sailing partner Eric Malling had bought the boat on Georgian Bay in 1997 and I offered to bring it to Toronto. As crew, I recruited another friend, sailing partner and former colleague, Stan Westall, who took this picture. I hoped that if Eric and I went cruising on Lake Ontario, it would help him to overcome a crisis in his life. Instead, tragically, he used the boat as a hideaway from his problems and died the following year.

On shore leave, in Sidney, Australia, 1944, in my best going-ashore uniform. Note the lean and hungry look after years on civilian rations and naval grub. I was probably heading for the nearest restaurant to see if it was true that the national dish was, unbelievably, a whole egg on a whole steak.

Sunday morning in a village in Devon, in the Spring of 1972. Jeannie and I were staying with friends, Jan Breyer, who took this splendid picture (and also the one on the cover), and his wife Barbara Buchanan, a well known journalist and our colleague when Jeannie and I first met at the *Bristol Evening World* in 1948.

Jeannie and I still laughing after half a century together. Appropriately, the picture was taken by Jeannie's oldest friend, Judith Inman, when she was visiting us in Toronto.

Walter Cronkite presented the 1970 National Newspaper Awards when I and two *Star* colleagues were among the winners: Tom Hazlitt, left, and Duncan Macpherson collecting his fifth NNA for cartooning.

With John Diefenbaker, in the trademark homburg, and his brother Elmer at the family homestead in Saskatchewan, during the 1965 election campaign. Val Sears, then of *The Toronto Star*, is asking the questions, I'm making notes, and the late Ron Collister, then of the *Toronto Telegram,* is looking worried. Val and I spotted a cradle in a wooden lean-to, but decided it was just a coincidence.

How times change us. Jean Chrétien was the young northern affairs minister when we toured his Arctic empire in the high summer of 1969.

On the boat to Canada, 1956: Jeannie with Tracy, six months. Not exactly your huddled masses, we had a stateroom on the main deck. But we had passed through a severe autumn gale; notice the windblown hairstyle.

Senator Richard Doyle, formerly my editor at *The Globe and Mail,* inducting me into the Canadian News Hall of Fame, 1992. My irreverent family said it should have been the Hall of Shame.

In my plain black gown, flanked by the Chancellor of Carleton University, retired Cabinet Secretary Gordon Robertson, with gold trimmings, and my former colleague George Bain, the distinguished columnist, in royal blue. I had introduced George when he received an honourary degree, which he has firmly in hand.

and banished to the country during the Cultural Revolution. In such company I was a dull fellow, as became embarrassingly clear at our London meeting when we were invited to talk about freedom of the press in our own country. I was explaining the freedoms and hazards of working in Canada when a journalist from the Middle East interrupted: "It must be very nice to be a journalist in Canada," he said. "In my country, if you write something they don't like the police take you into a backroom and beat you." I've often thought about that.

As an associate editor, I went to Boston in 1979 to supervise the first regular issue — featuring, naturally, my current interest, the rise of multinational corporations. Since then I have probably written more for the paper than anyone except founding editor Snow, who produced a monthly column until he moved on to other projects recently. But, intrigued as I was by the *WP* experiment, I soon concluded that there was a flaw in the idea. Of necessity, all the associate editors could speak and write in English, and several had worked or studied in Britain or the United States. They were familiar with the Western style of journalism, with what made news and how it should be written, so the *WP* reflected those norms, and did not speak as well as had been hoped in different voices with different values and ideas from around the world. As journalists, we shared an international culture of journalism. The *WP* proved quite popular with papers outside North America, but American papers which had agreed to carry it soon dropped out. Some said it was too expensive to print and distribute, but another reason, I suspected, was that editors did not like carrying a supplement in which the content was beyond their own control, and which was, anyway, an implied criticism of American journalism. Advertising also was a problem; it turned out that multinational corporations we had been expected to find the *WP* a cost-effective way to reach customers around the world tended to have local rather than global advertising strategies and budgets. But the *WP* struggled on, mainly due to the driving enthusiasm of Crocker Snow, changed its strategy, passed to new owners, and at last count was appearing in seven language editions in twenty-eight publications with a combined circulation of nearly 2 million.

My luck struck again as I was settling in at Carnegie: Canada-United States relations suddenly became more exciting. Announcing his presidential candidacy in November 1979, Ronald Reagan had advocated a "North American Accord" to promote the free flow of people and commerce. A few months later, Trudeau and the Liberals easily defeated Clark and the Conservatives, and returned to office. In his memoirs, Trudeau conceded that it was the most political campaign of his career. Instead of following his own interests and instincts, he followed the script provided by veteran Liberal Party strategists which included moderately nationalist policies. He promised, among other things, to broaden and strengthen the Foreign Investment Review Agency (FIRA), and to introduce a national energy policy that would sharply reduce the level of foreign control in the oil industry, both moves certain to annoy American business interests. The consensus in both countries, therefore, was that the two countries were on diverging paths, and that a crisis lay ahead. I thought this exaggerated, and one of my early activities at Carnegie was to organize a dinner meeting at which the new Liberal trade minister, Herb Gray, addressed a score of American business and government people. I had of course known Gray for years, and recognized that his study of foreign investment, which I mentioned earlier in this chapter, had provided the basis for many of the government's nationalist policies, notably FIRA. But I knew him also to be a pleasant and reasonable man with a reassuring, not to say soporific, style of speaking — a fog-producing talent for which he later became famous as Leader of the House of Commons. We had an enjoyable dinner and Gray explained the government's plans in a manner I thought would convince our guests that here was no flaming revolutionary out to remake the world, or worse, expropriate their investments in Canada. So I was surprised, when saying goodnight to the Americans, to hear that Gray had confirmed all their fears about the new government. I should have known after all those years as a journalist that people tend to hear and read not what is said or written but whatever will confirm the opinions they held previously.

I have often taken pride in being a contrarian, opposed to the conventional wisdom in politics, journalism, and even in private organizations in which I have participated and usually wound up as the loyal opposition, the house critic. At times this tendency may have warped my judgment, persuading me to take stands for the sake of being different. But that was not the case when I came to the conclusion that far from heading in different directions, Canada and the United States were in fact converging. The evidence was plain to see. Despite all the efforts of governments in Ottawa, a larger and larger share of Canadian trade was with the United States. Everybody knew that American investment capital was flowing into Canada, but my researches in Washington showed that Canadian capital was pouring into the United States. With federal support and protection, Canadian cultural industries were flourishing, even achieving some recognition in the United States, but American movies and magazines continued to be popular in Canada, while the spread of TV cable systems made more American programs available to more Canadians than ever before. The idea that the United States was a racial melting pot and Canada a home for two founding cultures, creating distinctly different societies, was crumbling. In the United States, minority groups — Latinos in particular — were demanding recognition and public services in their own language. There were projections that in time Spanish would replace English as the majority language. Schools in New York, and no doubt in other great gateway cities for new immigrants, were teaching not in two languages, but in ten or more while students attempted to master English. In Canada, multiculturalism had replaced biculturalism as the national policy. While relations between the two national governments were sometimes strained, agreements between Canadian provinces and neighbouring U.S. states were multiplying, and cross-border consultations between premiers and governors became routine. In private society, of course, there were scores of continental organizations, and travel between the two countries steadily increased. I set out some of this evidence and the argument that flowed from it in an article for *Foreign Policy*, the prestigious quarterly journal published by the Carnegie Endowment:

> The record of the past decade suggests that complete independence is not a realistic option for either country. Increasing interdependence should be recognized and its implications explored. Examining the state of their own confederation in the 1970s, Canadians came to the conclusion that Quebec could not enjoy both economic association and political sovereignty. As was often pointed out in the course of the debate, economic association requires joint decision-making that necessarily encroaches upon

sovereignty. In the 1980s Canadians may have to accept that the same logic applies to their own association with the United States.

That was the major article, among several, that I wrote while in New York, but I was limited by the space available in the journal, the need to address an American audience, and by the fact that my own ideas were still germinating, meaning that I was not ready to argue policy proposals. Nevertheless, I claim the article was ahead of the curve, and perhaps encouraged others to think about Canada-United States relations outside the nationalist frame.

When we were moving to New York, I had been concerned about how we would adjust to the change from a spacious house to a small apartment, but we found it suited us very well, so when the time came to return to Ottawa, we looked for an apartment to rent — and in fact have lived ever since in rented apartments. Jeannie quickly found us a delightful apartment in a renovated old building near the Rideau Canal, but declared that she herself would not move to frozen Ottawa in the middle of the winter. She returned for a few months to our place in New York. I went back to the classroom at Carleton in January, camped in our half-furnished apartment, and took occasional weekends in New York.

I was still thinking in terms of a bigger and bolder article on Canada-United States relations, but, as always happened when I returned to the university and the *Star* column, work overtook me. However, in 1983 I became eligible for a half-year sabbatical, and looked for a hospitable place to work back in New York. Carnegie said their was no room at their inn, so I turned to an old friend, Lansing Lamont, whom I had met when he was bureau chief in Ottawa for *Time*. Lamont developed a lasting interest in Canada, and by 1983 was running a Canadian Affairs program at the Americas Society in New York for David Rockefeller. The society had been concerned mostly with commercial and cultural relations between the United States and Latin America, but Rockefeller decided to expand its interests northwards. He liked to tell the story of how, when he was a young man unsure of what career to pursue, his father, John D. Rockefeller Jr., the American philanthropist and industrialist, sent him for advice to Prime Minister William Lyon Mackenzie King in Ottawa. King had once worked for the Rockefeller's industrial empire as a labour expert, and was apparently well regarded by his employer if not by the workers. King advised the young David that if he wanted to be more than merely his father's son he would have to be able to point to his own achievements, and that his best course might be to return to university and earn a PhD in economics. David took the advice and had been grateful for it ever since, which explained in part why his interest in Canada reached beyond the success of his own investments. Lamont soon made the Americas Society the best known forum in New York for discussion of Canadian affairs, and he invited me to be on his advisory committee. For that service I eventually received, with splendid irony, a copy of *The Canadian Encyclopedia*, published by Mel Hurtig, a fervent nationalist, and inscribed to me by David Rockefeller who must have ranked among Hurtig's arch imperialist villains. I count the encyclopedia as Hurtig's great contribution to Canada, and still refer to it constantly.

Anyway, when I needed an office in New York in 1983, I suggested to Lamont that what his program needed was a visiting associate from Canada. He agreed and I became the first in a series of visiting associates, mostly journalists and academics. The Americas Society was in a grand old mansion on Park Avenue, formerly the offices of the Soviet delegation at the United Nations, and where Nikita Khrushchev once made a famous appearance on the balcony. But there was no office for me there, so I was given space in the attic, more or less, of the building next door, where I was later surrounded by a fledgling organization called Women's World Banking. The small female staff were inventing the idea of guaranteeing tiny bank loans to women in developing countries to help them start a small business, perhaps by buying a sewing machine, or a weaving loom, or opening a store. It's now a familiar and highly successful technique to encourage economic development, but I was so intrigued by the concept — and admiring of the women who kindly tolerated my presence in their space — that I wrote a story about it for *The WorldPaper*.

As for my own work, I pounded out my magnum opus on the future of Canada-United States relations on a typewriter leant to me by Lamont, an ancient model that had served him well but belonged by then in a museum. To structure my argument, I chose to attack head-on Sharp's Third Option strategy, which still formed the basis for the government's policy toward the United States. Sharp, I said, had chosen the wrong option. Instead of seeking to reduce Canada's dependence on the U.S. market, he should have accepted that integration was inevitable, even desirable, and adopted his Second Option: "We can move deliberately toward closer integration with the United States," by which I meant free trade rather than the more ambitious common market. The article ran to about twenty thousand words, and concluded:

> The basic argument being made here is that Canadians, both as individuals and as a political nation, are more likely to prosper and fulfill themselves in free association with Americans than they are by seeking to protect themselves from U.S. competition and influence. The desire to escape from U.S. influence, the desire to put distance between Canada and the United States, arises in large measure from fear of absorption by the United States and from jealousy of U.S. wealth, power and vitality. But fear and jealousy are corrosive in national as in personal life; they feed the Canadian sense of inferiority, encourage parochial attitudes, and give rise in politics to nationalist policies that are bound to fail because they are against the tide of events and against the private aspirations of most Canadians who wish to enjoy the maximum freedom to trade, invest, travel and exchange ideas. Canadians have no reason to feel inferior to Americans, or to be fearful of the United States. They have built an orderly and progressive society that is in some ways an example to the United States, and as workers and producers they are surely equal to Americans. To the extent that size, climate and geography set Canada at a disadvantage in competing with the United States, that can be corrected only by public policy and private effort; protection at the border seeks only to hide such a problem and not solve it.
>
> Finally, what is required is not so much a change in Canadian policies as a change in Canadian attitudes. Canada, after all, is — through GATT — already committed to the abolition, virtually, of tariffs on trade with the United States, and to the maintenance of the free flow of information and entertainment, which together ensure the continuing integration of the two societies. But instead of regarding this prospect with foreboding, as a defeat for

Canadian nationalism and a threat to sovereignty and identity, Canadians should be encouraged to see it as an opportunity to knock down barriers, thereby enlarging their opportunities to compete and to demonstrate the virtues of their society. With a new association with the United States established by a treaty setting out the rules and limits of the relationship, Canada might at last get the aging monkey of nationalism off its back and be able to turn all its energies to solving the internal problems of economic management, social injustice and political reform.

In retrospect, I should have been clearer about the virtues of a free trade treaty. My research had shown that economic integration was continuing apace, despite nationalist policies, and GATT ensured that tariffs would continue to fall. Freer trade, therefore, was a certainty, and the choice was between trade regulated only by the market and trade regulated by a treaty. In the market, Canada would have no protection against the vagaries of U.S. trade policy dictated by powerful industrial lobbies; with a treaty, there would be legal procedures for arbitrating disputes.

My article was an awkward length; too short for a book, obviously, and too long for most magazines. But it found an appropriate home in the winter 1984 issue of *International Perspectives*, the journal in which Sharp's original Third Option had appeared a dozen years earlier. Ownership of the journal had passed from External Affairs into the private hands of Alex Inglis and John Munro. These were the two historians who had managed the remarkable feat of assisting two sworn enemies, John Diefenbaker and Lester Pearson, with their memoirs. As I mentioned earlier, I had been of some assistance to them when they completed Pearson's story after his death, and they had appointed as editor of their journal Gordon Cullingham, whom I had known as a CBC producer. So I was well-positioned to submit my opus, and, gratifyingly, they jumped at it, devoting almost an entire issue to the work — just as Sharp's thesis had occupied an entire issue. While *International Perspectives* had only a small circulation — and, regrettably, soon went out of business — my article attracted comment, and a reply from Sharp, which appeared as the leading article in the next issue under the headline "Sharp on Westell." Sharp referred to me as his friend — I had reported on him for years — but insisted that the Third Option had not been nationalistic, that he himself was not an economic nationalist, and that therefore I had attacked a strawman. However, he was apprehensive about free trade, and his Third Option strategy, "still represents a valid basis for Canada-United States relations, although it is admittedly difficult to implement." Years later, in his memoir, *Which Reminds Me ...* (University of Toronto, 1994), he conceded that it had been impracticable from the start:

> The Third Option had contemplated the adoption of policies to alter the industrial structure of Canada so as to diversify and strengthen our industries and thereby reduce our dependence upon the United States as an export market and as a source of imports. This was never seriously attempted and, in retrospect, was probably far too difficult an undertaking for any federal government of Canada, given the crucial role of the provinces with respect both to resources and industry.

Trudeau, also, in his *Memoir* conceded that the policy had failed to reduce dependence on the U.S. market: "I suppose the changing of individual decisions by thousands of exporters is likely to be beyond the power of any government."

I'm happy to say that my personal relations with Sharp were in no way damaged by this difference of opinion. Things were a little more difficult with Mel Watkins who wrote to *International Perspectives* to say he was downright angry with my article, not because of my advocacy of free trade, which he dismissed as old stuff, but because in describing our relations with the United States I had repeated "every tired and dangerous cliché of the cold war; that 'NATO seeks to deter the Soviet Union,' that 'NORAD seeks to deter Soviet attack.'" In his view, there were grounds to fear the United States. In fact, I had said in the article that a case could be made that the United States rather than the Soviet Union presented a threat to peace but that was not a factor in considering Canada-United States relations because public opinion did not agree. So, "Policy has to be based on the reality that Canada will almost certainly remain a close ally of the United States." When Watkins's path and mine next crossed we were both researching in London in 1987, and a mutual friend invited us to dinner. The hostess told me diplomatically that Watkins was hesitating to accept because he thought I might not want to meet him after his harsh attack on me in *Perspectives*, but no such thought had crossed my mind. I do not take political arguments personally, and Watkins and I have since had cordial relations.

Soon after my article was published, I had lunch with Donald Macdonald, who was preparing to publish the massive report of his Royal Commission on the Economic Union and Development Prospects for Canada Now. He invited me to write the popular digest of the report. Regretfully, because it would have been an interesting and lucrative commission, I declined, pointing out that it would tie my hands as a journalist by preventing me from commenting on the report in my *Star* column. But I did press upon him, at our meeting, a copy of my article in *International Perspectives*. So when his report appeared I was flattered to find that the section on free trade began, right there in the first line, by citing my piece as "a seminal article," and quoting from it. Fame at last! Obviously, I had served as the prophet of free trade, persuading the chairman of the royal commission by the power of my argument. Alas, not so. I discovered later that Michael Hart, a trade expert, had written the final version of the chapter, clarifying the economic research and argument that underlay the free trade proposal. He had chanced to read my article, liked it, and used it as the introduction to his draft. Some commissioners rightly questioned his use of the word *seminal,* which implied that I had planted the seed of a new idea. In fact, the free trade initiative had been germinating in the government for years — long before Prime Minister Brian Mulroney adopted it in 1985. The Economic Council of Canada, in a farsighted report in 1975, had urged wide-open free trade to compel Canadian business to adapt to the coming post-industrial economy in which intellectual capacity would be the most valuable commodity. The Conservative minority government elected in 1979 proposed a national debate on the possibility of free trade but was thrown out before it could act. The Standing Senate Committee on Foreign Affairs completed a seven-year study in 1982 by recommending free trade with the United States. That same year, Trudeau hinted at his own thinking when, asked by James Reston of *The New York Times* about the possibility of a North American common market, he replied:

I don't think that should be the first stage of our thinking. I think we should do more to create a commonality of views of North American countries first and perhaps eventually in the hemisphere ... I have suggested and even promoted with Presidents Portillo and Reagan trilateral meetings.

By then, his government had already ordered a review of trade policy. In *Decision at Midnight: Inside the Canada's Free Trade Negotiations* (BC Press, 1994), Michael Hart and his co-authors describe the ensuing conflict in the bureaucracy between those who still supported the Third Option and those who wanted to move to freer trade. The outcome, in 1983, was a discussion paper, approved by the Trudeau Cabinet, which found unconvincing the argument for full free trade with the United States, but proposed free trade in a few sectors. As it happened, the minister of international trade at the time was Gerald Regan who, as a Nova Scotian, was keenly aware that the Maritimes had enjoyed their greatest prosperity when there had been free trade with the United States before Confederation. He jumped the government gun by proclaiming the death of the Third Option when he announced negotiations for free trade in steel, urban transportation industries, agricultural equipment, and informatics. So Macdonald's report was only the last step in the process by which Ottawa moved from economic nationalism toward free trade. Interestingly, Macdonald had himself gone through a conversion, like so many other Canadians. As a young MP he had been a follower of Walter Gordon, and even managed the floor fight for Gordon's nationalist policies at a national Liberal party convention. But somewhere along the way he changed his mind, perhaps persuaded by the evidence of his commission's economic researchers. Before the report was finished, he indicated to a *Globe* reporter that it would probably propose free trade, saying it would be "a leap of faith," a phrase which, contrary to popular myth, never appeared in the report itself. And his report appears to have converted Prime Minister Mulroney, who had come to office opposed to free trade.

That was not quite the end of my involvement. When I retired from Carleton in 1991, I had leave due, and took it in Boston where I helped *The WorldPaper* organize a conference on the proposal to bring Mexico into the free trade agreement, by means of the North American Free

Trade Agreement. To report on the pros and cons, I wrot‹
a *WorldPaper White Paper* and, translated into Spanish, it be
debate in Mexico where it was widely distributed. Now
tioned, South American countries are moving toward
NAFTA as a model, so the ball I helped to set in motion is still rolling,
and I hope will continue and gather speed. Free trade is not in itself globalism, but it does encourage the breaking down of borders, the acceptance
of an interdependent world. I don't believe in that comfortable cliché
"The Global Village," which conjures an image in which we shall all be
neighbours living in picturesque cottages, with Miss Marples on hand to
solve any unfortunate crimes against the peace. But I do think we are
heading toward a global metropolis in which there will still be rich and
poor, highrises and homeless people, conflict and crime, and eventually,
one race, probably mud-coloured, sharing a common culture, and speaking English — but in so many dialects that we shall still not easily understand each other. But that will be better than living in national tribes
competing for advantage, sometimes economically, too often violently.
On the way to that future, I think it almost certain that Canada and the
United States will enter some form of federal union — probably within
the next thirty years. Will that mean a loss of Canadian identity and influence? The Scots fought the English for centuries but enjoyed their greatest success as a nation after the Treaty of Union in 1707, when they
helped to create and then administers the British empire — as, for example, prime ministers of Britain and Canada. To this day they have retained
their distinctive identity. Canadians may play a similar role in the
American empire. Indeed, many of them already are.

Chapter 14

Reinventing Canada

The School of Journalism at Carleton University, when I was there, was in the arts faculty, and our dean of arts was a feisty historian, Naomi Griffiths, who both mothered and intimidated her academic staff. I got on well with her and, to my complete surprise, she asked me in 1985 to become her associate dean. The job was mainly administrative, including finessing problems to which there were no acceptable solutions. There was, for example, never enough space and one of my first tasks was to negotiate with the dean of social sciences a swap of classrooms and offices that was supposed to make better use of what little space was available. With a mixture of threats and promises, I persuaded various departments to move, but whether anyone was better off in the end was questionable. In the course of the exercise, I discovered our music department tucked away in wholly unsuitable quarters — so much so that some students chose to rehearse in the toilets — and resolved that if I did nothing else I would get a better deal for them. When I left they were still in the same space. There was in the end no way around the fact that the university had outgrown its buildings.

So the position of associate dean was not likely to make one popular, and that may have been one reason Dean Griffiths asked me to become her associate; with no academic career at stake, I could make unpopular decisions more easily than those whose whole career was in the university. Another question is why I accepted a post for which I had no qualifications, and the answer, I fear, was vanity. I wanted to be able to say I was probably the only university dean in Canada who had never studied in a university. But I was keenly aware that there was something slightly absurd about asking me to preside over academic planning meetings. Many members of the faculty probably felt the same way because they summarily rejected the design for a new graduate program proposed by a small committee I chaired.

When Dean Griffiths was away, I took her place on the high level committees that in effect ran the university, and the experience did nothing to increase my confidence in academics as administrators, but I'll have more to say about that later. On one occasion I had to replace her at the convocation when students received their degrees. Most of my academic colleagues wore gorgeous robes in various hues, and some even had a medieval style of plumed hat. I wore a borrowed plain black gown and was reminded of a journalist with only an undergraduate degree who had become dean of another J-school and described his robe as "cotton stuff trimmed with rats' fur." But I managed to distinguished myself in quite another way at the convocation. As acting dean, it was my task to drape a hood over the head and around the neck of graduating students as they knelt before the chancellor. The students were supposed to arrive on the platform with the hood correctly folded over their arm, but some managed to get them inside out and/or upside down, and I had great trouble in getting the thing over their head and correctly draped without strangling them. The chancellor, Gordon Robertson, was tactful in keeping the kneeling student engaged in conversation for rather longer than planned while I struggled to figure out the geometry of the problem, but I'm sure I heard tittering in the audience.

The redeeming feature during this period was Dean Griffiths herself. When the going got rougher than usual, which was often, she would gather me up and drive me downtown for lunch at a decent hotel where we could talk about matters more interesting than faculty politics. But by 1987 I had had more than enough of deaning and insisted on taking the sabbatical leave due to me, despite her objection that my sentence had not been completed. In fact, I was conceiving another book, this time on the future of social democracy — if it had one when the neoconservative right seemed to be triumphing everywhere. The obvious place to do research was in Europe, the birthplace of socialism and social democracy, so Jeannie and I went first to London where I read in the library of the London School of Economics, and interviewed politicians and theorists. On a lighter note, a friend of a friend, Kathy Stinson, author of books for small children, came to Britain on an official trip to promote Canadian literature, and I was asked to show her around London. I mentioned to her, because it had to do with children's literature, that when we had lived in Surrey many years before we had taken our small son, Dan, on a visit to the big city, mainly to see the lions in Trafalgar Square. At Waterloo station, he managed to drop his second-best teddy bear onto the tracks between the carriage and the platform. Porters — there were such beings in those days — were summoned and discussed the problem. Dan was fascinated because his favourite books at the time were the Railway Series by the Rev. W. Awdry — *James the Red Engine, Edward the Blue Engine, Thomas the Tank Engine,* and the rest — and anyone connected with trains was obviously important, particularly if they wore a peaked cap. So he was much impressed when the porters found a long rod with a hook on the end and managed to recover teddy. I told this slight family story to Kathy as we wandered through London on a cold, wet day. It matured in her writer's imagination, and reappeared in 1988 as *Teddy Rabbit* (Annick Press Ltd., Toronto). Dan had become Tony, my name, his teddy had become a toy rabbit, the train had become the Toronto subway, and the destination the Toronto Islands rather than Trafalgar Square. But the bearded father on the cover is recognizably Dan the man, and the book was "Dedicated with thanks to Dan, for dropping his teddy bear and to his father for telling me." Of such is immortality made.

Anyway, when I had finished my research in London we moved to Paris which I used as a base while interviewing in France, Germany, Norway, Sweden, and Denmark. We lived in a modest apartment in the classy sixteenth arrondissement, off the tourist track but an easy walk from most of the attractions. It took me months to figure why Paris is such a visually enchanting city: unlike most European capitals, it wasn't much damaged during the Second World War, and there are few modern glass and concrete towers to spoil the streetscapes. We both fell in love with the city, despite our minimal ability in French. In fact, it was in a Paris street market that I suffered my worst and final defeat with the language. I had enough vocabulary to prepare and deliver sentences that seemed to be understood, but as soon as I began to hear a reply in French my brain froze. I convinced myself it was sheer nerves and that if I could force myself to listen to the reply I would recognize enough French words to get at least the drift of what was being said. So one day when shopping for fromage in the market, when the stall-keeper spoke to me I resolved to be calm and to listen, listen, listen. But still I could not understand a word, and eventually asked if she spoke English. "Yes," she replied in perfect English. "That's what I have been saying to you, 'I speak English.'" No wonder I couldn't catch those French words. Beyond that, the only real difficulties we had in getting by was with recorded instructions on the phone, and at the post office. Fortunately, French phones come with two earpieces so we could both listen to the message, over and over again if necessary, until we deciphered what we were supposed to do, and in the post office there was usually some impatient customer way back in the line to shout out in English what the clerk was trying to tell us in French. And then there was the day when a neighbour banged on our apartment door to say he could smell "gaz." The gaz men were summoned and arrived, an interested crowd gathered around the door speculating on where the leak was — or that was what it sounded like — until it was traced to our meter and fixed. We were the last to know.

We left Paris reluctantly when I had completed my research and was ready to write, but I knew that if I returned to Ottawa I would at once be overwhelmed with other business. So we went to New York and I began transcribing my interview notes and drafting a book plan. Then I made the mistake of dropping into the magnificent New York Public Library to check a quotation. One book led to another, and so on until my leave was up and it was time to return to Carleton. And in fact the book did not get written until I retired, and then in a different form that I had first intended. In *Reinventing Canada* (Dundurn Press, 1994) I explored the history and current crisis of social democracy. I am a journalist rather than a heavy-duty thinker, and I look for simple ways to explain complicated issues — that is to say, my interpretation of those issues. Without having studied the works of Friedrich Hegel (1770-1831), the impenetrable German philosopher, I was attracted to his familiar dialectic: thesis, antithesis, synthesis. He argued, as I understand it, that the level of consciousness determined the level of social organization, and that consciousness was raised over the centuries by the clash of ideas — not political debate as we know it, but the clash of civilizations, social systems, cultures. The prevailing consciousness, or thesis, was contradicted by another set of beliefs, the antithesis. In the ensuing struggle, they influenced each other and the outcome was not the triumph of one over the other, but a synthesis of the two — a new and higher level of consciousness. This consciousness became the new thesis, and was in turn contradicted, leading to a new and yet higher synthesis. Finally, all contradictions would be resolved in a union of man with God — or if you prefer, utopia.

Was he right? I don't pretend to know, but the dialectic seemed to me to be at least a useful way to organize our understanding of history. In the Western world, in the period, roughly, 1750-1850, the prevailing thesis of feudal society was contradicted by the antithesis of industrial society. In this vast process a new class of merchants and bankers challenged the aristocracy, democratic ideas attacked conservative autocracy, scientific and humanist values contradicted traditional religion. The synthesis that emerged was an early version of liberal democracy in which the means of production were privately owned and operated for profit — laissez-faire capitalism — and democracy was restricted to the middle and upper classes. In turn, it was contradicted by a new antithesis, socialism, and the struggle between capitalism and socialism was at the centre of political debate in the developed countries for more than a century. In most developing democracies in the nineteenth and twentieth centuries there were two main strains of socialism, revolutionary socialism and democratic socialism, and the struggle between them was often as fierce as the struggle with capitalism. Revolutionary socialism was based, in the main, on the theories of Karl Marx, who wanted to liberate man from the state, but thought that capitalism and then a revolution against the capitalist class to establish a workers' state would first be necessary. He was better at critiquing capitalism than at prescribing a workable alternative, and it's interesting to note that when he did write a simple political program, in the famous *Communist Manifesto,* he proposed a series of reforms, most of which have long since been adopted in whole or in part, in principle if not always in practice, in western democracies: "Centralization of credit in the hands of the state by means of a national bank ... Equal obligation of all to work ... Free education for all children in public schools ...Abolition of children's factory labour ..." etc. His impatient disciples tried to leap from feudalism to socialism in Russia, and made the fatal mistake of thinking that the goal justified using the means of the police state, thereby achieving the opposite of what Marx had intended. Marx's opponents in the socialist movement accepted much of his analysis of the internal contradictions of capitalism, but rejected the call to violent revolution. The struggle between them was about means, not ends. They mostly agreed that the goal was to replace capitalism with a wholly new economic system: socialism. The means of production would be publicly owned and operated in the public interest, and co-operation would replace competition. In Canada, the original democratic socialist party, the Co-operative Commonwealth Federation, declared in its founding manifesto in 1933: "No CCF government will rest content until it has eradicated capitalism and put into operation the full program of socialized planning which will lead to the establishment in Canada of the Co-operative Commonwealth."

But, as Hegel would have expected, the struggle between laissez-faire capitalism and socialism produced not a victory for one but a synthesis — social democracy, sometimes called the welfare state, or now, the Third Way. In this model of society, the economy remains largely in private ownership, driven by the capitalistic competition for profit, but the state regulates the market, imposes public ownership where markets do not work, and redistributes profits through taxation and social services to ensure some degree of both equality of outcome— a minimum standard of living — and of opportunity. Social democracy arrived by stages, but the crisis of capitalism in the great depression of the 1930s gave it enormous impetus. Social democratic ideas infiltrated almost all parties, whether they called themselves democratic socialists, reform liberals, or progressive conservatives. In fact, they first flowered in practice North America in the form of the Democratic Party's New Deal in the United States in the 1930s. In Canada, Conservative Prime Minister R.B. Bennett tried his own version of the New Deal, but was shortly defeated in an election. Eventually, his legislation was struck down as unconstitutional because it infringed on the jurisdiction of the provinces. But the goal in both countries was to use the power of the state to rescue capitalism from its own crisis, not to introduce a new society. However, in the Second World War democratic governments took control of their economies to plan production, and promised a new and better society as a reward for victory. The effect was to institutionalize social democracy as a replacement for liberal democracy based on laissez-faire capitalism. It became the dominant ideology throughout the western democracies, and beyond. Political debate became essentially about how best to run the welfare state.

The golden age of social democracy was approximately 1945-70. Economies grew, raising employment and incomes, and generating revenues to finance new and better social services. There were of course occasional setbacks, but national governments were confident of their ability to iron out the bumps by manipulating the big levers of economic management, public spending, taxes, and monetary policy. As I have written earlier, problems began to appear in the late 1960s, and by the 1970s it was apparent, not least in Canada, that they did not respond to adjustment of supply and demand. Unemployment and inflation rose together, producing what became known as stagflation, and the rate of increase in incomes slowed to a crawl. Millions of words have been written to argue about what went wrong, and why, and this is not the place to continue that debate. What we do know is that with social democracy in disarray laissez-faire ideas made a comeback, and right-wing governments — called neo-conservative in North America and neo-liberal in Europe — were elected in Britain and the United States, and later in Alberta and Ontario. But if we are to continue with the dialectic, this resurgence of the right cannot be seen as an antithesis contradicting social democracy. It was not a new level of consciousness, but a revival of an old one. In any event, the neo-cons never dared to deny the central tenets of social democracy, that the state is ultimately responsible for managing the economy and ensuring at least a minimum of social justice. They made mostly marginal changes in the way the state operated, privatizing some functions, deregulating others to place more reliance on markets, and while they succeeded in slowing the growth of government, they did not significantly reduce its responsibilities. Opinion polls in the major democracies continue to show that the public is essentially social democratic, holding governments responsible for the performance of the economy, and more interested in public services than in tax cuts. In Western Europe at the end of the twentieth century, fourteen of nineteen countries with 88 percent of the population were governed by social democratic parties, alone or in coalitions. In order to win elections, conservatives must now call themselves "compassionate," and promise to improve rather than abolish the welfare state.

The real challenge to social democracy based on national states is not neo-conservatism but "globalism," so-called. Production of goods and services has been reorganized, first on a continental basis and then globally. New technologies of communication and travel make this new order possible — and therefore necessary in competitive markets. National sovereignty continues to be eroded, and not only in the economic dimension. The flow of people between countries, both legal and illegal, increases, pop culture continues to spread around the world implanting social norms and expectations, and there is an increasing willingness on the part of the "international community," however defined, to intervene in the affairs of supposedly sovereign states to enforce international law and even ideas on how governments should behave toward their citizens. Governments find themselves in competition for business investment and trade advantages, and it became increasingly difficult for them to manage national affairs by regulating the national economy.

This is not to say that global capitalism has defeated social democracy. Political democracy, market economies, and social justice — social democracy to a greater or lesser degree — are now accepted values in most countries. The task now is to bring global capitalism into the service of global social democracy, just as national capitalism was made to serve national social democracy. That can be done only by international institutions — the World Trade Organization, the International Monetary Fund, the World Bank, the Organization for Economic Cooperation and Development, North American Free Trade Agreement, and others. Social democrats in Europe are working in that direction, but in Canada and the United States the left wastes its energy on futile efforts to turn the clock back to national protectionism. The motive has been to preserve the ability to manage the national welfare state and so protect the gains made under national social democracy. But economic nationalism no longer works, if in fact it ever did: John A. Macdonald's famous National Policy attempted to build Canadian industries behind tariff walls but resulted in inefficiently small and uncompetitive producers that eventually fell easy victims to American and other foreign corporations.

As I wrote in *Reinventing Canada*, the crisis of social democracy based on national states is particularly serious in Canada because we believe that our commitment to social democracy is what distinguishes us from the United States and justifies our separate existence. But resisting modernity makes any country, any political movement, irrelevant. We need instead to reinvent our national identity. It may be as part of the American empire, or perhaps as a collection of small states on the periphery of the empire. The great mistake is to think that the Canadian state as we know it today is part of the natural order of things, and unchangeable. History shows that empires rise and fall, nation states form, change their borders, merge and separate, and often disappear into larger states. The only certainty is that Canada as a state will change, and in *Reinventing Canada* I argued that if we want this process to be peaceful — that is, made by democratic consent — we need urgently to reform our flawed political system and renegotiate our dysfunctional federalism.

When I returned to Carleton in 1988, after my sabbatical leave, it was my turn to be director of the J-school. I say my turn because academic departments in a university are administered by members of the department who were hired in the first place not because they had training or experience as administrators but for their abilities as scholars and teachers. Some prove to be good administrators, many do not and among them I include myself. To be the chair or director is usually a thankless job, shunned by those who have more sense than ambition, and no misplaced notion of duty. In some perfect past age, universities were said to be communities of scholars. Now they tend to be divided and divisive organizations harbouring competing interest groups. No two universities are exactly alike, but in most the senior administration wants to enrol more students without raising costs. The faculty, organized in a trade union, wants fewer students in the classrooms, more time for research, and of course more pay. The experienced assistants and secretaries without whom departments would soon fall into chaos are underpaid. The students, naturally led by the aspiring militants among them, demand better teaching, more facilities, and lower fees. None of these groups has much leverage. Unlike the managers of a business, the administrators of a university can't discipline their workers, the members of faculty. Public opinion to the contrary, tenure is not really the problem because it never precludes firing for cause; the problem is often a union contract that provides for endless and costly arbitration of disputes in what all sides like to pretend is a participatory democracy. The faculty can and will go on strike, but that tends to punish their customers — that is, the students — more than their employers, the administration. The support staff are essential but not influential. Students can protest noisily, but not much more if they want to complete their program, obtain their degree, and start earning money to repay their frightening debts.

Caught in the middle of this unhappy situation, and pressured by all sides, is the hapless head of a department, amateur part-time administrator, teacher and researcher, taking his or her turn at a thankless job and looking forward to returning to the ranks. Or at least, that was my experience at Carleton. But if I sound bitter, I'm not. Most of my experience had been in journalism, which is oriented to action-this-day, in newsrooms which tend to be authoritarian in structure, and all I knew about administration, or thought I knew, was that I should try to clear my desk every evening. So I was singularly ill-prepared for the leisurely, politicized, participatory decision-making of the university, and frequently in conflict with my superiors. I had ambitious plans for expanding the school while they were struggling to balance a shrinking budget. I had problems also with student leaders who, one year, named me as the third most disliked member of the entire university faculty. Actually, the students were misinformed about my role in some issue, so I was not much disturbed, and when my dean expressed sympathy, I told her not to worry; I would be shooting next year for the top spot on the hate list. During my tenure of three and a half years as director of the school, we did create a new Master of Journalism program, launch an MA in Communication, and begin work on a PhD, but that was mainly because journalism is a marquee program at Carleton which the administration had an interest in expanding because it attracts first-class students from across Canada and beyond. A better and more diplomatic director could probably have achieved the same growth with far less turmoil.

Because I had to speak for the school, to the media, and at public and private events, I had to formulate in my own mind what I thought journalism education should be about — if only to answer, repeatedly, the question of why I, who had entered the news business as a sixteen-year old apprentice, should now be advocating undergraduate and graduate education for journalists. Although most of the major news organizations were recruiting from the J-schools, there were — still are — many successful journalists who were contemptuous of the very idea of schools of journalism. For some at least, that was because they had little or no idea of what went on at Carleton and, no doubt, at other good schools. They seemed to believe that schools existed to teach basic reporting skills, and they argued that students would do better to take a degree in some "useful" discipline such as economics or political science, and then learn reporting on the job. It's true that some schools are largely craft schools. In my view they exist mainly to relieve employers of the burden of training their own staff, and have no place in a university. Indeed, if training is the primary goal, on-the-job experience probably is the best method. But a good J-school offers much more.

At Carleton, to speak from my own experience, undergraduates took more courses than students in most other disciplines, combining journalism with other studies. Some students, in fact, took combined honours in journalism and another discipline, say economics or political science, and decided in the fourth year in which to graduate. In the J-school, craft courses offered training in print, radio, and TV journalism, plus such "academic" courses as media law, history, and communication theory. The goal, as I saw it, was not to teach journalism, but to educate students for a career in journalism — or, if they so chose, and many did, for a career in some other branch of the media, or even entirely outside media. As I explained to potential students, and to those who decided after a year or two that they did not want to be journalists, knowing how to research information, analyze, organize, and then communicate it in several media are useful skills in many occupations. Some students, even if they did not intend to become a journalist, seemed to find that building an undergraduate program around J-studies gave focus and purpose to their university years. As an apprentice reporter, I learned quickly how to gather news and write a formula story in the standard inverted pyramid style: the dramatic or important facts first, and the rest in declining order of importance so that editors could cut quickly from the bottom without fear of losing important elements, and readers could get the gist of the news in a few sentences. It took me years to question the conventions of the craft and the role of journalism in democratic society. Good J-schools do that for students, and the work of faculty is not easy. By the time I retired as director, I was worn out to the point at which my wife was worrying about my health. There are professors who take life easy, but many I knew worked damned hard.

When I say I retired, I do not mean I stopped working. I have continued to write occasional articles for the mainstream press, and for *The World Paper* in Boston, and to work as volunteer editor for *The Literary Review of Canada* in the hope that it will become in time our equivalent of *The New York Review of Books* or *The Times Literary Supplement* in London, a vehicle for the journalism of ideas. I have also written two books, *Reinventing Canada* and this one. So is this the end? While I was serving on the Board of Governors of the Canadian Journalism Foundation we launched a lifetime achievement award for journalists. In fact, I think it was I who suggested the award, and it occurred to me only later that it is a rather depressing notion for a recipient, implying there will be no more achievements, maybe no more lifetime. I hope I'm not there yet, so how to write End to this account of my life — so far? When news moved on telegraph wires, operators ended a message with three crosses, XXX. That was shortened to 30, and journalists began to use it to mark the end when they typed their stories. I should perhaps word process, say,

28

~ Index ~